# Doh Ray Me, When Ah Wis Wee

Ewan McVicar was born in Inverness. After working abroad, he returned to Scotland and was employed in various areas of social work before becoming a self-employed storyteller, author and songwriter. He has performed in over 200 schools and countless other venues across Scotland, as well as in Canada, the USA, Holland, Russia, Sweden and Uganda. He has written some 40 songs which have been commercially recorded, including 20 for the Singing Kettle children's show and a 1960s Top Twenty hit.

# *Doh Ray Me, When Ah Wis Wee*

❧

## Scots Children's Songs and Rhymes

## Ewan McVicar

BIRLINN

First published in 2007 by
Birlinn Limited
West Newington House
10 Newington Road
Edinburgh
EH9 1QS

*www.birlinn.co.uk*

ISBN 13: 978 1 84158 558 1
ISBN 10: 1 84158 558 0

British Library Cataloguing-in-Publication Data
A catalogue record for this book is available from the British Library

Typeset by Iolaire Typesetting, Newtonmore
Printed and bound by Cromwell Press, Trowbridge, Wiltshire

# Contents

# Acknowledgements

My grateful thanks and appreciation are given to the following people for aid in time of need.

Linda McVicar for unfailing encouragement, support, proofreading, glossary making and standard-keeping. Morris Blythman, Josh Macrae, Norman Buchan and Hamish Henderson for the example they gave and the standards they set.

Staff at the School of Scottish Studies, University of Edinburgh, for many acts of kindness and help, especially Emily Lyle, Margaret MacKay, Cathlin Macaulay, Katherine Campbell, Arnot McDonald and previous librarians, Ian MacKenzie, Stewart Smith, Morag Nicleod and others, and many fellow students at the school. Staff at East Tennessee State University for help with American material.

Ian Davison for the use of his manuscript collection. Rob MacKillop for the transcription of Kette Bairdie, librarians throughout the land for assistance and advice and for filing books where I could find them. Anna Lomax Wood, Nathan Salsburg, Don Fleming and others at the Association for Cultural Equity, New York, for access to the Alan Lomax archives and support. Tom Laurie of Glasgow Folk and Traditional Arts Trust, Pam Diamond of Moray Council, Susan Thores of West Lothian Council for organisational assistance. Steve Gardham and many others at the Ballad List and Mudcat Café for information and comment freely given. Paul Snow for the Alex Campbell book.

Head teachers, teachers and helpers, and most of all pupils in many Scottish schools, particularly in Glasgow and West Scotland, Moray and West Lothian, for help collecting song and rhyme. Culbokie Primary on the Black Isle, Boghall Primary in Bathgate, Bankton Primary in Livingston and Springfield After School Care Scheme in Linlithgow for help in organising photography.

Karina Townsend for kindly permitting use of photographs by her father, Raymond Townsend. Ian MacKenzie of Celtic and Scottish Studies, University of Edinburgh, for his excellent photographs.

Scottish Borders Council archives for help finding material about Robert Coltart and for permission to reproduce an extract from the *Galashiels Almanac and Directory*. Edinburgh City Libraries and Simon Radcliffe for permission to reproduce the modern postcard of Coulter's Candy.

My thanks are also due for the following permissions to reproduce published materials. Particular thanks are due to the University of Aberdeen for permission to include a substantial number of texts from *The Greig–Duncan Folk Song Collection*,

Volume 8, edited by Patrick Shuldham-Shaw, Emily B Lyle and Katherine Campbell and published by Mercat Press, based on the manuscript versions of the songs collected by Greig and Duncan in the early part of the twentieth century, held by Historic Collections in the University of Aberdeen. I was fortunate enough to undertake some of the editorial work on the children's lore part of Volume 8.

Harper Collins regarding material from *101 Scottish* Songs by Norman Buchan, Odyssey Productions on behalf of the Estate of Alan Lomax for material from *Singing in the Streets,* Conrad and Sue Wilson of Ramsay Head Press for material from *Murder Murder Polis*, Routledge and Kegan Paul by way of Thomson Publishing Services for material from *The Traditional and National Music of Scotland* and *Dae Ye Min' Langsyne?* Scots Language Dictionaries for definitions and descriptions from their various dictionaries.

Special grateful thanks for permissions for transcription and use of recorded material held in the School of Scottish Studies archive, particularly material collected and recorded by Hamish Henderson. This book would never have been begun without the interest and support of the School's staff, and could not have been written without the resources of the School's archive and library. The School's transcriptions of Alan Lomax's 1951 recordings in Scotland were of great help to me in various ways, as were many recordings that concentrated on Scots children's lore. But much of the School's massive archive of children's lore appears as a few items recalled by adults in the midst of other material, much less easy to access, so I must have missed mining many gems. Although I was educated alongside Gaels, I was unable to make use of archive Gaelic material. It was not possible to locate some informants, collectors or their heirs, or even to identify most of the children whose recordings are in the archive. I trust the many named and unnamed informants, and the following collectors, or their heirs, who deposited copies of their recordings in the archive, approve my use of what they gathered and I selected – Linda (Headlee) Williamson, Lynn Hendry, Elizabeth Neilson, Arthur Argo.

I have throughout the book sought to identify all my sources and to get permission to include any copyright material that is in quantity over the limits of general publishing practice. I apologise for any errors or omissions and would be grateful to learn of any necessary corrections. I am sure some of the small comic verses began life in publications or programmes for children – but which ones?

# 1
# *Introduction*

Doh ray me, when ah wis wee Ah used tae peel the tat - ties

Noo ah'm big an ah can jig An ah can kiss the lad - dies Ma

fai - ther built me a nice wee hoose Tae keep me frae the lad - dies But the

roof fell in an ah fell oot An ah fell in wi the lad - dies

*(Transcription: McVicar from personal recollection, Glasgow 1960s)*

Doh ray me, when ah wis wee
Ah used tae peel the tatties
Noo ah'm big an ah can jig
An ah can kiss the laddies

Ma faither built me a nice wee hoose
Tae keep me frae the laddies
But the roof fell in an ah fell oot
An ah fell in wi the laddies

*(McVicar from personal recollection: heard in Glasgow in 1960s)*

This little song is an encapsulation of many features of Scottish children's song and rhyme: vigour and bounce, direct language, the Scots voice, implied humour and the topics of childhood, home life, dance, parental actions that include an element of archaic control over women, courting, violent events and a surreal touch. The voice is female, and girls hold and transmit most of this lore. The energetic tune sounds familiar and simple, yet like 'Ye canny shove yer grannie' the tune has a complex history and is linked to an American gospel song.

Which of these recall to you the bedlam sound of the playground? Though you may well say 'He's got the words wrong'.

A B C
Ma grannie caught a flea
She salted it and peppered it
And had it for her tea

⁊

Auntie Mary had a canary
Up the leg of her drawers
It pulled a string and began to sing
And doon fell Santa Claus

⁊

Wha saw the 42nd?
Wha saw them gaun awa?
Wha saw the 42nd
Merchin doon the Broomielaw

Some o them had boots an stockins
Some o them had nane at aa
Some o them had green umbrellas
For tae keep the rain awa

⁊

One two three aleerie
I spied Mrs Peerie
Sittin on her bumaleerie
Eatin chocolate babies

⁊

Ma maw's a millionaire
Blue eyes and curly hair
She stots ma faither aff the wa
Like a wee cahoutchie ba
Ma maw's a millionaire

એ

Captain Cook was eatin soup
His wife was eatin jelly
Captain Cook fell in the soup
And burnt his rubber belly

Any Scottish adult can, when pressed, dredge up from deep memory a few such small songs they have not sung since they were kids, songs which they associate with playing in the street or school playground, used for ball-bouncing or skipping or insulting someone or amusing oneself.

In 1990 I was asked by Glasgow Folk and Traditional Arts Trust to teach for a week some of these old favourites to classes visiting the harsh bare classrooms of the Rennie Mackintosh-designed Scotland Street School Museum, since 'the kids don't sing songs in the playground any more'. I summoned up songs I recalled with affection from child-hood and others I'd heard sung in folk clubs. Midway into the first session, a small hand went up: 'We sing songs like that.'

'Tell me some', I said, and the floodgates opened. Every class who came in that day knew a couple of dozen. 1991 at Scotland Street Museum brought another exhilarating collecting and sharing week. Then I began collecting more and investigating published sources and archives for the backgrounds and related versions of what the kids sang and told me, eventually graduating to the hallowed halls of the School of Scottish Studies in Edinburgh University. While all the time teachers told me that the kids had no songs of their own any more.

I found many books and pamphlets. Some are collections of rhymes at particular times and give some variations in texts, others are selections from publications and collections and give only one version of each rhyme. There are individual recollections of childhood repertoires, regional collections and descriptions of the use of song and rhyme in games. Almost exclusively these publications deal with texts only, with infrequent identification of tunes and no discussion of them. There are a few commercial recordings, all limited in either time or location. And there are archive collections: the huge one in the School of Scottish Studies and those of a few private collectors.

What I wanted and did not find was a Scottish overview, selected thematically and systematically from the mass of material collected into print and archives in the last 150 years to show the development and interconnectedness of Scottish texts and to consider the processes of recreation and remaking that are crucial to the material. Such an overview should consider the music used and give a sense of historical developments and trends, including changes in usage and application of the material by children.

It should draw heavily on the UK wide work of Peter and Iona Opie. All the work of the Opies is invaluable. Their many books on aspects of children's play are standard reference works for anyone interested in the subject, and their scholarship is impressive. I could just about have written a version of this book by reorganising and rehashing material from a few of their books. Indeed, my initial interest in Scottish children's lore arose in part from a comment made by Peter and Iona Opie (1959) in their first major work on these kinds of song: 'Pluckings like these from the Scottish wool-bag of oral songs seem to be as numerous as they were in the eighteenth century.'

But the overview should also investigate an area little covered by the Opies because most informants were school teachers – the myriad bawdy or 'rude' texts in use, the 'fantasy' violence and aggression songs, the gang chants, football songs and rhymes and the anti-school songs known in every Scottish school. There is almost no representation in print of the materials created or updated in the past fifty years, including the many parodies of TV commercials and pop songs. Though there have been many laments for what has been 'lost' in children's song and rhyme play in Scotland, there has been little consideration of why and how this happens and little investigation of what replaces the abandoned material.

This book seeks to cover most of the above neglected areas, creating for Scottish lore – as the Opies have done with great and continuing success for British children's lore – a work of not only scholarly but general interest, since one thing that unites us all is our childhood experience and (usually vague) recollections of song and rhyme. The consistent response I get when sharing this material in presentations and conversations is fascination and recognition from people from right across the social and age spectrums.

I include nursery rhymes, skipping chants, dandling songs, guising pieces, ring game lyrics, what are termed 'street songs' though now they live instead in the playground, etc. The material is shared by everyone through memories of childhood, but there is an astonishing range and quantity of versions and uses of the songs and rhymes. They were and are learned informally at home, in the streets, back courts and playgrounds. Some are first heard as members of formal groups – Guides, Scouts, Boys Brigade, and especially Brownies – and in more recent years in nursery classes or even school assemblies.

The songs and rhymes have vigour, simplicity and strong character. In many the humour often has startling surreal qualities. Others are maudlin. Some employ words the children themselves consider 'rude' – sexy, bum, belly, fart – or are downright crude, relishing explicit toilet humour or sexual language. Occasionally they are frankly offensive to minority groups, or challenges to fight or absurd accounts of past street battles.

They are learned when aged seven to nine years and abandoned when aged twelve, although some people recover and use them when they need, as adults, to amuse children. When this is done the adult is alarmed to find the child usually does not recognise these relics, which to the adult are precious memories of being young and 'innocent'.

'But what songs do you use when you are bouncing a ball on the wall or skipping a rope?' asks the adult. On learning that such activities are unknown locally at present, the adult sadly concludes that 'children don't sing playground songs these days, and they only play computer games'.

Go into any playground, look and listen a little while. They are hotching with song. Not, I fear, any of the ones I thought to teach in Scotland Street School that 1990 day, but others bearing the same hallmarks of energy, humour and directness. The game ones are not at present used to accompany ball bouncing and seldom for rope jumping. In the 1990s they were employed for rhythmic movements using Chinese Ropes (which are made by linking rubber bands together, the continuous rubber line being entwined round ankles) and predominantly just now for hand-clapping routines. Rude songs seem to have got cruder in the last twenty years, or maybe children like adults are just being more honest about bodily functions nowadays. Songs about violence have got bloodier, as the films and TV have.

So this book is not a requiem for the vanished folklore of Scottish childhood, but an enquiry as to what has been going on over the years, and in some cases, centuries with these songs and rhymes.

Where do they come from? How old are they? How does the process of unpicking and recreating them happen? What makes some die out? Who makes the new ones? What are they for?

I have followed some song elements as they are made, unmade and remade, tried to identify the building blocks of their creation and investigated their histories.

I have chosen songs that seem to have a Scottish identity, but as we'll see these songs wander the world. A case can be made for 'Old King Coul' being originally Scottish. The tune of 'London Bridge is falling down' is undoubtedly Scottish, but the words are not. The song 'Johnny Todd' is claimed for Liverpool, 'Dance to yer daddy' for Tyneside and 'The Wind Blows High' for Ireland, but all have respectable Scottish ancestry, which is not to assert that they do not also have respectable ancestry in the 'Pool, Newcastle and Dublin. Some of these songs are true citizens of the world, with American tunes, old Scots words and relatives scattered from Australia to Sardinia.

When selecting what to include here I have at times begun with songs recalled from my own childhood. Immediately I hit a problem: often there are 'rude' versions alongside non-rude ones. When I was wee I thought that the 'Captain Cook was eating soup' rhyme was rude because it had the word 'belly' in it. I don't think that way any more, but there were frankly Rabelasian ones too.

I refuse to give an example just here. Not because of my own embarrassment, but because I fear the discomfort of some potential readers. Things in print somehow seem so much worse and more titillating than when heard. Anyway, the nastiest versions are perhaps just that, made extreme in order partly to shock, I think. I prefer the songs with clever wordplay and startling surreal imagery, but bawdry and honest vulgarity have their place in our world and lives. If you are easily offended, or cling to the belief that children are innocent lambs who have no interest in sexuality or amusement about bodily functions, avoid chapter 14.

I have not considered in detail all the puzzles that surround these songs, any more than I have included all the thousands of songs and rhymes I found.

What should I call them? A few of the songs I consider are termed 'nursery songs'. Were you raised in a nursery? Was anybody you know raised in a nursery, and sung these songs by a nanny? Songs sung when older can also be categorised by the place where they were sung. To call them 'street songs' is showing your age – cars have pushed them off the streets and 'playground songs' identifies where the songs and rhymes appear to live these days.

Another approach is to label them by the function the person recalls using them for – 'skipping' or 'jumprope' or 'ball' or 'clapping' or 'dandling songs'. Many of them were and are used for more than one game purpose, and many of the songs were not for formal game use, although the amusement songs seem to be part of the Game of Language. As in physical games the participants use purposeful repetition, development of verbal dexterity and competitive performance, while the formal rules and limits essential to physical games are mirrored in the fierce insistence with which children assert the correctness of their own version of song and rhyme texts, tunes and associated activities.

They are largely dividable along sex identity lines. While most kids in a class hold a few songs in common, the bulk of the games songs are collected, held and used by girls, while the boys have the rude, aggression and football ones.

When editing texts from various sources I have chosen to omit many commas and full stops within and at the end of lines, though I have kept question marks. I have also pruned down the forest of apostrophes that decorate older versions of texts, used by the original editors to identify 'missing' letters. In modern print usage, Scots is considered to be as old a language as English, so what would be a missing letter in English was and is not there in the first place in spoken Scots. The above statement may infuriate some pedants by its over-simplification and over-generalising. Fair play to them. Further, I have in the interests of clarity changed 'a' in the sense of 'all' to be 'aa', and changed many capital letters within lines and 'O's at the end of lines to lower case.

With thousands of songs and rhymes to choose from, and many thousands of variants, which should I give in this book? First of all, the 'best': the most interesting and amusing. Then, those that show the process of growth, change and decay: the oldest and the newest, the most startling and most puzzling, complexity distilled to simplicity, confusion creeping in then resolved. Next, I have preferred versions not currently or recently in print, so there are few of the fine versions of rhymes and songs selected by the Montgomeries, Ritchie, Fraser and the Opies. The mighty volumes of the *Greig–Duncan Folk Song Collection*, although in print, are harder to access, so I have included many of them. The old volumes compiled by Gregor, Maclagan and the Rymour Club are very hard to find, so I have drawn heavily on them. My other priority has been to report on what the kids have been singing since the last of the substantial reports in print was nailed down by Ritchie in 1965. Ian Davison's collecting in Glasgow schools in the 1960s and 70s and my own in the 1990s and 2000s have harvested some of the more recent crop.

I have chosen when possible to tell stories of linked versions and elements, and of the tunes involved with texts. Where I have no tale to explore, I have categorised texts in anthology style. The allocation of texts into categories of use and purpose is easy enough for most, but some songs and rhymes are or were used at need for skipping, entertainment, ball-bouncing and organised games, speeded up for movement or dramatically slowed down for declamation at Halloween. Adults who recall one specific use for a rhyme may not approve of how I categorise it.

General readers' responses to texts in this book will naturally in part be mediated by their own individual memories of the childhood lore in which we all have a share. They may even feel that their childhood memory of the 'right' text or tune is being challenged by the richness and variety of versions here. In this case – everybody is right!

# 2
# Wee Eerie Weerie

## Adult to child 'nursery rhymes'

Hushaba burdie, croon, croon
Hushaba burdie, croon, croon
The sheep are gane tae the siller wid
An the coos are gane tae the broom, broom

Let's begin with the problematic term 'nursery rhymes'. As noted in the introduction, few of the readers of this book will have been raised in a nursery, although many will have formed an acquaintance with songs and rhymes in this section through compulsory attendance at a day nursery or nursery school. However, the first major editor-collectors of the genre, Chambers and Halliwell, lived at a time when half the families in the land had servants, and it was fairly usual to have the individual attention of a nursery nurse or elderly family adherent. When, in 1826, Robert Chambers assembled *Popular Rhymes of Scotland*, 'chiefly collected from oral sources', he said 'Many others must have, like myself, cracked credit with their grandmothers, by inquiring after such homely and foolish things', but he gave only a few 'specimens' of children's lore. By the 1842 edition half the book was composed of such 'Rhymes of the Nursery', stories, riddles, games and songs. This version was kept in print for sixty years, and is much overdue for a modern reprint.

James Orchard Halliwell not only acknowledged Chambers as one of his sources when in 1849 his *The Nursery Rhymes of England*, 'collected principally from oral Tradition', was published, but followed 'in some respects, the plan adopted by Mr Robert Chambers, in his elegant work'. More recent collections labelled 'Nursery Rhymes' and 'Nursery Songs' often include pieces usually employed in the street or playground for games or activities, but also serviceable in nursery schools.

While most of the material in this book is passed from child to child with little involvement from adults, lullabies and manipulation songs are used by adults when caring for babies and small children, for the amusement of both parties, to soothe or entertain infants. Often the child is pre-speech, so the important content is tone of voice, rhythm and physical movement, while the words are there to entertain the adult.

Adults around the world need soft-sounding and rhythmic lullabies to hush and calm babies. Barbara and Michael Cass-Beggs have collected together lullabies in fifty languages, and they say: 'Lullabies are fundamental to our folk cultures. Mothers of every race and country have sung lullabies, made up by themselves, answering the needs of their own particular baby.' (Cass-Beggs 1969) As the infant develops language and motor skills, the repetition and comfort associated with such rhymes is both encouragement and learning support.

I can find numerically very few traditional Scottish lullabies, in comparison with the hundreds of pieces I have chosen from for all the other kinds of Scots children's song in this book. Many writers have penned lullabies, but they are usually far too wordy for the purpose and are sung by adults as performance pieces instead. I am reminded of blues singer Big Bill Broonzy's rendition of an Afro-American children's song about going fishing: 'You get a line and I'll get a pole, we'll go down to the crawdad hole.' The earnest BBC interviewer listened to Broonzy croon the first verse slowly, then heat the song up. 'Is that a lullaby, would a mother sing it to put the baby to sleep?' You could hear the smile in the polite interviewee's voice. 'Yeh, sure, but he'd go to wakin up again after the second verse!'

The baby needs the sound, not the sense of the mother's singing voice, so any soft tuning will do – pop hit, aria, rugby song, or half remembered and recombined scrap from childhood. See how the elements of soft sound, cuddly animal imagery, terrifying salutory tale and lament swirl and conjoin in the texts I quote. Nor is more than one verse needed, as the instruction for 'Baby Bunting' in *Tommy Thumb's Song Book* (1788) says, 'Encore 'till the Child's afleep.'

The favourite old Scottish term for a lullaby is the baloo. Chambers (1842) gives 'He-ba-laliloo!', 'the simplest of the lullaby ditties of the north'. He sniffs at the entertaining suggestion of Rev. Mr Lamb that this is from the French 'Hê bas! Là le loup!' (Hush! There's the wolf). Chambers goes on to comment that 'Ba loo la loo' was a Scottish lullaby at the time of James VI, since in 1621 in *Ane Compendious Book of Godly and Spirituall Sangs* the baby Jesus is comforted and praised with 'that richt Balulalow'.

Volume 8 of the *Greig–Duncan Folk Song Collection* is quite rich in baloos and other baby-calming fragments. The two wordless croons to soothing syllables that follow (Shuldham-Shaw et al. 2002, nos. 1548 and 1549) were 'noted by George F Duncan from mother, 1885'.

Hush - a - ba    loo loo-ee loo - ee loo-ee    Hush - a - ba    loo-ee    loo - ee

*(Shuldham-Shaw et al. 2002, no. 1548)*

Hush-a-ba loo loo-ee loo-ee loo-ee
Hush-a-ba loo-ee loo-ee

Oh hush-a-ba - loo, loo-ee loo-ee loo-ee    loo-ee loo-ee Hush-a-ba - loo loo - ee loo-ee loo

*(Shuldham-Shaw et al. 2002, no. 1549)*

Oh hush-a-ba-loo, loo-ee loo-ee loo-ee loo-ee loo-ee
Hush-a-ba-loo loo-ee loo-ee loo

After the wordless lilting come the words of comfort and assurance:

Ba - loo ba - lil - li, ba - loo ba - lil - li Ba - loo ba - lil - li, ba - loo    ba Gae a-

wa, pee-rie fai-ries, gae a - wa, pee-rie fai - ries Gae a - wa, pee-rie fai-ries fae    oor bairn noo

*(Buchan 1962)*

Baloo balilli, baloo balilli
Baloo balilli, baloo ba
Gae awa, peerie fairies, gae awa, peerie fairies
Gae awa, peerie fairies, fae oor bairn noo

Dan come boanie angels, ta wir peerie bairn
Dey'll sheen ower da cradle, o wir peerie bairn

Norman Buchan (1962) found this dreamy charm in *The Shetland Folk Book* vol. 1, which says it was 'noted by Mrs E.J. Smith, Sandness, Shetland, from her mother's singing'.

Some lyrics acknowledge the vulnerability of the infant, the lamb being a favourite image:

Baloo ma peerie lamb
Cuddle close to mammie
Mammie'll sing a bonny song
Ba ma prettie lambie

*(School of Scottish Studies archive: Neilson, Orkney, 1961)*

The best known lullaby expresses the dangers well, and one wonders how many small children have been alarmed to hear their mother inform a baby sibling that

> When the bough breaks, the cradle will fall
> Down will come baby, cradle and all

A fragment of the tragic ballad of 'Lord Randall', who is poisoned by his sweetheart, is turned through the folk process into a most alarming account of an infant informing its mother that its stepmother has killed it with a 'wee blue fish'.

Where hae ye been the livelong day, my wee little croodin doo?
I've been to see my stepmother, Mammy, mak my bed noo
And what did your stepmother give you to eat, my wee little croodin doo?
She gave me a wee blue fish, Mammy, mak my bed noo
And what did ye do to the bones of the fish, my wee little croodin doo?
I gave them to my wee wee dog, Mammy, mak my bed noo
And what did your dog when he'd eat of the bones, my wee little croodin doo?
He stretched his wee leggies and died, Mammy, as I do noo

This terrifying slur on stepmothers was collected by Lucy Broadwood in Sussex over ninety years ago, from a man who had learned it from his mother. She came from 'Glenfinlas and Glenbuckie, Braes of Balquidder'. The Cass-Beggs (1969) 'could not resist its charm and humour', though they felt 'it could not really be classified as a lullaby!' Moffat (1933) gives another version, guaranteed to terrify the wean into good behaviour, called 'Willie Doo'. Willie is fed a speckled trout caught among the heather hills, followed by another treat from his stepmother, who 'brewed some deadly hemlock stocks' for him to drink. Unsurprisingly, 'He turned his wee face to the wa, Willie's died now.'

Other 'lullabies' are reflections on the nature of motherhood, often complaining or lamenting. In 1960 traveller Lucy Stewart sang to American collector Ken Goldstein of a farmer's daughter who yearned for a baby and rocked her father's greyhound, singing 'If it wisnae fur your lang snoot, I wad gie you a pappie o.' Her tune is called 'The Rose Tree' or 'Johnnie's Grey Breeks'. There are many versions of this small song, but the 1960 recording is sweetly poignant, and it deserves its place at the start of the 2006 CD *Chokit on a Tattie*. Another version of the song, sung to the tune 'Cawdor Fair', changes the identity of the animal:

> Bonnie Jean o Fogieloan, she langed for a baby
> She took her father's grey cat and rowed it in a plaidie
> 'Hishie bishie bow row, lang leggies ow ow
> And twerna for your hairie mouthie I wad kiss you now now'
>
> *(Shuldham-Shaw et al. 2002, no. 1419A)*

Often a singer, adult or child, does not always attend closely to the full sense of the lyric they use. For a Stenness informant the dog becomes a father, changing the sense in a startling way.

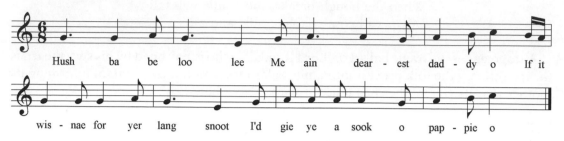

Hush ba be loo lee  Me ain dear-est dad-dy o  If it
wis-nae for yer lang snoot I'd gie ye a sook o pap-pie o

*(Transcription: McVicar; School of Scottish Studies archive, Neilson, 1961)*

> Hush ba be loo lee
> Me ain dearest daddy o
> If it wisnae for yer lang snoot
> I'd gie ye a sook o pappie o

*(School of Scottish Studies archive: Neilsen, Stenness, Orkney, 1961)*

This tune is the repeated first phrase of the reel 'The wind that shakes the barley'. 'Ba loo ma peerie lamb' above is sung to another version of this tune. In Chambers' 1842 version the girl thinks of offering not her breast, but a kiss:

> There was a miller's dochter
> She couldna want a babie oh
> She took her father's greyhound
> And rowed it in a plaidic oh
>
> Saying 'Hush-a-ba, hush-a-ba
> Hush-a-ba my babie oh
> An 'twere na for your lang beard
> Oh I wad kiss your gabbie oh'

Moffat, in *50 Traditional Scottish Nursery Rhymes*, gives the following Highland baloo to a 'Gaelic air', but its reminder of the high infant mortality rates of the past and savage incitement to rapine and cattle rustling seem hardly calculated to soothe the tiny breast. The complexity of the lyric suggests that it is an adult performance song made in the guise of a mother's comforter, like many to be found in Robert Ford's *Ballads of Bairnhood*.

Hee baloo, my sweet wee Donald
Picture o the great Clanronald
Thou'lt be chief o aa the clan
If thou art spared to be a man

Leeze me on thy bonnie craigie
An thou live thou'll lift a naigie
Travel the country through and through
And bring hame a Carlisle coo

Through the Lawlands, owre the Border
Weel, my babie, may thou further
Herry the louns o the laigh countree
Syne tae the Hielands hame to me

*(Moffat 1933)*

A more convincing lullaby-like approach to this theme is given in *Songs From David Herd's Mss* (Hecht 1904) and in *Nicht at Eeenie* (Shelmerdine & Greirson 1932).

Hey dan dilly dow, how den dan
Rich were your mither, gin ye were a man
Ye'd hunt and ye'd hawk, and keep her in game
And water your father's horse in the mill dam

Hey dan dilly dow, howden flowers
Ye'll lie in your bed till eleven hours
If at eleven hours ye list to rise
Ye'll get your dinner dicht in a new guise
Laverock's leg and titlin's tae
And aa sic dainties my mannie sall hae

In the *Greig–Duncan Folk Song Collection*, Vol. 8, several 'lullaby' lyrics seem to be fragments of adult songs. Two lyrics classified as lullabies are laments, one from a cuckolded husband, the other from an unmarried mother.

Hushie baa, ee-a-baa, naething to me ava
Hushie baa, ee-a-baa, baby lie still
Tho I'm nae your daddy, my wife she's your mammy
Oh wae's me she's gotten too much of her will

*(Shuldham-Shaw et al. 2002, no. 1559)*

And in the fine ballad lamenting the seductive charms of the ploo-boy lads, 'When I was nou but sweet sixteen', as sung memorably by Jeannie Robertson (Porter & Gower 1995), the last two verses utilise the North-Eastern version of hush-a-ba, 'heeshie-baw': 'Heeshie-baw, for ah'm yer maw, but the Lord kens fa's yer daddie.'

Next we have 'dandling and manipulation' songs. To dandle – to bounce the baby up and down – needs an accompanying rhythm, but there are very few rhymes specific to the purpose. There are more rhymes made for manipulating and naming the baby's digits and limbs, clapping its hands together and for other types of physical stimulation and amusement.

The best-known rhymes used to manipulate the fingers, hands, toes or body of the baby or infant are known throughout the English-singing world in standard texts, thanks to frequent printing in *Mother Goose* and her many offspring, so need no investigation here, though I have included a few I found in distinctively Scots garb.

Some examples of the standard ones I mean follow: for hands, 'Pat a cake, pat a cake, baker's man'; for hand and oxter, 'Round and round the garden like a teddy bear'; for toes, 'This little piggie went to market'. The latter is still instantly recognised when chanted in Shetland dialect:

> Dis peerie grice gaed tae market
> Dis peerie grice stayed at hame
> Dis peerie grice hed meat tae ate
> And dis peerie grice hed nane
> And dis peerie grice
> Said 'Wee wee wee wa a the wye hame'

> *(School of Scottish Studies archive: Neilsen, Lerwick, Shetland 1961)*

The Opies (1951) say the 'This little pig' version is 'the most common toe or finger rhyme in the present day'. Ramsay included a reference to it in Volume 4 of *The Tea-Table Miscellany* in 1740, but we cannot fairly claim it for Scotland: the language of it is too southern. The language of 'rhymes' used to name parts of the infant's body while touching them has more Scots.

> Brow brow brenty
> Ee ee winkey
> Nose nose nebbie
> Cheek cheek cherry
> Mou mou merrie
> Chin chin chackie
> Catch a flee, catch a flee

> *(Chambers, 1842)*

Or, if going up rather than down:

> Chin chappie
> Mou merry
> Nose nappie
> Cheek cherry
> Ee winkie
> Broo brinkie
> Ower the hills and awa

*(Rodger, nd)*

The fullest version, reported by the Opies in the *Oxford Dictionary of Nursery Rhymes* from oral collection in Scotland in 1944, goes from the toe to the top of the head. Versions of another rhyme for touching parts of the face, ending by the finger entering the infant's mouth, show the usual variation of remembered elements that typifies the oral process.

> Come ower the hillie
> Chap at the doorie
> Keek in
> Lift the sneck
> Dicht yer feet
> And walk in

*(Rodger, nd)*

The hillie is the crown of the head; the doorie is the forehead; keek in indicates peeping in the eyes; the sneck is the nose; the upper lip is used for dichting.

Do the little kids remember these later? Certainly not the baby lullabies and probably not much of the others. But they hear them employed for younger siblings, and the more maternally inclined eight year olds will use them. As with skipping and other action rhymes most of this material is known to and used by women. But some of the body manipulation pieces are used by men, e.g. 'This is the way the ladies ride', and father features frequently in lyrics.

'Dance to your daddy' has recently, through its use as the theme tune for a TV drama series, become exclusively associated with Newcastle-upon-Tyne. Here are Scots versions, which use it respectively as a manipulation song for the small male child, a lullaby for the baby and a menu to induce a small girl to entertain her father.

*(Transcription: McVicar from personal recollection, Glasgow 1950s)*

Dance to your daddie, my bonnie laddie
Dance to your daddie, my bonnie lamb
And ye'll get a fishie, in a little dishie
Ye'll get a fishie when the boat comes hame
And ye'll get a coatie, and a pair o breekies
Ye'll get a whippie and a supple Tam

*(Chambers 1842)*

*(Shuldham-Shaw et al. 2002, no. 1561)*

Hush-a-ba baby, dinna mak a din
And ye'll get a fishie when the boats come in

*(Shuldham-Shaw et al. 2002, no. 1561)*

Dance to your Daeddy, my bonnie leddy
Dance to your Daeddy, my bonnie lamb
An ye'll get a fishie in a little dishie
An a furly-giggie, an a souple Tam
An ye'll get a slicie o a dishie nicey
An a sweetie wiggie, an a mutton ham

*(Rymour Club 1928)*

*Nicht At Eenie* (Shelmerdine & Greirson 1932) gives a version that includes dance step directions:

> Dance to your Deddie, my bonnie leddie
> Jink through the reelie, jook round and wheelie
> Bob in the setting, my bonnie lamb

## Anthology: Lullabies, dandling and manipulation

*Lullabies*

> BA BA LAMMIE
> Ba ba lammie noo
> Cuddle doon tae mammie
> Trowies canna tak thoo
> Hushie ba lammie
> Me bonnie peerie bird
> Sleepin in me bosie
>
> *(Hendry & Stephen 1982: Orkney)*

> BA LAMB
> Ba lamb, ba lamb, beattie o
> Your mammy's away to the city o
> To buy a wee bit croby's skin
> To row about your feety o
>
> *(Maclagan 1901)*

> BALALOO LAMMY
> Now balaloo lammy, now baloo my dear
> Now balaloo lammy, ain mammie is here
> What ails my wee bairnie? What ails it this night?
> What ails my wee lammy? Is bairnie no right?
> Now balaloo lammy, now baloo my dear
> Does wee lammy ken that its daddie's no here?
> Ye're rockin fu sweetly on mammie's warm knee
> But daddy's a-rockin upon the saut sea
>
> *(Moffat 1933)*

BALOO LILLIE BEETIE
Baloo lillie beetie
Mammie's at the creetie
For tae plick an tae pu
For tae gather lammie's woo
For tae buy a bullie's skin
Tae rock wir bonnie bairnie in

*(Gossett, 1915: Orkney)*

THE BLACK DOUGLAS
Hush ye, hush ye, little pet ye
Hush ye, hush ye, dinna fret ye
The Black Douglas sall not get ye

*(Fraser 1975)*

Fraser notes 'These lines are from a lullaby said to have been sung to their children by women of the English garrisons during the War of Independence.'

CAN YE SEW CUSHIONS
O can ye sew cushions and can ye sew sheets?
And can ye sing Bal-lu-loo, when the bairn greets?
And hee and ba birdie, and hee and ba lamb
And hee and ba birdie, my bonnie wee lamb

Hee o, wee o, what would I do wi you?
Black's the life that I lead wi you
Owre mony o you, little for to gie you
Hee o, wee o, what would I do wi you?

*(Chambers 1842)*

This last was contributed by Burns to *The Scots Musical Museum* (Johnson 1797–1803). Chambers suggests that the change in rhythm and tune in the second verse shows the mother's anxiety for her other 'wee lambs', but it more likely shows that two distinct pieces have been welded together for adult performance. By the third edition of the *Museum* (1853) a second verse had been inserted that links this lullaby to various others in this section:

I've placed my cradle on yon holly top
And aye as the wind blows my cradle will rock
O hushaba, baby, o ba lillie loo
And hee and ba, birdie, my bonnie wee doo

Chambers (1842) also gives another, simpler air, from 'a manuscript collection of airs by the late Andrew Blaikie of Paisley', which may be the manuscript that Alfred Moffat drew on (see chapter 15).

HURR HURR DEE NOO
Hurr hurr dee noo, hurr hurr dee noo
Noo faa dee ower, my lammie
Hurr hurr dee noo, hurr hurr dee noo
Dere nane sall get my lammie
Hurr dee, hurr dee, mammie sall keep dee
Hurr dee, hurr dee, mammie is here

*(Hendry & Stephen 1982: Shetland)*

The authors say '"Hurr dee, hurr dee" refers to the whirr of the spinning wheel.'

HUSH-A-BA BABY LIE DOON
Hush-a-ba baby lie doon
Your mammy's awa tae the toon
And when she comes back ye'll get a wee drap
Hush-a-ba baby lie doon

*(Shuldham-Shaw et al. 2002, no. 1554)*

HUSHIE-BA, BURDIE BEETON
Hushie-ba, Burdie Beeton
Your mammie's gane to Seaton
For to buy a lammie's skin
To wrap your bonnie boukie in

*(Chambers 1842)*

HUSHABA BABIE, LIE STILL
Hushaba babie, lie still, lie still
Your mammie's awa to the mill, the mill
Babie is greeting for want of good keeping
Hushaba babie, lie still, lie still
Hushaba, babie, lie still and sleep
It grieves me richt sairly tae hear ye weep
Hee and ba lilliloo, down dilly dan
Sing hee and ba, birdie, my bonnie lamb

*(Moffat 1933)*

HUSH-A-BA BIRDIE, CROON
Hush-a-ba birdie, croon
The sheep are gane to the silver wood
And the coos are gane to the broom, broom
An it's braw milking the kye, kye
An it's braw milking the kye
The birds are singing, the bells are ringing
The wild deer come galloping by, by

Hush-a-ba birdie, croon, croon
Hush-a-ba birdie, croon
The gaits are gane to the mountain hie
And they'll no be hame till noon, noon

*(Chambers 1842; tune Moffat 1933)*

LOO LOOTIE LOO LAN
Loo lootie loo lan
Mammy's pet and daddy's hahn

*(Rymour Club 1911: Calder Ironworks, 1860s)*

A 'favourite lullaby'. The word 'hahn' is suggested to mean 'hen or cock'.

SLEEP BONNIE BAIRNIE
Sleep bonnie bairnie behind the castle
By! By! By! By!
Thou shalt have a golden apple
By! By! By! By!

*(Cass-Beggs 1969)*

The Cass-Beggs found this in AG Gilchrist's 1915 article, where it is titled 'Newcastle lullaby', but Gilchrist's informant learned it 'from her old Scotch nurse'.

### Dandling and manipulation

BA BIRDIE IN A BOG
Ba birdie in a bog
Doon amang a pickle fog
Ba birdie ran awa
An I socht him a day
And I fand him oot at last
Hidin in a craw's nest

An I took him by the powe
An I flang him owre the knowe
An tell'd him to rin hame
Cauld, wat an hungry wean

*(MacLennan 1909)*

The sequence and description of movements suggests to me a dandling rhyme. Surprisingly, it seems not to have been selected by the Opies. The Rymour Club (1911) has an 1830s or 1840s version, in which the birdie is found 'drookit in a wild-deuk's nest, and they bade it aye gang hame, cauld feet and hungry wame'.

BAIRN IN THE CRADLE
The bairn in the cradle, playin wi the keys
Tammy i the kailpot up tae the knees
Pussy at the fireside, sappin aa the brose
Doon fell a cinder an burnt pussy's nose

*(MacLennan 1909)*

THE BROO O KNOWLEDGE
Here's the broo o knowledge
Here's the ee o licht
Here's the bubbly ocean
Here's the pen knife
Here's the shouther o mutton
Here's the briest o fat
Here's the vinegar bottle
And here's the mustard caup

*(Rymour Club 1911: Forfar)*

Wilson (1993) gives

This is the bubbie gauger
This is the moo te bite

CHICKI NAIGIE
Up, Chicki Naigie, buy white breid
Tell the King the Cardinal's deid

*(Rymour Club 1919: Dunbar)*

'To a child dandled on nurse's knee or foot.'

CLAP CLAP HANDIES
Clap clap handies
Mammy's awa tee wall
Daddy's awa workin
For a new shawl

*(Rodger nd)*

Or

Clap clap handies
Mammie's wee wee ain
Clap clap handies
Daddie's comin hame
Hame till his wee bonnie
Wee bit laddie
Clap clap handies

*(Hendry & Stephen 1978)*

CLAPA CLAPA HANDIES
Clapa clapa handies, daddie's comin hame
Pennies in his pocket for a good wee wean

*(Margaret et al. early 1990s: West Lothian)*

DANCE A BABY DIDDY
Dance a baby diddy
What can mammie do wi ye?
Sit on her lap, give it some pap
And dance a baby diddy

*(Moffat 1933)*

DINGLE DINGLE GOWD BOW
Dingle dingle gowd bow
Up the water in a low
Far up i Ettrick
There was a waddin
Twa and twa pikin a bane
But I gat ane, my leefu-lane
Deuk's dub afore the door
There fell I
Aa the lave cried 'Waly waly'
But I cried 'Feigh, fye'

*(Chambers 1842: Perthshire)*

DIS IS DA WEY DA DOGS GAED
Dis is da wey da dogs gaed ta da hill
Aff a knowe and on a knowe
Dis is da wey da cats gaed ta da mill
Hame ageen, hame ageen spinnin spinnin

*(Saxby 1932: Shetland)*

The mother held the baby in her lap 'softly lifting one foot over the other'.

FEETIKIN FATIKIN
Feetikin fatikin fitikin tone
Lie wi me or lie i the loan

*(Rymour Club 1911)*

From Calder Ironworks in 1860s, a 'favourite lullaby'. 'A mother beating time with her infant's feet, one above the other in alternation.'

FETTIKEN FEETIKEN
Fettiken feetiken
When will ye gang?
When the nichts turn short
And the days turn lang
I'll toddle and gang, toddle and gang

*(Hendry & Stephen 1982)*

For 'working the feet'. See 'Wag a fit'.

HAILY PAILY
Haily Paily sits on the sands
Combs her hair with her lily-white hands

*(Rymour Club 1911: East Lothian)*

'Said by a mother when combing her child's hair.'

HEAT A WUMMLE
Heat a wummle, heat it weel
Bore it into Geordie's creel

*(Rymour Club 1911: from Bruce J Home)*

The finger is pointed at the fire, twirled at the little child, then 'bored' into its 'wame'.

I MAUN HAE MA GOUN MADE
It's I hae gotten a braw new goun
The colour o the moudiwort
I bade the tailyer mak it weel
An pit linin i the body o't
I bade the tailyer mak it weel
An pit linin i the body o't

I maun hae my goun made
Goun made, goun made
I maun hae my goun made
Like ony bigger lady

Side an wide aboot the tail
Side an wide about the tail
Side an wide about the tail
An jimp for my body

*(Rymour Club 1928)*

No. 1626 of the *Greig–Duncan Folk Song Collection* has 'ligger lady', or camp follower. One visualises the hands gently smoothing down the sides of the infant's dress, then making a sudden tickling grab at the little waist.

I GOT A LITTLE MANIKIN
I got a little manikin, I set him on my thoombiken
I saddled him, I bridled him, and sent him to the tooniken
I coffed a pair o garters to tie his little hosiken
I coffed a pocket-napkin to dight his little nosiken
I sent him to the garden to fetch a pund o sage
And fand him in the kitchen neuk kissing little Madge

*(Chambers 1842)*

There are many English versions. The Opies (1951) comment that 'Songs about impossibly small husbands are also popular in France.'

JOHN SMITH, FALLOW FINE
John Smith, fallow fine
Can you shoe this horse o mine?

Yes sir, and that I can
As weel as ony man
There's a nail upon the tae
To gar the pony speel the brae

There's a nail upon the heel
To gar the pony pace weel
There's a nail, and there's a brod
There's a horsie weel shod

*(Chambers 1842)*

Repeated while patting the baby's foot 'in various places'. A rhyme kent far and wide. One Aberdeenshire version includes a local setting on the 'hielan road' to Turra Town. (Shuldham-Shaw et al. 2002) That 'hielan road' verse seems drawn from a nine-verse poem by Robert Grant, born in Peterhead 1818. (Ford nd) It is unclear from the dates involved whether he created the initial verses or, far more likely and as Burns often did, expanded on an older collected item.

JOHNNIE NORRY
I'll tell you a story
Aboot Johnnie Norry
He gaed up twa stairs
And in at a wee doory

*(MacLennan 1909)*

MA MITHER'S KNIVES AND FORKS
There's ma mither's knives and forks
There's ma mither's table
There's ma sister's looking glass
And there's the baby's cradle
Rock, rock, bubbly-jock
Gies a piece an tracle

*(McVicar: St Geraldine's PS, Lossiemouth, 2006)*

THE MUIR O SKENE
There was a man i Muir o Skene
He had dirks, and I had nane
But I fell till'm wi my thoombs
And wat ye hoo I dirkit him, dirkit him, dirkit him

*(Rymour Club 1911)*

For 'dirking' the wean with your thumbs.

> PEEDIE PEEDIE
> Peedie Peedie
> Paddy Luddy
> Lady Whisle
> Lodey Whusle
> Great Odomonclod

*(Hendry & Stephen 1982: North Ronaldsay)*

Finger rhyme beginning with little finger.

> POUSSIKIE POUSSIKIE
> Poussikie poussikie wow
> Where'll we get banes to chow?
> We'll up the bog, and worry a hogg
> And then we'll get banes enow

*(Chambers 1842)*

Described as a 'Nonsense verse to sucklings.'

> TAM O MY BACK
> There was Tam o my back, an Tam i my lap
> An Tam o my knee, an Tam sookin me
> Tam fiddler, Tam piper, Tam wi the gleyt ee
> Tam here, Tam there, Tam o the lea

*(Shuldham-Shaw et al. 2002, no. 1632)*

There are ten Tams here, suggesting manipulation of fingers or toes.

> TEA'S IN THE POT
> Tea's in the pot, sugar in the cup
> Hi, Buckie Willie is your rhubarb up?

*(Sheena Wellington 1997)*

Wellington explains that this was 'sung while patting the back of a colicky infant to encourage it to bring up its wind (it works).'

> THIS IS THE MAN
> This is the man that brak the barn
> This is the man that stealt the corn

This is the man that run awa
This is the man that tell't aa
And puir Pirly Winkie paid for aa

(Chambers 1842)

Dis is da een at brük da barn
Dis is da een at stül da corn
Dis is da een at ran awa
Dis is da een at telled it aa
And dis is da peerie weerie winkie een
   at fell idda burn wi da hallow o
   straw, and peyed for aa

(Saxby 1932: Shetland)

THUMB BOLD
Thumb bold
Thibity-thold
Langman
Lickpan
Mamma's little man

(Hendry & Stephen 1982)

The authors say this is 'A finger count beginning with the thumb.'

TWA WEE DOGS
Twa wee dogs gaed awa tae the mill
Tae fecht aboot a lick o meal
The tane got a lick an the tither got nane
An the twa wee dogs cam toddlin hame

(Rymour Club 1911: Calder Ironworks, 1860s)

Twa peerie dogs, gaein to the mill
Trill trill trill
Tak a lick oot o this man's pock
An tak a lick oot the next man's pock
An tak a lick oot o tither man's pock
An hame again, hame again
Wiggly waggly, fill fill fill

(School of Scottish Studies archive:<br>Neilsen, Stenness, Orkney, 1961)

WAG A FIT
Wag a fit, wag a fit, whan wilt thou gang?
Lantern days when they grow lang
Harrows will hap and ploughs will bang
And every auld wife tak the tether by the tap
And worry worry worry till her heid fa in her lap

*(Rymour Club 1928: Dumfriesshire)*

The informant says this was said 'To a young child just about the walking stage.' See 'Fettiken feetiken'.

WAMIE TO WAMIE
Wamie to wamie, handie to back
Breestie to mouie, clap airsie clap

*(Rymour Club 1911: from Rev. W Findlay of Saline)*

Said 'to a child at the breast'. But in Finlay's own notes in the Rymour Club papers (1904–7) on the verse, line two begins 'Raw flesh to mouie'.

THE WAY THE LADIES RIDE
This is the way the ladies ride
Jimp an sma, jimp an sma
This is the way the gentlemen ride
Spurs an aa, spurs an aa
An this is the way the cadgers ride
Creels an aa, creels an aa
Dogs at their heels crying 'Bouf bouf bouf'

*(MacLennan 1909)*

The child is sat and bounced on the knee or on the foot while held by the hands.

The lady goes to market
Trit trit trit
The gentleman goes to market
Trot trot trot
But the farmer goes to market
Trit-trot, trit-trot, trit-trot

*(McVicar: Kilbarchan, 1920s)*

I learned this version in childhood from my father, who learned it in his childhood.

WHAT WILL WE ROW
What will we row his wee feetie in
His wee feetie in, his wee feetie in
What will we row his wee feetie in
In the cauld nights o winter?

Row them in a rabbit-skin
A rabbit-skin, a rabbit-skin
Row them in a rabbit-skin
In the cauld nights o winter

*(School of Scottish Studies archive:*
*Henderson from Joshua Shaw, Glasgow, 1957)*

# 3
# Coulter's Candy

## Lullaby, dandling, skipping or advertising?

> Here comes Coulter doon the street
> A big lum hat upon his heid
> He's been roon aboot aa the toon
> Singin an sellin candy

Some rhymes I have included in the anthology section for dandling were also used for play by older children, and for a few the texts suggest to me that their use was to dandle but my sources list them only as 'some rhymes'. What is now one of the best-known Scottish children's songs is widely thought of as a lullaby or as a body manipulation song, but it was made from earlier traditional elements by an adult as an advertising jingle.

'Coulter's candy' now ties with 'Ye canny shove yer grannie' for the title of the single best-known Scots children's song. However, until it was published with tune in 1960 in a weekly Scots newspaper, then commercially recorded, it was little remembered.

In late 1998 a phone enquiry to the School of Scottish Studies was referred to me. The English enquirer had first asked to be put into communication with either Marjorie Kennedy Fraser or Francis Collinson, but sadly neither of them was still with us. I felt honoured to be considered any substitute for two such eminent authorities, but I also quickly checked my pulse, just in case.

I had been nominated because the query had to do with a Scots children's song, 'Coulter's candy'. A Japanese TV company was seeking information on Coulter: was he still alive, where did he live, could they interview him? I thought their chances of an interview were fairly poor. I looked up the usual sources, beginning of course with Collinson (1966) himself and his *The Traditional and National Music of Scotland*. He described the song as a 'specimen of children's folk-song [. . .] which concerns itself with the Peeblesshire "sweetie" that was cried in the streets of the Border towns in the late years of the last century, and which has more recently become popular on the radio'. His version runs

Al - lie bal - lie  al - lie bal - lie bee  Sit - tin  on  your  mam - my's knee

Greet - in  for  an - oth - er baw - bee  To  buy some Coul - ter's  can - dy

*(Collinson 1966)*

> Johnnie Scott was awfu thin
> His banes were stickin through his skin
> Noo he's got a double chin
> Wi eatin Coulter's candy
>
> Allie ballie allie ballie bee
> Sittin on your mammy's knee
> Greetin for another bawbee
> To buy some Coulter's candy

I remembered Norman Buchan had a substantial number of verses in *101 Scottish Songs,* and more useful information:

> Ally bally, ally bally bee
> Sittin on yer mammy's knee
> Greetin for anither bawbee
> Tae buy mair Coulter's Candy
>
> Ally bally, ally bally bee
> When you grow up you'll go to sea
> Makin pennies for your daddy and me
> To buy mair Coulter's Candy
>
> Mammy, gie me ma thrifty doon
> Here's auld Coulter comin roon
> Wi' a basket on his croon
> Selling Coulter's Candy
>
> Little Annie's greetin tae
> Sae whit can poor wee Mammy dae
> But gie them a penny atween them twae
> Tae buy mair Coulter's Candy

> Poor wee Jeannie's lookin affa thin
> A rickle o banes covered ower wi skin
> Noo she's gettin a double chin
> Wi sookin Coulter's Candy

Buchan (1962) noted that

This song probably produced more correspondence than any other when I printed it in *The Weekly Scotsman* a few years ago. Robert Coltart, the Coulter of the song – made and sold his own candy round all the country fairs and markets in the Borders. Correspondents have described his arrival in a town with his 'big lum hat, his candy, and his song'. I first learned the song as having only two verses and I added another which now seems to have been absorbed into the song. Another, but imperfect, verse from a correspondent seems to give the best description of all:

> Here comes Coulter doon the street
> A big lum hat upon his heid
> He's been roon aboot a the toon
> Singin an sellin candy

Buchan 'first heard it from Scots actor, playright and folk-singer Roddy McMillan'.

Within a few weeks of the initial *Weekly Scotsman* appearance of the song, a noted Scottish folk group leader had recorded the song, including Buchan's new verse, and claimed all the copyright payments. I believe the new verse was the one about 'going to sea'. However, I'll later on show a connection between 'Coulter's candy' and a song about a sailor.

From Norman Buchan I had a new spelling of the name, and a county. Lastly I tried AS Fraser (1975): 'Robert Coltart, the 'Coulter' of the song, made his celebrated candy, flavoured with aniseed, in Melrose and sold it there and in Galashiels. He travelled round all the country fairs and markets in the Borders. Children used to troop after him as if he was a Scottish Pied Piper. He died in 1890 and is still remembered.'

I gathered up reference information about Melrose and contacted the London connection for the Japanese TV company. I found that they were engaged in the making of a series of half hour programmes on 'Lullabies of the world'. Their scriptwriter had encountered 'Coulter's candy' on some disc, and, on the strength of no more than the words of the song, flights and hotel rooms had been booked. They wanted more information about Coltart, were still hoping to interview some elderly person who remembered him, and visualised a scene in which 'A mother with a baby in arms sings the lullaby while father watches over'.

I agreed to do some more research. I drove down to Melrose, bought books on local history, talked to the local primary school about participation in the programme, took photos and generally did a large lump of work.

What about the word 'candy'? I had thought this was American terminology, not Scots?

The *Scottish National Dictionary* said that in Scotland the word candy is used in combinations which are not found in southern England: candybob, candy-broad sugar, candibrod, candy-glue, candyman, candy-rock. They quoted Jamieson's suggestion that the term and the article must have been imported from the Low Countries, since they make *kandy* in Belgium. French has *candir*, to grow white after boiling, applied to sugar. In Arabic *Qandi* means crystallised sugar. The word sugarcandy occurs in Aberdeen, Angus, Fife and near Roxburgh. So, a reasonable Scots ancestry exists for the word candy.

Down in the Borders again, I went to see what the Scottish Borders Archive and Local History Centre, based in St Mary's Mill, Selkirk, could tell me. First they produced a substantial book about the surname, *'A Coulhard!': The History of a Surname*, by Alfred J Coulhard. The family was said to have moved to Niddersdale from Cumberland in the sixteenth century. The author wrote of 'Robert Coltart of Melrose, a colourful travelling man. Once a weaver, then a wandering hawker. Possibly based Melrose, dying Galashiels 23/4/1880, aged 45.'

He quoted another verse, a very attractive one.

> Willie grat baith lang an sair
> Till he got a penny to ware
> Noo he's tumblin doon the stair
> To buy Colter's candy

Coulhard had found this verse in a book called *The Cleikum, being interesting reminiscences of Old Innerleithen*, by John A Anderson, published in 1933 by the *Border Telegraph* in Galashiels and drawn from a weekly column in the paper. *The Cleikum* was also on the Selkirk shelves. In addition to the above verse about Willie, Anderson gives all the verses printed by Norman Buchan (except for the seagoing one, hence my deduction that this was created by Buchan), though the texts vary in detail.

Anderson had seen Coltart and describes him as follows: 'He wore a tam o shanter or was it a Balmoral bonnet? With a pheasant's feather sticking straight up from a buckle above his ear. A shiny black bag slung over his shoulder held his stock of the famous candy.' Coltart 'adopted daft methods to increase his sale. The opening nonsensical lines of 'Alla Balla' were sufficient to bring out all the prospective customers within sound of his voice, and long before he reached his fourth verse he had the bairns of the village gathered round him.'

In another book, *Guid Auld Galashiels,* Margaret Lawson of Galashiels said 'Another old worthie in the town was called Colter. He rose very early in the morning and was always on the watch for the late comers on their way to the factory some time after 6 am. He sold candy and whenever he saw them coming he would rush forward and hand out a piece of his candy rock, singing

> Colter rises every morning
> Never gie's his wife a warning
> Doon the toon at six o'clock
> Who'll buy my candy rock?'

Wait a minute, was Coulter/Colter/Coltart a Melrose man or a Galashiels guy?

The Archive Centre staff answered this, finding Robert Coltart in the 1870 Galashiels Census. Robert Coltart, a weaver aged thirty-eight, lived at 48 Overhaugh Street, with his wife Mary (thirty-six) and their children: Agnes (eighteen) a birler; Betsy (fourteen) a yarn winder, Maggie (five) and Barbara (three). Coltart was born in Kirkcudbrightshire, his wife and all the children but Maggie in Selkirk. Maggie had been born in Innerleithen. I looked up the *Galashiels Almanac and Trade Directory* of 1880, which listed him in Henderson's Close under Confectioners and Fruiterers.

So I was led to the 1880 Census, which said that living in one room with a window at Henderson's Close were Mary Coltart, widow and woollen warp winder, Margaret (fifteen) a heddle maker, Barbara (thirteen) a scholar and Robert (nine) a scholar, plus a boarder called Margaret Ross (forty-six), another woollen warp winder, born in Kelso. All five of them in one room.

Then the Archive Centre surpassed themselves and produced not one but two obituaries for Robert Coltart:

### DEATH OF A PUBLIC CHARACTER

People resident in the towns and villages over the south-east of Scotland will hear with surprise of the sudden death of Coltart, the eccentric candyman, who for some years back had made himself such a conspicuous and well-known figure on public occasions. He died on Wednesday night, after a brief illness, of disease of the brain. A *post mortem* examination was made, when a tumour of considerable size was found on the right side of the head near to the base of the brain. It had been there for some years, and was sufficient to account for the eccentricities of conduct and peculiarity of character which marked Coltart's life in later years. In some respects Coltart was a very remarkable character. Apart from the grotesque figure he cut, there was considerable force of character about him, combined with a large amount of shrewdness and cleverness. It is not everybody that is able to set all the children from Peebles to Berwick, and from Dalkeith to Dumfries, a-singing of a new nursery rhyme, and many of the elder folks made to wonder at 'candy' verses which had both sense and sweetness in them; and the author of 'alli, alli, lalli balli be' will be missed by thousands.

(*Southern Reporter*, 29 April 1880)

I noted with no little alarm the lyric quotation 'alli, alli, lalli balli be'. Could it be the newspaper got it right, and everyone else since has it wrong?

COLTART THE CANDYMAN

This well-known Borderer and frequenter of most of the places of public resort has somewhat unexpectedly been cut down, and his remains were buried on Sabbath last in the burial ground of the town in which he has for a long time resided. Coltart, however . . . hailed from Rhondhouse, or, as it is provincially termed in Galloway, *Ronus* . . . There is not a Border town but will feel the blank on gala or market days, when his whistle or his song seemed to electrify and enliven every one. Coltart's mirth had specially charming attractions for the 'bairns', who seemed heartily to agree with the author of the melodies that there was 'naething like the candy' as the infallible antidote to all their ailments.

(*Kelso Chronicle*, 30 April 1880)

The house where the family lived in 1880, at Henderson's Close, is no longer there. In Coltart's time there were only three houses in the close, but later there were eighteen houses. Number 1 was occupied by Thos Henderson, master carpenter. He had one new apprentice, George Meikle Kemp, who was given a lift to work on his first day by Sir Walter Scott, who was passing in his carriage. Kemp eventually designed and created the mighty Sir Walter Scott Monument in Princes Street, Edinburgh.

I was able to visit the house at 48 Overhaugh Street where the family lived in 1870. It now holds offices, and the kitchen range where he would have made his aniseed flavoured candy has gone.

The Japanese TV company filmed the site of Coltart's Galashiels grave and went home. Galashiels was said to be excited about a famous son they didn't know they had. A newspaper report said official discussion had begun on how to initiate the making and marketing of Coulter's Gala Candy.

I remained interested in the song and began to find links to others, such as the following verse from *Walkin' The Mat: Past Impressions of Aberdeen*, compiled by Andrew Cluer with help from Stanley Robertson:

> Mummy, gie us a penny doon
> Here's a manny comin roun
> Wi a basket on his croon
> Selling okey pokey

Did the 'Coulter's candy' tune hold any clues? It is one of a family of tunes which include the well known 'Johnny Todd'; its Scots version, 'Johnnie Johnston'; 'Whistle o'er the lave o't'; 'The hills of Connemara' and a song used to help teach the alphabet. The tune shares its initial phrase with 'Twinkle twinkle little star'.

AS Fraser (1975) says 'Surnames of the actual players were used' in

Mrs Johnstone lives ashore
With a knocker on her door
When a sailor comes ashore
He knocks at Mrs Johnstone's door

'The girl with the surname Johnstone joined the girl in front, who was presumably the sailor, and they swung round together while the other girls sang'

Alla balla alla balla bee
Alla balla A B C
Alla balla alla balla bee
Married to a sailor

The words as well as the tune lead us to the Scots song 'Johnnie Johnston'.

John - nie John-ston's ta'en a no - tion For to go and sail the sea

He has left his own true lo - ver Wee - ping by the wil - low tree

*(Rymour Club 1911)*

Johnnie Johnston's ta'en a notion
For to go and sail the sea
He has left his own true lover
Weeping by the willow tree

I will buy you beads and earrings
I will buy you diamonds free
I will buy you silks and satins
Bonnie lassie, marry me

What care I for beads and earrings
What care I for diamonds free
What care I for silks and satins
When my love's forsaken me?

*(Rymour Club 1911)*

Norman Buchan (1962) gives a version from *Kerr's Guild Of Play* in which the girl weeps 'on the Greenock Quay'. The *Greig–Duncan Folk Song Collection* (Shuldham-Shaw et al. 2002) has a first verse which provides another part of the link between Sailor Johnnie and Coltart the Candyman:

> Johny Johnstone took a notion
> For to sail across the sea
> Then he left his own dear (Minnie)
> Greetin on her mammy's knee

*(Shuldham-Shaw et al. 2002, no. 1583A)*

As does Maclagan (1901):

> Hullaballa, hullaballa, sitting on his mother's knee
> Crying for a wee bawbee to get some sugar-candy
> My wee lad's awa to sea, he'll come back and marry me
> Silver buckles on his knee, my wee lad's a sailor

This in turn of course links to the song 'Bobby Shafto':

> Bobby Shafto's gone to sea
> Silver buckles on his knee
> He'll come back and marry me
> Bonnie Bobby Shafto

*(McVicar from personal recollection:*
*Dingwall, 1940s, learned in school)*

In 1824 Sir Walter Scott in *Redgauntlet* quotes what he calls an 'old Northumbrian ditty', although we know how these songs wander back and forth over county and national lines:

> Willy Foster's gone to sea
> Siller buckles at his knee
> He'll come back and marry me
> Canny Willie Foster

How these little couplets have interwoven and interbred! The Liverpool version of this song, 'Johnny Todd', became famous when the tune was used for a black and white TV cop show called *Z Cars*. The Liverpool version was collected by Kidson and printed in 1891. It begins

John-ny Todd he took a no-tion For to go a-cross the sea

And he left his love be-hind him Weep-ing by the Li-ver-pool sea

*(Kidson 1891)*

> Johnny Todd he took a notion
> For to go across the sea
> And he left his love behind him
> Weeping by the Liverpool sea

*(Kidson 1891)*

Kidson says 'The words appear old, though some blanks caused by the reciter's memory have had to be filled up'. The Opies give a version from Washington DC in 1886, and Alice Gomme in 1898 gave versions from Fochabers, Laurieston and Perth. In Maclagan's Tullynessle version of 'Glasgow Ships' the boy is named as 'Jamie Tod'. So, the Scottish antecedents are well entrenched. Frank Shaw (1970) says that a Johnny Todd was hanged in a Liverpool gaol just before Kidson's 1891 date – whatever that proves. Frank Shaw says that in 1970 the tune was 'a sort of Scouseport anthem' being played 'weekly at Everton football games'. The Opies (1985) refer to 'the belief that children customarily skip to it in the streets of Liverpool. Several attempts to collect it from children [in Liverpool] have, however, failed.'

And anyway, if Scots author Neil Munro is to be believed, the song was, in the 1870s, 'very popular on gabbarts [shallow draught sailing vessels] before the steam puffer came in', and the chorus was

> Young Munro he took a notion
> For to sail across the sea
> And he left his true love weeping
> All alone on Greenock Quay

*(Para Handy)*

As with George MacDonald Fraser's account of the regimental origins of 'Auntie Mary Had A Canary' detailed later, one cannot rely on authors. The 'Greenock Quay' song is given on page one of the first story about master mariner Para Handy, and the appearance of the author's own name in the lyric – he began to publish these stories in 1905 under the pseudonym Hugh Fowlis – suggests a clue planted for the knowledgable reader of the *Glasgow Evening News* as to the writer's identity. Another literary connection stirs the dustcloud higher. Scots poet and tragedian William McGonagall wrote a poem, published in 1890, 'Young Munro the Sailor', that clearly works off Para Handy's song, locating it in Dundee and in fourteen turgid verses testing the girl's faithfulness to her absent swain. Unusually for McGonagall all ends happily.

While tunes related to Robert Coltart's rhymes were easy to trace, his descendants proved more elusive. The only information I had found about his five children – Agnes, Betsy, Margaret, Barbara, and Robert – was that one of the girls married Robert Pearson and that couple emigrated to Winnipeg, Canada. There are no Coltarts in the Borders phone book now, but there are several in the Edinburgh and Lothians phone book. In 2006 I mentioned my work on this book to the daughter of Hettie Smyth, joint owner of Blastoff Books, a children's bookshop in Linlithgow. I was startled to learn that Hettie's husband, Sid, was on his mother's side a grandson of Coltart, through Barbara Coltart. Although Coltart was referred to in the Smyth family as the 'Candy Man', they knew little of him till I supplied gratefully received copies of a draft of this chapter and the census information.

# 4
# *Caw the ropey*

## Skipping, ball-bouncing, clapping

> Bluebells, duma-duma shells
> Eavy, ivy, over
> Charlie Chaplin went to France
> To teach the ladies how to dance
> First the heel and then the toe
> Then you do big birlie o
> Big birlie o

The types of rhymes given in the following anthology section are sung or chanted while skipping with ropes, bouncing one or more balls with synchronised movements or hand clapping with one or more partners. There is much purposeful activity to be seen in the playground, with cooperation, elements of performance and the need to develop and demonstrate coordination skills. Are the rhymes central? No, they are an aid, support and accompaniment.

Ask a child what songs they sing in the playground and the response will be puzzled denial that they ever sing there, or a rendition of a recent pop song, or what they have been learning in class or are practising for the school show. Sing them a few of the lyrics in this book, especially 'A sailor went to sea', then ask what other ones like that they use for playing and you will begin to learn. Responses will be slow to start with: the words are so allied to movement and the outside environment.

When I asked a class in plush Bearsden in 1992 for songs I got a surprisingly good response, but after the bell had gone four girls gathered round me, remembering more. As they excitedly shared, each unconsciously put a hand into a pocket, brought out and held as an aide memoire her string of rubber bands linked together to make 'Chinese ropes'. In that school at that time the rhymes were being used to assist rhythmic movements as the ropes were twined round two pairs of feet and intricate footwork entangled then disentangled them. At other times the physical reminder could have been a ball or rope, or the instinctive movement of clapping hands.

The pieces I give in this anthology section are not exclusively used for any play purpose. Many given under the current heading are or have been also used for performance purposes. Equally, many, many songs and rhymes given under later headings, particularly Performance and Narrative, have been reported in use for rope, ball or clapping games.

While researching for this book I found skipping back in favour in many playgrounds. Rather than being passed on by older children, it is more likely another revival, the use of ropes and ways of skipping and singing having been reintroduced by teachers or travelling 'fitten up our kids' projects. It is perhaps most likely of all, I think, that it was non teaching staff playground supervisors who reached back to their own childhood and shared their lore with the kids. If so, it was the child inside the adult passing knowledge and expertise on to the child in the playground.

In 1951 Alan Lomax interviewed teacher and author JTR Ritchie and pupil Peggie MacGillivray, both of Norton Park School in Edinburgh, and asked about skipping.

Ritchie said 'Now "bumps" means this: that the rope passes twice and the girl's feet are up in the air and when we made this film, you know she actually is in the air.' Alan Lomax asked 'Well, you go up to four times if you're good, don't you, Peggy?' Peggy replied, 'You can do more than four . . . They can't keep up very long but I've seen them up to about seven or eight.'

Then Lomax asked about kinds of skipping: 'French, the German and the Dutch and oh, there's lots and lots of them. Some people give different names for ones – there's usually an argument which one's which.' She described French skipping. 'It's two ropes – you hold one in each hand. There's two people, one at each end. You hold these two ropes and then one turns round. When the one's coming down the other's coming up over the top. It's hard to describe, but that's it.'

Lomax asked 'And what about the Dutch?'

'That's the opposite: it's out the way instead of in.'

'And the German?'

'One rope along the ground and the other rope coming over and the person mustn't jump on the rope on the ground: they must keep going over, back and forward over the rope and still jumping through this rope that's coming over.'

'And then there are all sorts of different ways of doing each one of those, I guess.'

'Uh-huh.'

(This interview material is drawn from *Singing in the Streets*.)

I quote the above to show why in this book I do not investigate games in all their rich complexity. Many books have been written on aspects of movement and use of things in children's play. I have enough to say just about the lyrics used. The 1951 film *The Singing Street*, made by Ritchie and two fellow Norton Park teachers and still available to view, shows some of the ways rope and ball can be used. There are no hand-clapping games in the film. The Opies (1985) tell that 'the fashion for hand-clapping seems to have reached a peak during the late nineteenth century and up to the First World War'. Then it became rare, till 'the wave of sparkling and spirited chants came over from America', a few of them featuring in commercial Hit Parade recordings.

I have in this anthology section subdivided rhymes by lyric subject: characters, courting, movements and others. Here I'll look at a few families of lyrics linked to type of play use.

Quote the first line of a kids' song, and people may answer 'Oh, I know that one.' Never accept this, if you want to expand your knowledge. Say 'But what comes next?' Consider the following. I say 'One two three aleerie'. Do you continue:

> One, two, three, aleerie
> Four, five, six, aleerie
> Seven, eight nine, aleerie
> Ten, aleerie, postman

Or do you say

> One, two, three aleerie
> I spy Mrs Clearie
>    (or Mrs Peerie, or Jean McLearie,
>    or Jock McClearie)
> Sitting on her bumaleerie
> Eatin chocolate babies (or chocolate biscuits)

Or even, if you are old enough, what children in Craigmillar, Edinburgh, played to in 1954:

> One, two, three, aleerie
> I saw Wallace Beery
> Sitting on his bumaleerie
> Kissing Shirley Temple

*(School of Scottish Studies archive:*
*Henderson, Craigmillar, 1954)*

Mind you, if you are the right age you might sing with the kids of Glenrothes in 1981:

> One, two, three, aleerie
> I saw Tom Baleerie
> Sitting on his bumaleerie
> Kissing Margaret Thatcher

*(School of Scottish Studies archive:*
*Hendry, Glenrothes, 1981)*

If you thought of the number sequence, do you finish line four with 'postman', or with 'over ball' as I recall from childhood, or even make line four 'Early in the morning'?

If you do remember the 'postman' version, can you continue with 'Open the gate and let him in, sir'? Or do you remember the verses that contain ball-bouncing or rope-jumping instructions, abandoning the aleerie word?

One, two, three, a leggie
Four, five, six, a leggie
Seven, eight, nine, a leggie
Ten, a leggie, overboard

Followed by some containing the following: a clappie, a bluebottley, a whirly, a wallie, a stampie, front britches, back britches, Gibralter, big birley. If you do – what on earth kind of a movement was 'a bluebottley'?

There are other ways 'One, two, three, aleerie' can proceed. A group of pensioners in Castlemilk, Glasgow, sang a surprising stanza commenting on gender roles:

One, two, three, aleerie
Hand me a whip tae I spin ma peerie
Oh I cannae spin ma peerie
I wish I wis a laddie

*(Ma Maw Says* late 1980s)

Elsewhere in Glasgow the name element can become

One, two, three, a-leerie
My husband's name is Harry
If you think it's necessary
Look it up in the dictionary

In Strichen in 1960 'bumaleerie' was turned into basket cheerie (chairie), the old type of invalid's wheelchair. Or, maybe the basket cheerie came first and was subverted into bumaleerie?

Here is a more extended example, decribed by Eleanor Locke (1981) as an 'Anglo-American ball bouncing rhyme collected from children in Santa Cruz, California, in 1978'.

One, two, three O'Leary, I saw little Mary
Sitting on a dromedary, eating choc'late fishes

One, two, three O'Leary, I saw little Mary
Sitting on a basketery eating jelly babies

One, two, three O'Leary, I saw little Mary
Sitting on a missionary eating ladies' fingers

One, two, three O'Leary, I saw little Mary
Sitting in a cemetery eating plastic flowers

Shortly before I found the above, which – with its clever wordplay suggestive of the use of a rhyming dictionary – feels as if it has been reworked by an adult hand, I was expounding to Mark Trewin, a music lecturer in the University of Edinburgh, on the near total absence of versions of 'One two three aleerie' in England. His mother-in-law happened to overhear us and told me of a ball-bouncing verse she had learned as a London evacuee in Gorse Island, Wales, in 1940, from other London evacuees. Her tune was not the one I have heard used in Scotland.

> One, two, three, alairie
> My ball's down the airay
> Don't forget to give it to Mary
> Not to Charlie Chaplin

(McVicar Collection: Edinburgh 1998)

Other repronunciations turn up in literature. Frank Shaw (1970) reports a Liverpool verse that rhymes 'a leara' with 'Anty Sarah' and 'bumalaira'. In Leila Berg's autobiographical *Flickerbook* (1997) she recalls singing of her Auntie Clara 'sitting on a pomdelara' and ponders pomdelara, suggesting it is 'one of those big fat round things with a belt round the middle'. There are lots of us about.

The meaning and ancestry of 'aleerie' is startling. The word 'leerie' is defined in the *Scottish National Dictionary* as 'A child's word for bouncing a ball under one leg . . . Orig. echoic.' The dictionary goes on to suggest a possible association with the sung syllables used to teach bagpipe tunes. Indeed, the invariable Scottish tune for 'One two three aleerie' is the second strain of the popular Gaelic song 'Chan 'eil mo leannan ann a' seo'. But the latter tune is also used for a Scots 'night visiting' song that begins 'Ah'm the laird o Windy Wa's, and ah've come here withoot a cause'. Scots or Gaelic, which used the tune first?

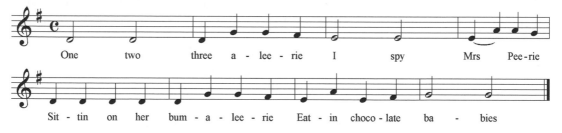

(Transcription: McVicar; Ma Maw Says late 1980s)

*(Transcription: McVicar from personal recollection, Glasgow 1950s;
tune: 'Chan 'eil mo leannan ann a' seo')*

Other dictionaries give meanings for 'leerie' to do with Edinburgh lamplighters or untrustworthy types in general, but not anything to do with bending the knee to bounce a ball under it.

However, an American scholar, Sister Mary Jeremy, has pointed out (reported in Knapp and Knapp 1976) that 'O'Leary', spelled 'a-lery', is found in a 1370 manuscript of *Piers Plowman*. 'Somme liede here leggis a-lery, as such losellis cunne' (some made their legs crooked, as such losers will). The sturdy beggars at the town gate held their legs crooked to suggest they were disabled. Aleerie seems a true archaic survival, held only within a children's song. The rhyme is still in use for skipping in West Lothian schools:

> One, two, three, aleerie
> Four, five, six, aleerie
> Seven, eight nine, aleerie
> Ten, aleerie, Welshman

*(McVicar: Springfield After Care, Linlithgow, 2007)*

One of the most famous children's rhymes is also claimed for antiquity, without proper grounding. People have often recounted (with a straight face) how 'Ring a ring a roses' is a memory of the Great Plague.

> Ring a ring a roses
> A pocket full of posies
> Tishoo tishoo
> We all fall down

Apparently people went around with a ring of roses around their neck, and when the smell of the plague overcame the rose scent they stuck their noses into their pockets where they kept a reserve supply of strong medicinal herbs. But if they sneezed at all – they died. Or else, a series of red marks appeared on your body, as a symptom of the illness. If the red marks met in a ring around your waist, the sap stopped rising in your body and – you died. Well, it might be true.

How likely is it? The Opies (1985) say 'We ourselves have had to listen so often to this interpretation we are reluctant to go out of the house.' They then carefully, politely and thoroughly demolish the notion, saying it 'has not been found in the work of any commentator before the Second World War'.

Ring a ring of ros-es,    Cup a cup of shells The   dog's a-way to Ham-il-ton To   buy a new bell

*(Transcription: McVicar from personal recollection, Glasgow 1950s)*

There are of course Scottish 'Ring a ring a roses' relatives. In Argyllshire 100 years ago the girls played 'Cheeses' by whirling round on the spot so their long skirts would fill out with air, then sinking down suddenly so the skirts made the shape of a cheese. As they played they sang

> Roon, roon rosie, Cappie, Cappie shell
> The dog's away tae Campbeltown tae buy a new bell
> If ye'll no tak it I'll tak it mysel
> Roon, roon rosie, Cappie, Cappie shell

*(Maclagan 1901)*

The lyric for this game of making a round object is full of round shapes – a rose, a shell, a bell, and cappie means 'cup-shaped'. In Edinburgh a few years later they sang

> Ring a ring of roses, Cup a cup of shells
> The dog's away to Hamilton, To buy a new bell . . .

*(Rymour Club 1919; tune McVicar from personal recollection, Glasgow, 1950s)*

In more modern Glasgow times the dog's task falls to another: 'The duck's away to Hamilton to buy a new bell.' (Sinclair 1986) The puzzling 'cappie cappie shell' and 'cup a cup a shell' look like 'nonsense', but we can choose to seek a sensible source from which children more interested in the game than in the words might have derived such a phrase, then garbled it. Our old friend Chambers (1842) provides a source, used to tease 'the presumedly prettiest young maiden of the party'.

> I ken something that I'll no tell
> Aa the lasses o our town are cruppen in a shell
> Except the Flower o (Hamilton), and she's cruppen out
> And she has a wee bairn, wi a dish-clout [etc.]

'Cruppen in a shell' means creeping in a shell like a snail. Chambers says the above is a Lanarkshire version, and gives also one from Berwickshire:

> I've found something that I'll no tell
> Aa the lads o our town clockin in a shell
> Aa but (Willie Johnson) and he's cruppen out
> And he will have (Susie Kerr) without ony doubt [etc.]

This time the lads are clucking in their shells like hens. Both of these rhymes go on to develop a narrative. The Lanarkshire rhyme tells of what happens to the bairn, the Berwickshire rhyme tells of the courtship, which includes the boy paring the girl's nails. The above rhymes raise a number of interesting little puzzles meandering off in directions tangential to the 'Ring a roses' quest, which is already complex enough, so I have omitted all but the first four lines of each.

Chambers gives another rhyme, this time used when waving a lighted stick before an infant to distract it from some upset, creating the appearance of 'a semicircle of red fire before the child's eyes'. This 'fireside phenomenon' is called a 'dingle dousy'.

> Dingle, dingle dousy
> The cat's at the well
> The dog's awa to Musselburgh
> To buy the bairn a bell

> Greet, greet, bairnie
> An ye'll get a bell
> If ye dinna greet faster
> I'll keep it to mysel

This rhyme manages to combine elements of 'Ding dong dell, pussie's in the well' with our 'bell' lines. Mactaggart (1824) gives different words, about a lousy cat and flea-ridden dog. *The Oxford Dictionary of Nursery Rymes* (Opie & Opie 1951) offers another version from an 1805 manuscript, which sends the dog off to Bellingen – a more likely place by far to find a bell foundry?

In more modern times in Edinburgh we get

> Clap-a-clap-a-handies
> Mammie's at the well
> Daddie's away to London
> To buy wee baby a bell

(Ritchie 1965)

We began with Maclagan, in Argyllshire, and end with another couplet reported by him that ties all these variants up into a tangle:

> I ken something, I'll not tell
> All the birdies in the town cam to ring the bell

I sometimes suspect all the birdies in Scotland must sing their songs a little differently from each other, just for the individuality of it. Certainly the kids in different parts of Scotland manage to vary the detail of what they sing and chant while holding to the overall identity of songs and rhymes.

Another paper chase for variants began for me when I looked at violence in courting rhymes.

> My boyfriend gave me an apple
> My boyfriend gave me a pear
> My boyfriend gave me a kiss on the lips
> And threw me down the stair
>
> He threw me over London
> He threw me over France
> He threw me over the USA
> And he lost my underpants

(McVicar Collection: P7a, St Robert's Primary School, Glasgow, 1996)

When I first heard the St Robert's version I immediately took it to be American. I found that versions of it are extremely popular in Scotland at present:

> My boyfriend gave me a apple
> My boyfriend gave me a pear
> My boyfriend gave me a (kiss kiss kiss)
> And he threw me down the stair
>
> I gave him back his apple
> I gave him back his pear
> I gave him back his (kiss kiss kiss)
> And I threw him down the stair

I threw him over Scotland
I threw him over France
I threw him over (kiss kiss kiss)
And he lost his underpants

His underpants were yellow
His underpants were blue
His underpants were (kiss kiss kiss)
So I flushed them down the loo

*(McVicar Collection: Whitdale Primary School, Whitburn, 1997)*

The (kiss kiss kiss) sound is done with the flat of the forefingers against the lips. In the West Lothian schools in 2007 they added

I took him to the sweetie shop
To buy some bubble gum
And when he wasn't looking
I shoved it up his bum

And in Fettercairn, Angus, in 2004 they finished with

He took me to the cinema
To watch a dirty film
And when I wasn't looking
He kissed another girl

I was sure of US ancestry, right until I found the following, collected by Alan Reid from 'girls attending the Public School at Gorgie, a working-class district in the extreme west of Edinburgh', and printed in 1911.

Jingle bells are ringing, Mother let me out
My sweetheart is waiting, he's going to take me out
He's going to give me apples, he's going to give me pears
He's going to give me a sixpence to kiss him on the stairs
I wouldn't take his apples, I wouldn't take his pears
I wouldn't take his sixpence to kiss him on the stairs
At last I took his apples, at last I took his pears
At last I took his sixpence and kissed him on the stairs

*(Rymour Club 1911)*

The Gorgie tune is not the relative of the near-ubiquitous square 4/4 'A sailor went to sea' tune that children in Glasgow and Whitburn had sung me, but a pleasant and bouncy 6/8 tune, regarding which Alan Reid comments, 'Evidently this air is an adaptation of "Hey rickety ba-loo, cock-a-doodle doo", used as a pantomime song about 1879.'

*(Rymour Club 1911; tune: 'Jingle bells are ringing')*

I should like to know more about the enchantingly named pantomime lullaby 'Hey rickety ba-loo', but I need to stick with the kissing on the stairs. Versions of the 'Jingle Bells' song were sung in Aberdeenshire and in Golspie around a hundred years ago. In Aberdeenshire (Shuldham-Shaw et al. 2002, no. 1623) the first lines were 'Six o'clock bells ringing, My ma won't let me out.' In Golspie (Nicholson 1897) the song begins with a clunking lack of rhythm: 'Mother, the nine o'clock bells are ringing'.

The song was also known in England, but in less formulaic shape. Alan Reid of the Rymour Club said in 1910

> First he gave me apples, Then he gave me pears
> Then he gave me sixpence To take me through the fairs
> Next he gave me bacon, And eggs to fry in a pan
> And nobody to eat them But me and my young man

Edward Nicholson gives what he calls 'a very funny Cheshire variant (or parody?)':

> Eight o'clock is striking
> Mother, may I go out?
> My young man is waiting
> To take me round about
>
> He will buy me apples
> He will buy me pears
> He will buy me everything
> And kiss me on the stairs

Ten o'clock is striking
Mother, may I come in
My young man has left me
He's an awful sting *(stingy one)*

He won't buy me apples
And he won't buy me pears
He won't buy me anything
Nor kiss me on the stairs

All in all, English versions feel as though they were derived from a pleasant old light ballad, while the Scots ones are fitted to game purposes. The Opies have observed (1985) that Scottish versions of games songs are often closer to American versions than they are to English ones, and the song is known and used for hand-clapping games in the US. The violent rejection of the boyfriend may have come over here from the US:

My mother gave me peaches
My father gave me pears
My boyfriend gave me fifty cents
And kissed me up the stairs

My mother took my peaches
My father took my pears
My boyfriend took his fifty cents
So I kicked him down the stairs.

*(Bronner 1988)*

Though this version comes from only 1968 in Kokomo, Indiana, Bronner says 'This is the common contemporary form of an old skipping rhyme':

Nine (or twelve, or seven) o'clock is striking, Mother may I go out?
All the boys are waiting for to take me out
One will give me an apple, one will give me a pear
One will give me fifty cents to kiss behind the stair

The message gets subverted in the USA too:

Johnny gave me apples
Johnny gave me pears
Johnny gave me fifty cents
And kissed me on the stairs

I'd rather wash the dishes
I'd rather scrub the floor
I'd rather kiss the iceman
Behind the kitchen door

*(Freemont & Barbaresi 1992)*

And on a commercial recording in 1928 the renowned Carter Family of Virginia sang a song called 'Chewin chawin gum' and threw in this verse, which uniquely presents the boy's (rather than girl's) voice.

First she gave me peaches, then she gave me pears
Then she gave me fifty cents to kiss her on the stairs.

*(The Carter Family, Anchored in Love, track 13)*

So, is the song Scots, English, American? I see no way of telling.

## Anthology: Characters, courting, movements, others

*Characters*

AWAY UP IN HOLLAND
Away up in Holland
The land of the Dutch
There is a wee lassie
I love very much
Her name is Suzanna
But where is she now?
She's up in the Highlands
Milking the cows

*(McVicar Collection: Glasgow, 1993)*

Suzanna is a popular name in these songs, perhaps because of the Stephen Foster song 'Oh Suzanna'.

Davison's version has a second verse:

Away up in Scotland, the land of the Scots
There lives a wee lassie who makes porridge oats
She makes them for breakfast, for dinner and tea
She makes them for mammy and daddy and me

*(Ian Davison Card Index: Rottenrow School; tune: 'Queen Mary')*

BATMAN AND ROBIN
Batman and Robin
Were lying in bed
Batman moved over
And Robin was dead

*(Ian Davison Card Index: Rottenrow School)*

CASEY THE COWBOY
Casey the Cowboy all dressed in red
Went to the graveyard, there lost his head
There was blood on the saddle, blood on the ground
Great big blobs of blood all around

Casey the Cowboy all dressed in blue
Went to the graveyard, there lost his shoe
Casey the Cowboy all dressed in white
Went to the graveyard, there lost his sight

*(Children's Singing Games: Webb, Dingwall PS, 1976)*

Webb found this rhyme in use for skipping.

CHICKA TONY
Chicka Tony went to London
Just to ride a pony
He stuck a feather in its cap
And called it macaroni

*(Alan Lomax archive: Cedar Place children, Aberdeen)*

CHINESE GOVERNMENT
Chinese government
Black man's daughter
Tra la la la la la la
The wind blows high
From the sky
And out comes (Jeannie) with the big black eye

*(Alan Lomax archive: Peggy MacGillivray, Edinburgh)*

CHINESE MEN ARE VERY FUNNY
Chinese men are very funny
This is the way they count their money
Oocha oocha, Chinese booska

*(McVicar Collection: Glasgow, 1990s)*

At 'booska' you bump bottoms. Other nationalities also feature:

> German boys are so funny
> This is the way they count their money
> Woop a lala, woop a lala
> Woop woop woop

*(School of Scottish Studies archive: Hendry, Glenrothes, 1981)*

> CINDERELLA AT THE BALL
> Cinderella at the ball
> Fell in love with Henry Hall
> Henry Hall at the table
> Fell in love with Betty Grable
> Betty Grable is a star
> S-T-A-R

*(Children's Singing Games: Webb, Noblehill Jun Sch, 1960)*

Webb found this rhyme in use for skipping.

> CINDERELLA DRESSED IN YELLA
> Cinderella dressed in yella
> Went upstairs to kiss a fella
> By mistake she kissed a snake
> And guess how many kisses she made
> One, two [etc.]

*(McVicar Collection: Dalkeith HS, 1997)*

> Cinderella dressed in yella
> Went upstairs to kiss a fella
> How many kisses did she get?
> Five, ten [etc.]

*(School of Scottish Studies archive: Hendry, Glenrothes, 1981)*

Cinderella dressed in yella
Went to the ball with a handsome fella

*(Ian Davison Card Index, Rottenrow School)*

Cinderella dressed in blue
Went to a party and lost her shoe

*(Ian Davison Card Index, Bellahouston School)*

COCA COLA WENT TO TOWN
Coca Cola went to town
Pepsi Cola shot him down
Dr Pepper fixed him up
Turned him into Seven-Up

*(McVicar Collection: St Geraldine's PS, Lossiemouth, 2006)*

DOWN IN ABERDEEN
Down in Aberdeen
I met my Auntie Jean
She gave me a tanner to buy a banana
Down in Aberdeen

Down in Aberdeen
There lives a fairy queen
Her name is Aggie, she's awfy raggy
Down in Aberdeen [etc.]

Her name is Mary, she's got a canary [etc.]

Her name is Alice, she lives in a palace [etc.]

*(Ian Davison Card Index: Rottenrow School; tune: 'Knees up Mother Brown')*

THE GARDEN WALL
Over the garden wall
I let my baby fall
My mother came out
And gave me a clout
Over the garden wall

*(Ian Davison Card Index: Rottenrow School; tune: 'Knees up Mother Brown')*

I HAD A LITTLE MONKEY
I had a little monkey, his name was Charlie Sim
I put him in a bathtub to see if he could swim
He drank all the water, he ate all the soap
We had to get the doctor before he could choke

In came the doctor, in came the nurse
In came the lady with the big fat purse
Out went the doctor, out went the nurse
Out went the lady with the big fat purse

*(Ian Davison Card Index)*

Other versions name babies called Tiny Tim (McVicar Collection, St Robert's, Glasgow, 1997) or Sunny Jim, who sometimes 'died last night with a bubble in his throat'. In this case the doctor is replaced by the 'man in the sugar allie hat' – the undertaker in his tall black hat. The lady with the purse is perhaps a 'green lady', a health or social worker, and she sometimes sports 'an alligator purse'.

I LOST MY LEG
I lost my leg in the army
I found it in the navy
Dipped it in some gravy
And had it for my tea

*(Ian Davison Card Index)*

I C TIARA
I met a little Spanish girl called I C Tiara
And all the boys on the football pitch said I See Tiara
How's your boyfriend? All right
Died in the fish shop last night
What wis he eatin? Raw fish
How did he end up? Like this

*(McVicar Collection: Boghall, 2007)*

This was performed as hand-clapping with integrated mime actions.

I WENT TO A CHINESE RESTAURANT
I went to a Chinese restaurant
To buy a loaf of bread bread bread
They wrapped it up in a five-pound note
And this is what I said said said
My name is Ina Wina
I come from China
Do us a favour
Push off

*(McVicar Collection: Erskine, 1992)*

After the first four lines it can go many ways:

My name is Ella Bella
Chicken chop chella
Chinese chopsticks, Indian fella
Whooooooo, How!

*(McVicar Collection, Moray, 2006)*

Or:

> My name is Ellie Ellie
> Chickalie chickalie
> Um pum poodle, silly willy noodle
> Chinese chopsticks, Indian cheddar
> Huff Puff Wow

*(McVicar Collection: Moray, 2006)*

Or:

> My name is Andy Pandy
> Sugary candy
> Roly poly, chocolate dip
> I can do the can can, I can do the splits
> I can do the hula hoop just like this
> Bow to the king, push to the queen
> Show your knickers to the football team
> Gonny hypnotise you, paralyse you
> Turn around and shoot

*(McVicar Collection: Bankton PS, Livingston, 2007)*

In the Bankton version the five-pound note has become ten pounds – inflation strikes.

> MADEMOISELLE WENT TO TOWN
> Mademoiselle she went to town, parlez-vous
> To buy herself a wedding gown, same to you
> All the people in the town
> Thought it was a lovely gown
> Inky-pinky parlez-vous, same to you

*(Ian Davison Card Index: Rottenrow School;*
*tune: 'Mademoiselle of Armentieres')*

> MARY HAD A LITTLE LAMB
> Mary had a little lamb
> She put it in the bunker
> A wee bit coal got in its eye
> And made it do the rhumba
> Oompah cha cha cha

*(Ian Davison Card Index: Rottenrow School)*

Mary had a little lamb
She sat it on the bunker
Pretty Polly came along
And made it do the rhumba
North south east west
I can do the rhumba best
I can do the rhumba best

*(Children's Singing Games: Webb, Noblehill JS, 1960)*

Mary had a little lamb
It climbed right up a pylon
Fifty volts went up its jolts
And turned wool into nylon

*(McVicar Collection: Dalkeith HS, 1997)*

MARY QUEEN OF SCOTS
Mary Queen of Scots got her head chopped off
Her head chopped off, her head chopped off
Mary Queen of Scots got her head chopped off
On the 14th of November

*(School of Scottish Studies archive: Henderson, Campbeltown, 1956)*

ME ME CHINAMAN
Me me Chinaman
Me feel ill
Me go to doctor
Me get pill
Me go home again
Me go to bed
Me never ever
Have sore head

*(Ian Davison Card Index: Rottenrow School)*

MISS POLLY
Miss Polly had a dolly who was sick sick sick
And she called for the doctor to come quick quick quick
The doctor came with his bag and his hat
And he knocked at the door with a rat tat tat
He looked at the dolly and he shook his head
And he said 'Miss Polly, put her straight to bed'
He wrote out a letter for a pill pill pill
'I'll be back in the morning with a bill bill bill'

*(Sinclair 1986)*

MY GRANNIE CAUGHT A FLEA
1, 2, 3, my grannie caught a flea
She roasted it, and toasted it
And had it for her tea

*(McVicar Collection: Glasgow, 1991)*

1, 2, 3, ma mammy caught a flea
She peppered it and salted it
And had it for her tea
She didn't like it
So she gave it to her son
He didn't like it
So he threw it up the lum

*(Ian Davison Card Index: Rottenrow School)*

1, 2, 3, my mither got a flea
She peppered it, and salted it, and put it in her tea
When she put the sugar in, it floated on the top
And when she put the milk in, it went pop pop

*(Rymour Club 1911)*

MY MOTHER SAID
My mother said that I never should
Play with the gypsies in the wood
And she said if I did
She'd break my head with the teapot lid

*(Rymour Club 1911: Bruce J Home)*

Home said this was used 'for "deedling" at dancing.'

MY NAME IS MACNAMARA
My name is MacNamara
I'm the leader of the band
My wife is Betty Grable
She's the fairest in the land
Oh she can dance, she can sing
And she can show her legs
The only thing she cannae dae
Is fry ham and eggs

*(Ian Davison Card Index: Sir John Maxwell School; tune: 'MacNamara's band')*

Mrs Macaroni
Here comes Mrs Macaroni
Ridin on a pretty pony
Ridin through her house-aroanie
This is Katie's washing day

Rump stump, stoodle addie
Rump stump, stoodle addie
Rump stump, stoodle addie
This is Katie's washing day

*(School of Scottish Studies archive:*
*(Headlee) Williamson, from Betsy Whyte, Montrose, 1976)*

My name is Elvis Presley
I went to a Chinese restaurant, to buy a loaf of bread
He wrapped it up in a five-pound note and this is what it said
My name is Elvis Presley, I'm a movie star
I do the hippy hippy shakey and I play the guitar
The boys are hunky and the girls are sexy
Sittin in the back street, drinkin Pepsi
Where's yer faither? Roun the corner
In the harbour drinkin lager
He feels a bit dizzy and he draps doon deid

*(McVicar Collection: Glasgow, 1994)*

A full-blown account, often performed with actions. Truncated versions are common:

I went to a Chinese restaurant
To buy a loaf of bread
The lady gave me a five-pound note
And this is what I said
My name is Elvis Presley
Girls are sexy
Sitting in the back seat
Drinking Pepsi
Having a baby
In the Royal Navy
Boys go (kiss kiss)
Girls go wooooo

*(McVicar Collection: Dalkeith HS, 1997)*

This last text joins together slices of two songs. In Rosyth in 2007 'Girls are sexy' has become 'Girlfriend Lesley'.

NOT LAST NIGHT
Not last night but the night before
Three wee monkeys came to my door
One with a banjo, one with a drum
One with a pancake stuck to its bum

*(McVicar Collection: St Robert's PS, Glasgow, 1997)*

Elsewhere other items adhere.

OLD MRS REILLY
Old Mrs Reilly at the pawnshop door
Baby in her arms an a bundle on the floor
She asked for ten bob, she only got four
An nearly pullt the hinges aff the pawnshop door

*(School of Scottish Studies archive: Argo, Glasgow, 1960, from singer Ray Fisher)*

ON THE MOUNTAIN
On the mountain stands a castle
And the owner Frankenstein
And his daughter Pansy Potter
She's my only Valentine
So I call on Linda dear
Linda dear, Linda dear
So I call on Linda dear
And out pops Jane till the next New Year

*(Ian Davison Card Index: Rottenrow School)*

On the mountain stands a lady
Who she is I do not know
All she wants is gold and silver
All she wants is a nice young man

*(Ian Davison Card Index: Rottenrow School)*

PADDY ON THE RAILWAY
Paddy on the railway, pickin up stones
Along came an engine and broke Paddy's bones
'Well,' said Paddy, 'That's no fair'
'Well,' said the engine man, 'You shouldny uv been there'

*(School of Scottish Studies archive: Hendry, Glenrothes, 1981)*

Known in Glasgow in the 1940s.

RABBIE BURNS
Rabbie Burns was born in Ayr
Now he's doon in George's Square
If you want to see him there
Take a bus wi a fourpenny fare

*(Ian Davison Card Index: Rottenrow School)*

The last line was sometimes 'Hop on the bus and dodge the fare.'

RIN TIN TIN
Rin Tin Tin swallowed a pin
He went to the doctor
The doctor wasnae in
He chapped the door
And the nurse came oot
Thumped in the belly
And the pin fell oot

*(Ian Davison Card Index: Rottenrow School)*

SALVATION ARMY
Salvation Army free from sin
Went to heaven in a corn mutton tin
The corn mutton tin began to smell
Salvation Army went to hell

*(Ian Davison Card Index)*

UP A BOGIE LANE
Up a bogie lane
Ta buy a penny whistle
The bogie man came up to me
An stole ma penny whistle
I asked him fur it back
He said he hudny got it
Ha ha ha, hee hee hee
I see it in your pocket

*(McVicar Collection: Glasgow, 1993)*

UP AND DOWN THE HOOSE
Up and down the hoose
To buy a mickey moose
If you catch it by the tail
Hang it up on a rusty nail
Send for the cook
To make a bowl of soup
Hurrah boys hurrah
How do you like ma soup?
I like it very well
Apart fae the smell
Hurrah boys hurrah
How do you like ma soup?

*(McVicar Collection: Glasgow, 1993)*

In the version Ian Davison found in 1970s Glasgow, after 'To make a bowl of soup' came

Aye, Sir, Aye, Sir
How d'ye like yer soup?
I like it very much
Kings and queens and jellybeans
And (we) all jump out

*(Ian Davison Card Index)*

WEE CHINKY CHINKY MAN
Wee chinky chinky man
Tried to milk a cow
Wee chinky chinky man
Didny know how

*(McVicar Collection: St Robert's PS, Glasgow, 1997)*

WEE SAM
Wee Sam, a piece an jam
Wee Betty, tin a spaghetti
Wee Linda, bottle o ginger

*(McVicar Collection: Glasgow, 1993)*

Wee Sam a piece and jam
Went to London in a pram
The pram broke and that's the joke
Wee Sam a piece and jam

*(Ian Davison Card Index)*

Where was Johnny?
Where was Johnny when the lights went out?
Up Sauchiehall Street smokin a dowt
The dowt was wee an so was he
Where was Johnny when the lights went out?

*(Sinclair 1986)*

## Courting

Down in Germany
Down in Germany
This is what they say
Eesha asha, you're a wee smasher
(or Saturday, Sunday, school on Monday)
Down in Germany – Ole

*(Ian Davison Card Index: Rottenrow School; tune: 'Knees up Mother Brown')*

Far away
Far away across the sea
Is a lad who's dear to me
I wonder if you'll ever see
The lad from Bonny Scotland

*(Ian Davison Card Index: John St School)*

Hard up
Hard up, kick the can
(Sadie's) got a fancy man
If you want to know his name
His name is (Willy Thompson)

*(McVicar Collection, Edinburgh, 1999)*

Hard up, kick the can
(Jane Thomson's) got a man
If you want to know his name
His name is (Peter Burgess)
Ah widnae get married if Ah wis you
Ah widnae get married if Ah wis you
Ah widnae get married if Ah wis you
Ah'd rather stay wi ma mammy

*(Ian Davison Card Index: Rottenrow School; tune: 'Bee baw babbity')*

HI JASON DONOVAN
Hi Jason Donovan, how about a date?
I'll meet you round the corner at half past eight
I can do the burley, I can do the splits
The only thing I canny dae is kiss you on the lips

*(McVicar Collection: Glasgow, 1991)*

An update of a rhyme that has in its time featured The Beatles, Roy Rogers – and
Coronation Street character Ena Sharples:

Hey Ena Sharples, how about a date
I'll meet you at the Wagon Train at half past eight
I can do the rhumba, and I can do the splits
And I can lift my petticoat up to my hips

*(Ian Davison Card Index)*

I LOVE MY SCOUT
I love my scout
He takes me out
He buys me chips
To grease my lips
He takes me to the
P-I-C-T-U-R-E-S

*(Ian Davison Card Index)*

I'M A TEXAS GIRL
I'm a Texas Texas Texas Girl
I live over there not far away
I can jump, I can shoot, I can do the hula-hoop
Cowboys comin to town, yee ha

There's a boy over there who's lost one eye
He says he loves me but he's tellin a lie
He's got curly hair and his boots don't shine
Cowboys comin to town, yee ha

I'm a Texas Texas Texas Girl
My mama left me when I was three
She walks like a wiggle and a wiggle and a woo
So let's do the Texas wig-wam

*(McVicar Collection: Dalkeith HS, 1997)*

Another child in the class had the following alternative lines:

> There's a guy over there and he blinks one eye
> He's got curly hair and his boots don't shine
> He ain't got money and he ain't got mine

The last two lines are derived from the popular song 'Tennessee wig walk', the rest perhaps from another pop song or two. The next version takes the story in a different direction:

> I'm a Texas girl, I'm a Texas girl
> I come from the land of the cowboys
> I can dance I can shoot
> I can do the hula-hoop
> Yippee it's Mr Whippy

*(Ian Davison Card Index: Rottenrow School)*

### My boyfriend's name
My boyfriend's name is Tony
He lives in Macaroni
With a cherry on his nose and three black toes
And this is how my story goes
One day when I was walking
I saw my boyfriend talking
To the prettiest girl in the whole wide world
And this is what he said to her
I am I really love you
I K-I-S-S kiss you
I jump in a lake and saw a snake
I tiddley I tie
Drop dead

*(School of Scottish Studies archive: Hendry, Glenrothes, 1981)*

### Up a tree
(Christopher) and (Norma) up a tree
K-I-S-S-I-N-G
First comes love, then comes marriage
Then comes a baby in a golden carriage

*(McVicar Collection: Dalkeith HS, 1997)*

*Movements*

A, B, C, HIT IT
A, B, C, hit it
Karate chop
Lick the lolly, push the trolley
A, B, C, hit it

*(McVicar Collection: Moray, 2006)*

A B C TOGETHER
A B C together, up together, down together
Back to front, knee to toe
Wiggle your bum and round you go

*(McVicar Collection: Glasgow, 1991)*

A B C together, up together, down together
Back to front, heel to toe
Wiggle your bum and round you go
A B C, hit it
That's the way uh uh, I like it uh uh
That's the way uh uh, I like it uh uh
Pull the chain and start again
Boys got the muscles, teacher canny count
Girls have got the sexy legs, you better watch out
Hypnotise you, paralyse you, until you faint

*(McVicar Collection:
East Calder Primary, 2007)*

APPLE ON A STICK
Apple on a stick will make me sick
Will make my heart go 2 4 6
Hey boy, do you want a fight
Not because you're dirty, not because you're clean
Not because you kissed me behind the old scene
You can walk, you can talk, you can do anything
Bet you can't do it with your eyes closed

*(McVicar Collection: Moray, 2006)*

While handclapping, second time with eyes closed.

AUNTY ANNA
My Aunty Anna plays the pianna
24 hours a day
Do the splits

My Uncle Ryan keeps on cryin
24 hours a day
Do the splits

*(McVicar Collection: Moray, 2006)*

BLUEBELLS, DUMMY-DUMMY SHELLS
Bluebells, dummy-dummy shells
Eavy, ivy, over
Charlie Chaplin went to France
To teach the ladies how to dance
First the heel and then the toe
Then you do big burley-o
Big burley-o

*(Alan Lomax archive: Peggy MacGillivray, Edinburgh)*

BOYS HAVE GOT THE MUSCLES
Pepsi Cola, Pepsi Cola
Irn Bru, Irn Bru
Boys have got the muscles
Teacher's got the brains
Girls have got the sexy legs
So we won the game (or 'And you've got nane')
I'm gonna hypnotise you
Paralyse you
Turn around and faint

*(McVicar Collection: Dalkeith HS, 1997)*

CHRISTOPHER COLUMBUS
Christopher Columbus was a very old man
And he sailed through the ocean in an old tin can
And the waves grew higher and higher and over
5, 10, 15 [etc.]

*(McVicar Collection: Glasgow, 1993)*

More often he was 'a very brave man'.

### Gem, gem

Gem, gem, ba, ba
Twenty lasses in a raw
No a lad amang them aa
Gem, gem, ba, ba

*(Rymour Club 1919: Professor R Wallace)*

### High low

My name is
High low chucalow
Chucalow high low
High low chucalow
Chucalow high

*(McVicar Collection: Dalkeith HS, 1997)*

### Hokey pokey

Hokey cokey penny the lump
The mair ye ate the mair ye jump
The mair ye jump ye're sure tae faa
Hokey cokey that's it aa

*(McVicar Collection:*
*St Geraldine's PS, Lossiemouth, 2006)*

### Horsey horsey

Horsey horsey don't you stop
Just let your feet go clippety clop
Your tail go swish and your wheels go round
Giddy-up to London Town

*(Ian Davison Card Index: Rottenrow School)*

Horsey horsey living in a stable
Does not know his two times table
The teacher says you're not able
Horsey horsey living in a stable

*(Ian Davison Card Index: Rottenrow School)*

### I AM A GIRL GUIDE

I am a girl guide dressed in blue
See all the actions I can do
Stand up at ease, bend your knees
Salute to the king, bow to the queen
Show your knickers to the football team

*(McVicar Collection: Glasgow, 1993)*

### I HAVE A BONNET

I have a bonnet trimmed with blue
Do you wear it? Yes I do
I always wear it when I can
Going to the ball with my young man
My young man has gone to sea
When he comes back he will marry me
Tip to the heel and tip to the toe
That's the way the polka goes

*(Sinclair 1986)*

An assemblage of text elements, used for clapping or movement.

### I PAULA TAY

I paula tay paula tasca
Paulatay, paula toe
I paula tay paula tasca
Paulatay, paula toe
O alla tinka, to do the rhumba
Paulatay, paula toe
O alla tinka, to do the
Rhumba umba umba umba ay

*(Alan Lomax archive: Peggy MacGillivray, Edinburgh)*

### I WAS GOING TO THE COUNTRY

I was going to the country
I was going to the fair
I met a senorita with a curl in her hair
Oh shake it senorita
Shake it all you can
Rumble to the bottom
Rumble to the top
Turn around till you make a stop

*(McVicar Collection: Glasgow, 1991)*

In Davison's versions one senorita has curlers in her hair and is told:

> Shake it like a milktop
> You'll get a handsome man

Another goes to 'walkie talkie' with 'bubbles in her hair'.

> IN LIVERPOOL
> In Liverpool there is a school
> And in that school there is a class
> And in that class there is a desk
> And in that desk there is a book
> And in that book there is an
> A, B, C, D, E, F, G [etc.]

> *(Ian Davison Card Index:*
> *Rottenrow School)*

Rottenrow also gave Davison the following on the subject of Liverpool:

> Down in Liverpool
> The Beatles go to school
> Ringo cannae do his sums
> But he can do his drums

> *(Tune: 'Knees up Mother Brown')*

> JELLY ON THE PLATE
> Jelly on the plate, jelly on the plate
> Wiggle waggle, wiggle waggle
> Jelly on the plate

> Sausage on the pan, sausage on the pan
> Turn them over, turn them over
> Sausage on the pan

> Baby on the floor, baby on the floor
> Pick him up, pick him up
> Baby on the floor

Ghostie in the house, ghostie in the house
Kick him out, kick him out
Ghostie in the house

Apples on the tree, apples on the tree
Pull them off, pull them off
Apples on the tree

*(Alan Lomax archive: Cedar Place children, Aberdeen)*

The first verse was still current in Dalkeith in 1997.

A KEPPIE, A CLAPPIE
A keppie, a clappie, a furlie-ma-jockie
Heel, toe, through you go
Salute to the king, bow to the queen
An turn your back on the Kaiser

*(Wilson 1993)*

Though his gloss suggests the first line means 'A catch, a bowl, an ornament', they sound like movements.

LITTLE BUBBLE CAR
I had a little bubble (or 'bumpy') car, Number 48
Turned it round the corner
And crashed it through a gate

*(Ian Davison Card Index)*

Ah had a little bumper car
Number 48
Ah took it round the coooooorner
And then ah pult ma brake

*(McVicar Collection: Glasgow, 1993)*

I'm a little bubble car, number 48
I raced round the coooooorner and pressed on my brakes
How many miles can the bubble car go
5, 10, 15, 20 [etc.]

*(McVicar Collection: Moray, 2006)*

A LITTLE SHORT SHIRT
Oh what a little short shirt you've got
You'd better pull down the blind

*(Ian Davison Card Index: Bellahouston School; tune: 'Lincolnshire poacher', chorus)*

NELSON
Nelson in the army, lost one arm
Nelson in the army, lost the other arm
Nelson in the army, lost one eye
Nelson in the army, lost the other eye
Nelson in the army, lost one leg
Nelson in the army, fell down dead

*(Ian Davison Card Index)*

NOT LAST NIGHT
Not last night but the night before
Twenty-five robbers came to my door
As they walked out they said to me
Spanish dancers turn around
Spanish dancers touch the ground
Spanish dancers do the high kicks
Spanish dancers do the high splits

*(McVicar Collection: St Roberts PS, Glasgow, 1997)*

OFF THE CARPET
Off the carpet two and out
Miss a beat and you are out
I like coffee, I like tea
I like sitting on Cheyenne's knee

*(Ian Davison Card Index: Rottenrow School; tune: 'Katie Bairdie')*

THE OLD GREY MARE
The old grey mare she ain't what she used to be
Ain't what she used to be, ain't what she used to be
The old grey mare she ain't what she used to be
Ever since the old man died – paralysed

The old grey mare she cannae dae a birlio [etc.]

The old grey mare she cannae dae a jibbio [etc.]

*(Ian Davison Card Index: Rottenrow School)*

OLIVER TWIST
Oliver Twist you can't do this
So what's the use of trying
Number 1 touch your tongue
Number 2 touch your shoe
Number 3 touch your knee
Number 4 touch the floor
Number 5 take a dive
Number 6 do the splits

*(Ian Davison Card Index: Rottenrow School)*

PK
PK penny packet
First you chew it, then you crack it
Then you stick it on your jacket
PK, penny packet

*(Alan Lomax archive: Cedar Place children, Aberdeen)*

Davison found this still in use twenty years later in Rottenrow School.

THE POSTMAN'S KNOCK
Early in the morning
Past eight o'clock
You should hear the postman knock
Up jumps Jane running to the door
To catch a one-a-letter, two-a-letter
Three-a-letter, four

*(Ian Davison Card Index: Rottenrow School)*

RONALD DONALD
Ronald Donald deshca peshca
Ronald Donald deshca peshca
I've got a boyfriend peshca
He's so sweet peshca
Sweeter than a cherry tree peshca
Icecream soda with the cherry on the top
Icecream soda with the cherry on the top
Down down baby, down by the roller coaster
Sweet sweet baby, I will never let you go
Shimmy shimmy coco pops
Shimmy shimmy I
Shimmy shimmy coco pops
Shimmy shimmy I

*(McVicar Collection: Bankhead, 1992)*

Often Ronald MacDonald. The following is similar:

Down down baby, down by the roller coaster
Sweet sweet baby, Mama never let you go
Shooby shooby shooby shooby shooby oh-ah
I like coffee, I like tea
I like the big boys and they like me
Sitting by the fire, peeling my potatoes
Waiting for the clock to go
Tick tack BOOM

*(McVicar Collection: Erskine, 1992)*

As is:

Down down baby
Down by the roller coaster
Sweet sweet baby
I'll never let you go
Shoomy shoomy coco pop
Shoomy pow
Shoomy shoomy coco pop
Shoomy shoomy pow
Grandma, grandma, sick in bed
She called for the doctor and the doctor said
Let's get the rhythm of the head
Ding dong
Let's get the rhythm of the head
Ding dong
Let's get the rhythm of the hands
Clap clap
Let's get the rhythm of the hands
Clap clap
Let's get the rhythm of the feet
Stomp stomp
Let's get the rhythm of the feet
Stomp stomp
Get the rhythm of the ho-o-o-o-t dog
Put them all together and what dae ye get?
Ding dong clap clap stomp stomp ho-o-o-o-t dog
Put them all backwards and what do you get?
dog hot stomp stomp clap clap dong ding

*(McVicar Collection: Dalkeith HS, 1997)*

A Dalkeith classmate added on

> My old granny sleeps in bed
> This is what the doctor said
> She'll be all right in a week or two
> No more school for me, just you

*(McVicar Collection: Dalkeith HS, 1997)*

A 2007 Bankton School, Livingston, version was a little garbled:

> My name is
> Down down baby
> Down by the roaster
> Sweet eats pizza
> I will never let you go
> Shooby doo, shooby doo
> Shooby doo wah
> My old grannie went to bed
> This is what the doctor said
> You'll be in bed for a week or two
> No more school for you or you

> SKIP THE LADDER
> Skip the ladder, high high high
> Up to the top of the pale blue sky
> I like coffee, I like tea
> I like sitting on a cowboy's knee.

*(Ian Davison Card Index: John Street School; tune: 'Katie Bairdie')*

> TEDDY BEAR
> Teddy bear, teddy bear
> Touch the ground
> Teddy bear, teddy bear
> Birl around [etc.]

> Show your shoe [etc.]
> That will do [etc.]

> Run upstairs [etc.]
> Say night prayers [etc.]

> Switch off the light [etc.]
> Say goodnight [etc.]
> Goodnight, teddy bear

*(School of Scottish Studies archive: Henderson, Campbeltown, 1956)*

Almost the same words were sung in Dalkeith in 1997.

UP AND DOWN, UP AND DOWN
Up and down, up and down
All the way to London town
Swish-swosh, swish-swosh
All the way to King's Cross
Leg swing, leg swing
All the way to Berlin
Heel toe, heel toe
All the way to Jericho

*(Alan Lomax archive:*
*Peggy MacGillivray, Edinburgh)*

WAVY WAVY
Wavy wavy, turn the rope over
Mother's at the butcher's buyin fresh meat
Baby's in the cradle, playin wi a radle (rattle)
One two three, and a porridgee

*(Rymour Club 1919: Dirleton, 1913)*

Interviewing Edinburgh informant Peggy MacGillivray in 1951 Alan Lomax asked her the meaning of 'porridgy', suggesting it meant 'hot'. She said 'Well, I think it should be hot. It goes awfully fast.' Here it indicates a movement, but what? Dictionaries do not advise us.

*Others*

APPLES AND PEARS
Apples and pears, they make you six
They make my heart beat twenty-six
Not because they're dirty, not because they're clean
Not because they kissed a boy behind a magazine
Hey girls, do you wanna have fun?
Here comes Eve with her knickers on fire
She can dae the wibble wobble, she can dae the splits
But I bet you ten bucks that she can't do this
Just close your eyes and count to ten
If you mess up, just do it again

*(McVicar Collection: Culbokie PS, 2006)*

The rhyme and actions are indeed repeated with eyes shut.

### CAT'S GOT THE MEASLES
Cat's got the measles, dog's got the flu
Chicken's got the chicken pox and so have you

*(McVicar Collection: Moray, 2006)*

### EENIE MEANIE DESTANEENIE
Eenie meanie destaneenie
You are the one and only
Education, liberation
I like you
Down down baby, down by the roller-coaster
Slippin, slidin, no place to go
Caught you with your boyfriend, naughty naughty
Didn't do the dishes, lazy lazy
Jump out the window, flippin crazy

*(McVicar Collection: Culbokie PS, 2006)*

### ENGLAND IRELAND
England Ireland Scotland Wales
Inside outside, monkeys' tails

*(McVicar Collection: Dalkeith HS, 1997)*

Scotland England Ireland Wales
All went out to fish for whales
Some got heads and some got tails
Scotland England Ireland Wales

*(Rodger nd)*

### FIRECRACKER
Firecracker, firecracker, boom boom boom
The boys have got the muscles, the teacher's got the brains
The girls have got the sexy legs, an we won the games

*(School of Scottish Studies archive: Hendry, Glenrothes, 1981)*

### HOUSE TO LET
House to let, apply within
Lady put out for drinking gin
Drinking gin, it's an awful sin
Mary goes out and Ethel goes in

*(Rodger 1974)*

A house to let, no rent to pay
Just chap the door and run away

*(Ian Davison Card Index: Sir John Maxwell School)*

HOW MANY?
How many boys were in your bed last night?
1, 2, 3, 4, 5 [etc.]

*(Ian Davison Card Index: Bellahouston School)*

How many times did you wet the bed?
1, 2, 3, 4, 5, 6 [etc.]

*(Ian Davison Card Index: Bellahouston School)*

LADIES IN THE TIGHT SKIRTS
Ladies in the tight skirts can't do this
Can't do this, can't do this
Ladies in the tight skirts can't do this
Can't do this

*(Ian Davison Card Index: Rottenrow School)*

MADEMOISELLE
Mademoiselle she went to the well
To wash her hands to dry them
To comb her hair to say her prayers
To catch a ball in the basket

*(Ian Davison Card Index: Bellahouston School)*

MY MOTHER, YOUR MOTHER
My mother, your mother live down the street
18, 19, Marble Street
And every night they have a fight and this is what they say
Boys are rotten, made of cotton
Girls are sexy, made of Pepsi
Boys come from Jupiter to get more stupider
Girls come from Mars to get more bras
Itsy bitsy lollipop
Itsy bitsy bee
All the boys love me

*(McVicar Collection: Whitdale PS, 1994)*

OM POM PAY
Om pom pay bonnalay, bonna lassie
Om pom pay bonalay
Academic so funny
Academic puff puff

*(McVicar Collection: Whitdale PS, 1994)*

# 5
# *You are het*

## What language was that? Counting and choosing

> Eeny meany acha racha ex pert dani nacha
> Oot skoot pocks a leen jecks
> You are not het

There are many short, rhythmic pieces for counting out or counting in or eliminating, for choosing sides in games of football or cops and robbers, or choosing who is 'het' (it) – who is to be chaser in a game of tig.

While children continue to be proud of feats of memory, they seldom now maintain the old long strings of words and lines, some connecting together in a narrative or wordplay fashion, some to be learned as 'nonsense' and performed to demonstrate strength of memory and ability to tongue twist.

Most children, and most adults, in the land can finish the chant 'One potato, two potato', or '1, 2, 3, 4, 5, 6, 7, All good children'. Many could summon up a couple more ways of selecting, but they would not agree about the words, unless they were school playmates. Which of the following rings your bell?

> Eetle ottle black bottle
> Eetle ottle out
> If you want a piece and jam
> Please step out

*(McVicar from personal recollection: Dingwall, 1950s)*

Or, alternatively, it might end 'Just call oot'. (Hendry & Stephen 1982) How about this?

> Eetle ottle black bottle
> Eetle ottle out
> Shining on the mantelpiece
> Like a shining threepenny piece
> Eetle ottle black bottle
> Eetle ottle out

*(Alan Lomax archive: Norton Park schoolchild, Edinburgh)*

Or even

> Me and the minister's wife coost oot
> Guess ye what it was aa aboot
> Black pudding, dish-cloot
> Eerie orie, you are oot

*(Hendry & Stephen 1978)*

The rhyme can move far away in elements, but take a dish-cloot with it:

> Ibble obble
> Chocolate bubble
> Ibble obble out
> Pack your case and step right out
> Turn a dirty dishcloth inside out

*(McVicar Collection: Glasgow 1991)*

Although in some chants children take what they do not understand and remake it, in other rhymes they celebrate what seems nonsense. Counting out rhymes attract 'nonsense' lines like jam attracts wasps. Abblesey bibblesy, terry erry ram tam, eachie peachie, eenie meenie – there are lots more attractive rhythmic syllabic sounds in the anthology section. One family of puzzling rhyme has attracted quite a lot of discussion, and a few scholars have spun long threads out of what is termed Shepherd's Counting.

Here is one version from Ross-shire, from the childhood of my grandfather-in-law, Roderick MacLennan, who was himself a shepherd:

> One ery two ery
> Tackery teeven
> Kiloma crackery
> Tenory leeven
> Wish wash, bang a wish
> Little wee sting horse

*(McVicar Collection: per Ishbel Mackenzie,*
*recalled from Easter Ross, 1920s)*

It is claimed that this rhyme family originated in a shepherd's sheep counting rhyme, known as the 'Anglo-Cymric Score'. Versions have been found in northern English and southern Scottish counties, and in Wales. Here is a Lincolnshire text:

Yan, tan, tethera, pethera
Pimp, sethera, lethera, hovera
Dik, yan-a-dik, tan-a-dik, tethera-dik
Petheradik, bum-fit, yan-a-bumfit
Tan-a-bumfit, tethera-bumfit, pethera-bumfit, figgit

*(Bett 1924)*

Bett traces this family of rhymes to origins in the Welsh language, in which the first five numerals are 'un, dau, tri, pedwar, pump', though the Scottish version he quotes is so far adrift, 'Aina, peina, para, peppera, pen, hasee, nasee, nusee, nottical, hen', that he says 'One is impressed [. . .] with the hopeless corruption of some numbers'. Now for some of the richer Scots versions – eentie is perhaps a child's version of een or one.

Eenertee, feenertee, fichertie, feg
Ell, dell, dolman's egg
Irkie, birkie, starry rock
Ann tan two's Jock
Black puddin, white troot
That shows you're oot

*(Rodger nd)*

Eenty, feenty, figgery fell
Ell, dell, dominell
Auntie, Tantie, torry-row
An, Tan, Teesy Jo
You are out

*(Ma Maw Says late 1980s)*

Inty, tinty, heathery, blethery, bamfalourie
Hootery, scootery, ding dong, long tong
Salmonella (or 'semolina') fill your pipe
And you are out

*(Margaret et al. early 1990s)*

These link on to somewhat clearer narratives:

Eenti teenti terry merry, am tam tosh
Look under the bed and catch a wee fat mouse
Cut it up in pieces, fry it in the pan
Mind you leave some gravy for the wee fat man

*(Margaret et al. early 1990s)*

There are more counting rhymes in the anthology section, but there is a class of rhyme sometimes said to be for counting out, but so long and complex that playtime might well be over before sides were chosen. For example, Miss Bell Robertson, one of Gavin Greig's best informants, who contributed texts for over four hundred and twenty items, gave him the following twelve-line version. Greig described it as a 'counting out rhyme', but Bell Robertson seems to have heard it sung to the tune 'The craw's taen the pussie o', which is better known as 'Green grow the rashes o'.

> As I gaed owre yon heich heich hill
> To meet my father, he'd gane will
> He had mony bonnie things
> He'd a chillie, he'd a chase
> He'd a bonnie blue gless
> He'd a dog amon the corn
> Blawin Billy Buck's horn
> Billy Buck had a coo
> Black and fite aboot the mou
> They ca'd her Belly Bentie
> And she lap owre the Brig o Dee
> Like ony covilintie

*(Shuldham-Shaw et al. 2002, no. 1640C)*

What should we make of this sequence? Not any connected narrative, but a memory challenge, as many disconnected pieces of rhyme as can be strung together. Yes, used for counting out, but also for some child's ceremonial purpose like the way the 'Cobbling grace' was used to embarrass a classmate, or as a performance piece.

As an adult recalling what seemed in part nonsense as a child, Miss Robertson noted down words and phrases that she might not have understood: 'a chillie', 'a chess', 'he'd gane will', 'covilintie' and a dog blowing a horn. Lines 9 and 10 have floated in from Katie Bairdie. Others develop a clearer meaning when we turn to Chambers (1842), who gives six pieces he has not been able to classify by usage, saying 'Those which follow are of no particular application. They are often heard among children.' Two of them are

> I've a cherry, I've a chess
> I've a bonny blue glass
> I've a dog amang the corn
> Bah, Willie Buckhorn

and

As I gaed up by yonder hill
I met my father wi good-will
He had jewels, he had rings
He had mony braw things
He had a cat wi nine tails
He had a hammer wanting nails
Up Jack, down Tam
Blaw the bellows, auld man
The auld man took a dance
First to London, then to France
Etc. Etc. Etc.

*(Chambers 1842)*

While lamenting gently for what is lost within 'Etc. Etc. Etc.', we find 'chillie' becomes 'cherry', 'he's gane will' becomes 'wi good-will'. The dog relinquishes his horn-blowing. Chess is unexplained – the *Concise Scots Dictionary* says it is a window sash or window frame, which does not fully convince.

Chambers helps again with another rhyme, introducing it by saying 'The snail is saluted in the following couplet by the boys of Forfarshire': 'Willie, my buck, shoot out your horn / And you'll get milk and bread the morn.' The last two lines, 'The auld man took a dance / First to London, then to France', put one in mind of the well-known 'Charlie Chaplin went to France / To teach the ladies how to dance.' But it's an obvious rhyme to use, so perhaps there's no connection.

Another nineteen-line version of the rhyme, given to Greig by Rev. John Strachan, has 'Covenanter' instead of 'covilintie', and uses 'chase' instead of 'chess'. (Shuldham-Shaw et al. 2002, no. 1640A) A chase is a 'section of fruit', the editors of *Greig–Duncan* tell us. But this version introduces many more linguistic puzzles than it solves, and possible translations and interpretations of it would take several paragraphs while proving little.

Mrs D Lyall added another six lines to Rev. John Strachan's version, stating that her husband 'explains that they used these long nonsense rhymes when they were spinning, to count how many threads for the hank'. (Shuldham-Shaw et al. 2002, no. 1640E) Believe that if you choose. And the lines she 'adds' are mostly re-rumples of lines Rev. Strachan reported.

James Cassie gave Greig another variant, twenty-three lines long. The first fifteen lines share ideas with the Rev. John, except that a line about a haddock becomes more grammatical if no more sensible, 'Took a haddock by the heels', and a cow becomes a cat. Then more puzzles ensue:

She widna ate tobacco
She widna ate the beef
She widna ate the lang kale
For spoilin aa her teeth
But she ate the bonnie birdie
That sat upon the tree
And down the burn, David lad
And I'll follow thee

*(Shuldham-Shaw et al. 2002, no. 1640B)*

These lines seem parts of two songs, as do the last two lines of the nineteen-line piece learned by Ella Hamilton Boyd from 'an old nurse who came from Strichen': 'Away to Fisherfew, to see the boats come in'. (Shuldham-Shaw et al. 2002, no. 1644B) Many lines in this and/or *Greig–Duncan* no. 1644A are to be found tumbling about in the sixty-four-line 'Dreg Song' collected by David Herd and printed in 1776. Hamish Henderson collected from renowned North-Eastern singer Jimmy MacBeath some related lines Jimmy had learned in about 1902 in 'the playground of Portsoy School'. Henderson links (1992) the lines about the 'mannie' and the 'fairy boatie' to a couplet from Herd (1776), 'Hey hou Harry Harry / Mony a boat skail'd the ferry', and finds a possible hint of 'Hairy, alias Clootie' being invoked by seamen.

Mary Annie, sugar cannie
Bumbee bedlar
Saxteen saidler
A mannie in a hairy caipie
Rowin at the fairy boatie
Fairy boatie ow'r dear
Ten pounds in the year
Jock Fite had a coo
Black and white aboot the moo
Hit can jump the Brig o Dee
Singin Cock-a-linkie

*(Henderson 1992)*

Greig received the following epic from an anonymous correspondent in Inverugie. In his notes on it he commented 'It is a problem how these rhymes originated; and it is equally remarkable that, albeit whimsical, disconnected, and illogical to a degree, these should inhere in the memory for a lifetime.' (Shuldham-Shaw et al. 2002, Vol. 8)

The carle sits upo the sea
A his canles on his knee
Ye's three an I's fower
Shaw's the gate tae Aiberdour
Aiberdour an' Aiberdeen
Cragleith upo the green
Cragleith and Wullie Fair
Fat's gweed for a deer?
For a deer an a dog
Cam to warn Wullie Tod
Wullie Tod an Wullie Tey
They were baith born in May
Lunon is a hard gate
Quo the eel unto the skate
Quo the haddock to the eel
Crook ye your tail weel
As weel micht ye be
As the sheep o Lunnerty
Lunnerty an jeelie fike
Staw the rumples fae ma tyke
Fae ma tyke an fae ma turn
Gie me siller, gie me some
Gie me gowd, gie me nane
Ca ma mither Jerry King
Jerry King and Jerry Couth
Staw a pair o gingers
Ten pair o fite feet
Kent ye Thrumlie?
Thrumlie had a mear
Foo mony bags did she bear?
Ten an the monyfauld
Kent ye John Auld
John Auld and Jeelsie
Rang the bell o Dousie
Dousie and Dulzie
Happiky an Hulzie
Rotten geese an almond waters

*(Shuldham-Shaw et al. 2002, no. 1644A)*

There is enough in the Inverugie version to fill a monograph of speculative inter-pretations about placenames, personalities, odd animals and queer fish. For two more richly puzzling texts gathered in by Gavin Greig, see 'I'll tell ye a talie' and 'Eerie Orie, Virgin Mary' in the following anthology section.

The Rev. William Findlay found this kind of rhyme in use by a boy's pals to humiliate him publicly for breaking wind – see the two versions of 'The cobbling grace' in my discussion of boys' favourite topics. Findlay gives a third 'variant' which draws not on the same ground as the first two he quotes, but instead on the same sources as the cooked up mishmash above:

> Jock, John, Jellie, Jam, he cam linkin owre dam
> Owre dam, owre dyke, trip o my taillie
> Taillie and richt knot, dear bocht, dear saul (sold)
> She keepit sheep o green faul (fold)
> As sheep sae did she swine, they ca'd her faither Lord Lyne
> Lord Lyne, tilly tackit, hairy hal his mither nakit
> Mither nakit tho she be, tho a the limbs a limmer tee
> Limmer tee, limmer ta, Jeannie Fyke stoo'd the tail fae my tyke

*(Rymour Club 1911)*

In Rymour Club (1928) Joseph L Waugh gives a thirteen-line version from Dumfriesshire that throws in a piece of 'Johnnie Hielandman', quoted elsewhere. The Rymour Club first published the work of their members in parts, which were later collected into three volumes. Volume 3 (1928) holds the last ten years of parts. When they were emptying out the cupboards before they closed shop, they printed a final selection of Miscellanea, including thirteen lines more (Rymour Club 1928) that muddy the tracks even further, labelling the piece 'one of many variants'. It gives one the beginnings of a headache just trying to think in a straightish line through such wordy thickets. Enough.

## Anthology: Counting and choosing

ABBLESY BIBBLESY
Abblesy bibblesy
Kebblesy dibblesy
Ebblesy fibbleysey
Wy sedan

*(McVicar Collection: Sandy Duncan of Saltcoats, 1950s)*

This is in performance introduced as 'the alphabet said very fast'. It is in a way based on the letters A to F.

ANNIE BELL
Annie Bell, she kens hersel, she lives below the steeple
And every time she rings the bell, she wakens all the people

*(Rymour Club 1919: Kingarth School, Bute, 1911)*

As I was in the kitchen
As I was in the kitchen
Doing a bit of stitching
Old Baldie Humle
Cam an stole ma thumle
I up wi a wee cherry stone
An struck him on the knuckle-bone
You are out, out goes one and out goes she

*(Maclagan 1901)*

Counting out rhyme, see 'Grannie in the kitchen'.

As many bawbees
I've as many bawbees as I can spend ava
And gin ye need a shillin, man, it's I could gie ye twa

*(Rymour Club 1919)*

Black bau
Black bau, grey clüd
Green grass, tap rüd
Stand du der fur do's oot

*(Saxby 1932: Shetland)*

Black sugar
Black sugar white sugar strawberry jam
Tell me the name of your young man

*(Rodger nd)*

Buckie Baker
Buckie Buckie Baker
Your name's in the paper
What is your name in the paper for?
(Love/Marriage/ Murder) (If murder:)

Who did you murder?
I murdered (name)
(Named person goes out)

*(McVicar Collection: Glasgow, 1991)*

CATCH THE NIT
It bit, catch the nit
You are not it

*(McVicar Collection: Glasgow, 1993)*

COWBOY JOE
Cowboy Joe fi Mexico
Hands up, stick them up
Drop your guns and pick them up
O, U, T, spells out

*(McVicar Collection: Dalkeith HS, 1997)*

DONKEY IN THE GRASS
There's a donkey in the grass
With a bullet up his ass
Pull it out, pull it out
Be a good Boy Scout
And if you do what colour would the blood be?

*(McVicar Collection: Glasgow, 1993)*

The rhymer picks a colour and spells it out round the group.

EACHY PEACHY
Eachy peachy hallagolum
Pitchin tatties up the lum
Santa Claus got one in the bum
Eachy peachy hallagolum

*(Ian Davison Card Index)*

EENERTEE FEENERTEE
Eenertee feenertee fichertie fag
Ell dell dolman's egg
Irkie birkie starry rock
Ann tam toosh Jock
Black puddin, white troot
That show's you're oot

*(Hendry & Stephen 1982)*

EENIE MEENIE
Eenie meenie, clean peenie
If you want a piece and jelly
Just walk out

*(Maclagan 1901)*

Eenie meenie macca racca
Eenie meenie macca racca rah ray
A dominaca lollypopa
Don doon doosh out

*(McVicar Collection: Glasgow, 1991)*

Eenie meenie maka naka
El do dona macka
Sugar lolly popa
Rumdum squash

*(McVicar Collection: Glasgow, 1991)*

Eenie meenie macca racca
Day daw dominacca
Chicken poppa, lolly poppa
An O-U-T spells out

*(McVicar Collection: Moray, 2006)*

In East Calder, 2007, the last line was 'Rum dum doo'.

Eenie meenie acha racha
Ex pert dani nacha
Oot skoot pocks a leen jecks
You are not het

*(McVicar Collection:
St Robert's PS, Glasgow, 1997)*

Eenie meenie macca racca
Om pom pacca racca
Eenie meenie macca racca
Om pom push

*(School of Scottish Studies archive:
Hendry, Glenrothes, 1981)*

Eenie meenie makaraka
Diri diri dominaka
Pom pom push
Chinese ju-ju 1, 2, 3
Alla walla webstick
Out she goes

*(Ian Davison Card Index: Temple School)*

**EENIE MEENIE MINEY MO**
Eenie meenie miney mo
Sit the baby on the po
When it's done, clean its bum
Eenie meenie miney mo

*(McVicar Collection: Dalkeith HS, 1997)*

Eenie meenie miney mo
Sit the baby on the bo
Out pop 1, out pop 2
Out pop another one
And that means you

*(McVicar Collection:
St Robert's PS, Glasgow, 1997)*

Eenie meenie miney mo
Sat the baby on the po
When it's done wipe its bum
Fling the paper up the lum
You are out with a dirty dish clout
Right over your shoulder just like this
Penny on the river, tuppence on the sea
Threepence on the ocean and out pops she

*(Ian Davison Card Index: Bellahouston School)*

**EENTY FEENTY**
Eenty feenty halligolun
The cat went out to get some fun
He got some fun and tore his skin
As eenty feenty halligolin

*(Maclagan 1901)*

*[handwritten margin note:]* Eenie, meenie miney mo / Catch a nigger by the toe / If he squeals, let him go / Eenie meenie miney mo

*Our version 1940's – 50's*

EENTIE TEENTIE
Eentie teentie, tippenny bun
The cat geed oot tae get some fun
She got some fun, she played drum
Eentie teentie, tippenny bun

*(Hendry & Stephen 1982: '19th century')*

EERIE ORIE
Eerie orie, Virgin Mary
Aa the keetles in a tearie
Tak up your fit and gie's a pu
Seven weeks have I been fu
Seven more shall I be
By the weeks of Marie
Marie an St John
Aa the tailors in the tron
Up the bank and doon the brae
Lang fit and short tae
Gie his tail to the pleuch
My tail's lang eneuch

*(Shuldham-Shaw et al. 2002, no. 1642)*

A relative of the long rigmaroles in the previous chapter. A Mintlaw version from Annie Shirer is a little smoother:

Tak up your fit an gie's a pu
Sax ouks hae I been fu
Sax mair I shall be
By the land and by the sea
Aa the tailors in the toon
Up the bank, syne doon

*(Rymour Club 1919)*

EERIE ORRIE
Eerie orrie, eekerie am
Pick me, mick me, shick me sham
Orum scorum, pick-ma-norum
Shee sho sham shutter – you're out

*(Rymour Club 1919:*
*'Old Edinburgh rhyme')*

### Ezeenty teenty

Ezeenty teenty figgery fell
Ell dell dominell
Arky parky taurry rope
Ann tan toosey joke
Jock went out tae sell his eggs
Who did he meet but bandy legs
Bandy legs and tippy toes
That's the way the ladies go
You are out

*(Ian Davison Card Index)*

### Freddie

One, two: Freddie's coming for you
Three, four: You'd better lock the door
Five, six: Get a crucifix
Seven, eight: You'd better stay up late
Nine, ten: Never sleep again

*(Ian Davison Card Index: Bellahouston School)*

### Hurley burley

Hurley burley, tramp the trace
The coo shet owre the market place
East or west? The craw's nest?
Where does this poor man go?

*(Rymour Club 1919: Dunfermline)*

### Ickerty pickerty

Ickerty pickerty pie-sel-ickerty
Pompa lori jig
Every man that has no hair
Generally wears a wig
One two three, out goes he
Ickerty pickerty pie-sel-ickerty
Pompa lori jig

*(Rymour Club 1911: Edinburgh)*

### Iggoty piggoty

Iggoty piggoty
Iso liggity
Umpah pygo jig
Every man in China
Ought to wear a wig

*(Ian Davison Card Index: Bellahouston School)*

IF YOU'D HAVE BEEN
If you'd have been
Where I have been
The fairy queen
You'd have been out
Out goes one, out goes two
Out goes another one
And that means you

(Ian Davison Card Index: Rottenrow School)

First two lines are a fragment of 'The braes of Killiekrankie'.

I'LL TELL YE A TALIE
I'll tell ye a talie
Aboot the fit and the failie
And the brunt bridle o Killiemeer
That nae man weel feart
I took my fit in my hand
And I hit it owre to Ireland
And fat saw ye there?
I saw the maiden at the window
Kaimin her hair
And by cam the cock
And snappit the kaim fae 'er
And he took gate and she took gate
And throw the meer they ran
And fair fa ye Blue-breekies
Saw ye my guidman?
I saw your guidman
And I'll tell ye fu
He brunt a hole in's breeks
And fat maks that to you?

(Shuldham-Shaw et al. 2002: no. 1635)

INGLE ANGLE
Ingle angle, silver bangle
Ingle angle, A, B, C, D,
E, F, G, H, I, J, K, L,
M, N, O, P, Q, R, S, T,
U, V, W, X, Y, Z Zombie
Ingle angle, silver bangle

(McVicar Collection: Glasgow 1991)

IP DIP

Ip dip dog shit
You are no it

*(McVicar Collection: Glasgow, 1991)*

IPPITTY SOOPITTY

Ippitty soopitty, ippetty sap
Ippetty soopittie, cunella cunapp
Cunellow up, cunellow down
Cunellow into Chinatown

*(Alan Lomax archive:*
*Kathleen & Jack Mearns, Aberdeen)*

JOHNNY'S HEAD

All over Johnny's head
The bugs are playin leapfrog
1 2 3 and over, 1 2 3 and over
They play so merrily in every little corner
1 2 3 and over, 1 2 3 and out

*(Ian Davison Card Index:*
*Rottenrow School; tune: 'Poppa Picolino')*

MAISTER MUNDY

Maister Mundy, how's your wife?
Very sick an like to die
Can she eat any meat?
Just as much as I can buy
She makes her porridge very thin
A pound of butter she puts in
Black puddin, white troot
Eerie-orie, you're oot

*(MacLennan 1909)*

MAMMY DADDY

Mammy Daddy tell me true
Who should I be married to?
Tinker tailor soldier sailor
Rich man poor man
Beggarman thief

*(Ian Davison Card Index: Rottenrow School)*

MARY AT THE COTTAGE DOOR
One two three four
Mary at the cottage door
Eating cherries off a plate
Doon fell the summer seat
I've a kistie, I've a creel
I've a barrelie fu o meal
To ser my bairnies till't be done
Come teetle, come tottle, come twenty-one

*(Rymour Club 1911)*

'A prime favourite among Forfar children.'

MY HERT'S IN THE HEILINS
My hert's in the Heilins, my claes is in the pawn
And my wife's awa to Paisley wi anither wife's man

*(Rymour Club 1919)*

MY MOTHER YOUR MOTHER
If my mother and your mother
Were hanging out the washing
And my mum punched your mum right on the nose
What colour would the blood be?

*(McVicar Collection: Glasgow, 1993)*

The rhymer picks any colour and spells it out between the people, and the last letter points to the person who is out. Note the perverse use of 'washing' rather than the usual rhyme 'clothes'.

My mother and your mother
Were hanging out some clo'es
My mother gave your mother
A dunt on the nose
What colour was her blood?
Red.
R-E-D stands for RED and O-U-T spells OUT

*(Alan Lomax archive:*
*Cedar Place children, Aberdeen)*

NIEVIE-NIEVIE
Nievie-nievie nick-nack
Which hand will ye tak?
Tak the right, tak the wrang
I'll beguile ye if I can

*(Chambers 1842)*

ONE POTATO
1 potato, 2 potato, 3 potato, 4
5 potato, 6 potato, 7 potato more
Penny in the river
Penny in the sea
Penny in the ocean
And out pops she

*(Ian Davison Card Index)*

ONE'S NANE
One's nane, two's some
Three's a pickle, four's a pund
Five's a dainty, six is plenty
Seven's a horse's meal

*(Maclagan 1901)*

OOR WEE JEANIE
Oor wee Jeanie had a nice clean peenie
Guess what colour it was
Red
R-E-D spells RED, and O-U-T spells OUT

*(School of Scottish Studies archive: Henderson, Glasgow, 1957)*

OOZIE OOZIE ARNS
Oozie oozie arns, you're withoot the harns
Up and doon aa the toon, glowerin at the starns
Eeksie peeksie, turn aboot
One two, you are oot

*(Rymour Club 1919: Perthshire)*

ORANGES, ORANGES
Oranges, oranges, four for a penny
My father was drunk from eating too many
Be bo Baldy Snout
I am in and you are out

*(Maclagan 1901)*

P-I-G SPELLS PIG
P-I-G spells PIG
T-I-G spells TIG
You are out
With a dirty washing clout
Right over your left ear
Just like this

*(Ian Davison Card Index)*

SING A SONG
Sing a song, a ming, a mong, a carlin and a kit
And them at disna like butter, put in their tongue and lick

*(Rymour Club 1919: Annie Shirer, Mintlaw)*

SOUR-MILK JENNY
Sour-milk Jenny, a pint for a penny
Stop your horse and give me a drink
Sour-milk Jenny, you are out

*(Rymour Club 1919: Kingarth School, Bute, 1911)*

THREE WHITE HORSES
Three white horses in a stable
Pick one out and call it Mabel
If it's Mabel, set the table
Three white horses in a stable

*(Alan Lomax archive: Peggy MacGillivray, Edinburgh)*

Six white horses in a stable
Pick one out and call it Mabel
Maypole butter maypole tea M-A-Y-P-O-L-E

*(Ian Davison Card Index: John Street School, tune: 'Bobby Shafto')*

A ruder version is quoted in Chapter 14.

TWO WAN
Two wan picks a man
1, 2, 3, 4, 5, 6, 7, 8, 9, 10
11, 12, 13, 14, 15, 16, 17, 18, 19, 20
Twenty-one picks a man and who should that very lucky man be?

*(McVicar Collection: Glasgow, 1991)*

# 6
# *For the want of the Golden City*

## Singing games

> How many miles to Babylon?
> Three score and ten
> Will we be there by candlelight?
> Yes, and back again
> Open your gates and let us through
> Not without a beck and a boo
> There's a beck and there's a boo
> Open your gates and let us go through

More has been written about singing games than the other kind of lyrics I cover. Games with a structure are more visible in the playground because of their organised group nature and formalised movements and if they have song involved they are more obviously audible. The disappearance of most of them from active use is much lamented by adults.

These games are repeatedly published, in scholarly surveys or in practical handbooks for people who work with children. Through these handbooks standard texts have been informally agreed and widely disseminated, although as ever the child players subvert the norms when outwith adult control. The games are much more available in print than other glories of Scots children's lore, so there is little need for me to give all of them here, nor shall I describe the games that lyrics are attached to – my concern is with the lyrics and tunes, not the movements.

I've subdivided my anthology section into two, one on the theme of courting, the other about movement. In their standard text, *The Singing Game* (1985), the Opies have 19 categories for 161 separate singing games.

Many of the games are played throughout the British Isles and former dominions, in richly diverse versions. I have chosen to show here detailed texts only for those games for which I can find strong Scottish connections or evidence of origin, or at least distinctive versions, north of the border, or where the text language is attractively Scots. But I owe it to the casual reader to give an aide memoire list of some of the best-known games I have not detailed: 'The big ship sails on the eely ally o', 'Bobby Bingo',

'The farmer's in his den', 'The grand old Duke of York', 'Here comes a bluebird', 'In and out the windows', 'King William', 'Lady on the mountain', 'The muffin man', 'Nuts in May', 'Old Roger', 'Oranges and lemons', 'Poor widow of Sandilands', 'Pop goes the weasel', 'Romans and English', 'Spanish lady', 'Tennessee wig-walk', 'Tisket a tasket', 'Two little sandy girls', 'We are all King George's men' and 'When I was a lady'.

As usual in the playground there was and is much swopping and amalgamating of stanzas and elements; it is the initial verses and the game actions that distinguish one from another, for which see the Opies and Gomme, who give multiple versions and histories. Scotland was at the forefront of collecting games and rhymes, with key early collections by Chambers, Nicholson, Gregor and Maclagan. Why this early interest? Was it because of the richness and vigour of game playing in Scotland? As usual the tale of these games and texts is tangled.

One aspect of child lore is the occasional preservation of skeletal versions of songs, games or customs that were formerly the preserve of young or full-grown adults. I gave earlier a couple of blood-curdling ballads that were reduced to 'lullabies'. The Edinburgh 1950 film *The Singing Street* shows fourteen-year-old girls playing street games that twelve year olds would now reject as too young for them. In the annual fair events of lowland Scottish towns the variously titled fair queens were formerly strapping teen-agers, but now are eleven year olds.

In *The Singing Game* the Opies select 'The merry matanzie' to be the first of their Wedding Rings games:

> Here I gae round the jingie ring
> The jingie ring, the jingie ring
> Here I gae round the jingie ring
> And through my merry-metanzie

They say the game was first mentioned in 1821 being played by Edinburgh children and the description first given in print by Jamieson in his dictionary of 1825, but the view of lexicographers, quoted below, that the song name is a 'corrupted phrase' suggests greater antiquity.

The *Scottish National Dictionary* gives a number of spellings of merry matanzie, describing them as 'various forms of a corrupted word or phrase found in the refrain of a children's ring game. The last element is probably a child's adaptation of dance.' Six other incidences of the phrase in print are given, ranging from the *Aberdeen Shaver* in 1837 to poet W Soutar in 1933. A shaver and a soutar – from a barber to a cobbler.

Versions of the game tend to include the choosing of a lover, guessing of a beloved's name, and preparation of the house for the return of the newlyweds. There are occasional felicities, like the following from Robert Chambers (1842):

Honey is sweet, and so is he, so is he, so is he
Honey is sweet, and so is he, about the merry-ma-tanzie

Apples are sour and so is he [etc.]

He's married wi a gay gold ring [etc.]

A gay gold ring's a cankerous thing [etc.]

Now they're married, I wish them joy [etc.]

Father and mother they must obey [etc.]

Loving each other like sister and brother [etc.]

We pray this couple may kiss together [etc.]

A couple of versions in print complicate matters quite a lot. In an article on 'Edinburgh Rhyme-Games and Airs' first printed in a Rymour Club Part of March 1908, then in Rymour Club Vol 1 (1911), Alan Reid gives an odd hybrid singing game called 'The galley, galley ship'. He comments that the first four verses, set to a familiar-sounding tune, are 'a quatrain evidently borrowed from "The gowden vanitee" or "The mermaid"'. The next five stanzas are sung 'to the air ' "Merry-ma-tanzie" ':

Three times round goes the galley, galley ship
And three times round goes she
And three times round goes the galley, galley ship
Till we sank to the bottom of the sea

'Pull her up, pull her up,' cried the sailor boys
'Pull her up, pull her up,' cried he
'Pull her up, pull her up,' cried the sailor boys
Till we sank to the bottom of the sea

'No, I won't, no, I won't,' cried the sailor boys [etc.]
'Yes, I will, yes, I will,' cried the sailor boys, [etc.]

Choose your neighbours, one or two
One or two, one or two
Choose your neighbours, one or two
Around the merry-ma-tanzie

> Shake your tails till the bride comes in [etc.]
> A guinea-gold watch to tell her name [etc.]
> A treacle scone to tell his name [etc.]
> Now it's time to show your face [etc.]

(Rymour Club 1911)

Reid says the game 'begins again, *de novo*, with the "Galley, Galley Ship" [. . .] I have never heard the correct words, "Gallant, gallant ship," used in the game.' What are we to make of the shaking of tails, and the offer of a treacle scone? I would be tempted to consider this as a possible corrupted, confused and facetious late survival of 'The merry matanzie', if it were not in fact fairly contemporaneous with other versions that show a clearer acount of proceedings. And if, also, there was not an account of a closely related but much more elaborate version given by Edgar L Wakeman in the *Weekly Scotsman* of 16 Oct 1893, reported by Alice Gomme (1894) who describes it as 'a wonderful music-drama of childhood'. In this variant the 'neighbours' become 'maidens', 'shake your tails' becomes 'sweep the house', an action which occupies 'several stanzas', and there are then 'from a score to a hundred stanzas, with marching and various imitations of what the lucky bride accomplishes or undergoes'. At the end the bride's first-born is christened:

> Next Sunday morn to church she must gae
> A babe on her knee, the best of aa
> And down goes Merrima Tansa

Up to one hundred stanzas! One hundred! Not one for a fifteen-minute playtime, then?

The professional day-nursery people have taken a butcher's knife to this game. Tinies are now invited to hip, hop and hie-de-ho, walk, skip and swing. Only three lines are left from traditional variants. Such maltreatment of the venerable Jingo Ring makes me feel rather ill.

How Scottish is 'The merry matanzie'? Almost exclusively so. As regards its age, there is a record of it in 1821 and a report of it being known earlier than 1816. A School of Scottish Studies file card records the following from the Crombie Mss, against a text of Jingo Ring collected by Dr Cramond: 'According to Dr Cramond, believed to have been introduced into Cullen from Aberdeen by Mary Guthrie in 1816, or perhaps reintroduced, after being forgotten.'

What interests and puzzles me most about this song is the title phrase. Robert Graves has pointed out that Matanze is a festival in Mallorca. The *Scottish National Dictionary* suggests 'tanzie' is derived from 'dance'. A friend of Robert Chambers seems to have started this particular hare: 'A friend has suggested to me that the name seems to be Mit mir tanzen, literally 'Dance with me', leading to the idea of a German origin for this piece of puerile amusement.'

'Here we go round the dance with me'? Or 'Here we go round the with me dance'? Doesn't really convince, does it? It is even less likely that they dance merrily round the tansy or common ragwort. I have a wildish theory of mine own.

'Merry' is merry, plain and simple. Ma occasionally becomes May in variants. Further, in the *Dictionary of the Older Scottish Tongue*, which considers the state of the Scottish language prior to 1700, ma can be may or mai. What if tanzie is a corruption or diminutive of tannel, which the *Scottish National Dictionary* says is 'a bonfire lit to burn garden or other rubbish or to celebrate some popular event . . . as on May-day, Midsummer Eve or Halloween'. The *Scottish National Dictionary* goes on to quote accounts of 'making merry' or dancing about the tannel.

Around the merry May bonfire. Seems reasonable enough. However, I know that in linguistics reasonability is not always a helpful guide, so I consulted a language expert informally after a lecture. He felt that the shift from tannel to tanzie was by no means impossible. He asked that I write to him with details if I wanted him to consider the matter properly. I have not yet done so. I suspect I would rather keep my nice little theory than have an expert assessment that may say 'Na, na, son, yer no on!'

Argyllshire children preserved the word 'tansie' in an unclear context that suggests it was a drink – 'Cuddie' here is not a horse, but a diminutive of 'Christina':

> Sandy likes in tansie o
> But my delight's in brandy o
> Sandy likes in a red red nose
> Caller on my Cuddie o
>
> Hey ho for Cuddie o
> My bonny bonny Cuddie o
> All the world that I wad gie
> If I had my Cuddie o

*(Maclagan 1901)*

What about the meaning and derivation of the Jingo Ring? 'By jingo' was a disguised swear phrase in the nineteenth century, surely not relevant, though Oor Wullie was too inclined to explete 'jings'. In *A Dictionary of Slang and Unconventional English* Partridge considers 'jings' probably comes from the Basque word meaning God, 'j(a)inko', via the Basque harpooners on British whalers. He also tells of 'jinkgoving, which is a way of clapping their hands on the mouth of two jars'. Too far out to be useful, I fear.

The game word can be jingo, jingle, jing-go, jing-a, ging-a, ging-go. Might it be linked to jing-bang? The *Scottish National Dictionary* cites an earliest printed reference in 1835, but casts no light on what kind of ring it is.

The tune usually employed for 'The merry matanzie' is also used for 'The mulberry bush' and 'Nuts in May' and requires detailed investigation. The 'merry matanzie' tune, most often known as 'The mulberry bush' or 'Nancy Dawson', has a long history, but, through consideration of two other Scottish game songs, 'Bee baw babbity' and 'Who'll come into my wee ring', I have been able to push the history of the tune further back still.

Although I refer to the tune as 'Bee baw babbity', I could as well call it 'Babbity Bowster'. Both songs are widely sung and are clearly close relatives, deriving from the older 'Bab at the Bowster'. Chambers (1842) gives a 'Babbity Bowster' text which is concerned with social skills:

> Wha learned you to dance, Babbity Bowster, Babbity Bowster
> Wha learned you to dance, Babbity Bowster brawly?
> My minnie learned me to dance, Babbity Bowster, Babbity Bowster
> My minnie learned me to dance, Babbity Bowster brawly
> Wha ga'e you the keys to keep, Babbity Bowster, Babbity Bowster
> Wha ga'e you the keys to keep, Babbity Bowster brawly?
> Ma minnie ga'e me the keys to keep, Babbity Bowster, Babbity Bowster
> Ma minnie ga'e me the keys to keep, Babbity Bowster brawly

Alan Reid in a 1913 article for the Rymour Club gives a 'match-making' text for 'Bee baw babbity':

> Bee baw babbity, babbity, babbity
> Be baw babbity, babbity, bounce the ballie
>
> Kneel down, kiss the ground, kiss the ground, kiss the ground
> Kneel down, kiss the ground, kiss a bonnie wee lassie
>
> I wouldn't have a laddie, o, a laddie, o, a laddie, o
> I wouldn't have a laddie, o, I'd have a bonnie wee lassie
>
> Choose, choose, who you'll take, who you'll take, who you'll take
> Choose, choose, who you'll take, I'll take a bonnie wee lassie
>
> *(Rymour Club 1919)*

In the Skene manuscript of the 1620s is a tune called 'Who learned you to dance and a towdle'. Defeated by the lute tablature, I was relieved to find in *Scottish Fiddlers and Their Music* by Mary Anne Alburger a transcription that turned out to be a fanciful and flighty playing of the usual *Babbity Bowster* tune. What was a towdle? Alburger got the transcription from William Dauney's *Ancient Scotish Melodies*, 1838, and says that in Dauney 'another eight bars follow this section' – maybe those eight bars were the towdle.

The tunes of 'The merry matanzie' and 'Babbity Bowster' are combined together for the game song 'Who'll come in tae ma wee ring'. This latter song was recorded in 1991 by a group of pensioners in Castlemilk, Glasgow, when they were recalling children's songs from childhood. Their text utilises the matchmaking elements of 'Bee baw babbity' given by Reid and others, and they add a stanza of 'Bee baw babbity' on to their singing of 'Ma wee ring'.

(Transcription: McVicar; *Ma Maw Says* late 1980s)

Who'll come in tae ma wee ring, tae ma wee ring, tae ma wee ring
Who'll come in tae ma wee ring, tae make it a wee bit bigger?
I'll come in tae your wee ring, tae your wee ring, tae your wee ring
I'll come in tae your wee ring, and make it a wee bit bigger
Choose, choose, wha ye'll tak, wha ye'll tak, wha ye'll tak
Choose, choose, wha ye'll tak, a lassie or a wee laddie?
I wouldnae hae a lassie-o, a lassie-o, a lassie-o
I wouldnae hae a lassie-o, I'd raether hae a wee laddie
Bee baw babbity, babbity, babbity
Bee baw babbity, a lassie or a wee laddie, laddie, laddie

(*Ma Maw Says* late 1980s)

    This game is known to me from childhood and to other singers I have consulted, and the Opies (1985) give a Paisley text and description from 1851. The two musical strains are linked in Charles D'Esteve's 1883 *Jing-Ga-Ring Easy Quadrille* dance arrangement of sixteen 'Songs and Nursery Rhymes Sung by Children'. He invites the dancers to sing when they reach 'Jing-ga-ring', and follows it immediately with 'Bab at the bouster', as follows:

*(D'Esteve 1883)*

This leads us into one of the most famous tunes of our islands, 'Greensleeves'. Hang on, surely 'Greensleeves' is not a game-type tune, but a lugubrious ditty, penned by Henry VIII in a depressed half hour? Not so. The oldest record of 'Greensleeves' has it registered with the Stationer's Company as 'A new northern dittye' in September 1580. In the seventh edition of *The Dancing Master* (1696) the tune is called 'Green sleeves and pudding-pies'. Both Emmerson (1971) and Fuld (1966) emphasise that the tune only became known as a slow and stately tune within the twentieth century; it was known as a sprightly jig in the time of Shakespeare and later. Not only that, it could be a rowdy song. In 1776 David Herd noted three stanzas for 'Green sleeves and pudden-pyes', the second of which is basic and bawdy enough to startle most companies. Boswell gave a 'Jacobite song' verse in his journal, and other political lyrics were set to the tune in England, because of the 'merry swing of the tune'. (Chappell 1859)

Emmerson quotes a verse of 'Green sleeves and pudding pies' sung to Johnson and Boswell in 1773 by the daughter of Alexander Macdonald of Kingsburgh, and said by her to be the only song sung by her father, a man who had entertained Flora Macdonald and the Young Pretender in his house and possibly sang his one song for them:

> Green sleeves and pudding pies
> Tell me where my true love lies
> And I'll be with her before she rise
> Fiddle and aw together

Comparison of the well known 'Greensleeves' tune and 'Who'll come in tae my wee ring?' shows that 'my wee ring' is essentially a major key version of the minor key 'Greensleeves'. This was a 'Northern' ditty when first listed in 1580. Northern could mean North England, or else Scotland. Which is it? Is 'Greensleeves' a Scottish tune? Could be.

There are as usual surprising reworkings of the puzzling text parts of 'Bee baw babbity'. Maclagan (1901) gives

> B O Babbity, babbity, babbity
> B O Babbity, babbity, busty barley

Mactaggart (1824) gives a text known to him in Galloway early in the nineteenth century as 'An old dance, the dance which always ends balls':

Wha learn'd you to dance, you to dance, you to dance
Wha learn'd you to dance, a country bumpkin brawly?
My mither learn'd me when I was young, when I was young, when I was young
My mither learn'd me when I was young, the country bumpkin brawly

The easy variability of the last line of the identifying stanza even permits 'Cockibendy', quoted elsewhere, to make a possible guest appearance. An article on 'Scottish Folk Rhymes' in Rymour Club (1911) gives as a song:

> Wha learned you to dance, you to dance, you to dance?
> Wha learned you to dance, Cocky Breeky brawly?
> My minnie learned me to dance, me to dance, me to dance
> My minnie learned me to dance, Cocky Breeky brawly

Busty barley, country bumpkin, Cocky Breeky, these syllables trip off the tongue to add to the lightness of the dance step. The bouncing open rhythm of 'The wind blows high' has long made it a favourite throughout Britain, though since it was a minor hit for Irish group the Dubliners under the title 'I'll tell my ma', it is considered by many to be Irish in origin. You should know about the Scots versions.

The *Greig–Duncan Collection* (Shuldham-Shaw et al. 2002) has three rich North-East texts dated from 1900 to 1910. This was from a 1900 schoolgirl in Durris:

> The wind, the wind, the wind blows high
> The rain comes pattering from the sky
> (Jenny Johnson) says she'll die
> For the lad of the rolling eye
>
> She is handsome, she is pretty
> She is the flower of the golden city
> She's got lovers, one two three
> Pray and tell me who they be
>
> (Johnny Gammie) is her lover
> Now and then he's waiting for her
> Lash the whip and away we go
> Up the Castle Races oh

> *(Shuldham-Shaw et al. 2002, no. 1578A)*

She sang it to a simplified version of the following, which was noted in 1906 by Greig from one of his fellow teachers in the small Whitehills school where he was head master.

The wind, the wind, the wind blows high    The rain comes spar-kling    down the sky

says she'll die    For    the lad    wi the rol-ling    eye

*(Shuldham-Shaw et al. 2002, no. 1578B)*

Sometimes 'snow' comes 'dashing' or more prosaically 'falling', or she pines for the 'boy with the tartan tie', 'for the want of the golden eye' or even 'for the want of the golden city' itself; sometimes she is the 'belle' of the golden city. The Opies (1985) tell us of a Shetland version circa 1900 that hints at a far older song. It 'begins "Rain, rain high, and the wind doth blow" and ends "Down she comes all dressed in silk With a rose in her bosom as white as milk. She pulls off her glove and shows him the ring. Tomorrow, tomorrow the wedding will begin."'

In Glenrothes in 1981 they played a full-throated full tilt game with special relish for the insult about her looks while the playground roared around them:

> The wind, the wind, the wind blows high
> Snow is fallin from the sky
> Tell me, tell me, who she loves
> For the one and two and three
>
> She is handsome, she is ugly
> She is the one from the golden city
> Tell me, tell me, who she loves
> For the one and two and three

Then they chose someone to go out into the middle and decided who their boyfriend was:

> Gavin Ford says he loves you, etc.
> Stamp your feet if you hate him, etc.
> Clap your hands if you like him, etc.

*(School of Scottish Studies archive: Hendry, Glenrothes)*

The sweet, simple tune used in Glenrothes in 1981 is also that used for the following, making the link with the 'I'll tell my ma' element of the Dublin version:

Weary weary waiting on you
I shall wait no longer on you
Three times I've whistled on you
Are you coming out?

I'll tell mamma when I get home
The boys won't leave the girls alone
They pull my hair and break my comb
I'll tell mamma when I get home

*(Rymour Club 1911)*

These two verses do not obviously live together, unless you visualise a girl complaining to her pal about a) another pal who will not come out when called, and b) boys in general.

On first meeting this next game song you might confidently assume from the opening that it is sung to the carol tune 'I saw three ships', but the air used is in fact 'Sheriffmuir'.

Glasgow ships come sailing in
Come sailing in, come sailing in
Glasgow ships come sailing in
On a fine summer morning

You dare not stamp your foot upon
Your foot upon, your foot upon
You dare not stamp your foot upon
Or Gentle John will kiss you

Three times kiss you
Four times kiss you
Send a piece of butter and bread
Upon a silver saucer

Who shall we send it to?
Send it to, send it to
Who shall we send it to?
To (Mrs McKay's) daughter

She washes her face, she combs her hair
She leaves her lad at the foot of the stair
She wears a gold ring and a velvet string
And she turns her back behind her

*(Maclagan 1901)*

'Gentle John' is sometimes 'Uncle John'. This was an exclusively Scottish game, and Maclagan says 'The same game exactly is played in (Tullynessle) Aberdeenshire.' That lyric substitutes 'a gill and a wee drap mair' for the ring and string, and names the boy as Jamie Tod. The Tullynessle tune, shown in Chapter 15, was ironed out to be 4/4 rather than 6/8.

The Rymour Club (1919) has the following variant last verse, collected by the Duchess of Sutherland in Helmsdale and Portgower Schools:

She washed her face and combed her hair, she left her lad at the foot o the stair
She gave him a glass and a little more, and shut the door behind him

These lines could be read either as a rejection of the lad, or an acceptance of him into her bedchamber. Speaking of beds, Glasgow in 1978 produced a surprisingly late version of 'Best bed's a feather bed', a game the Opies (1985) say 'always belonged to the north-east', and 'continues to be suggestive of blowzy eighteenth-century merrymaking'. Like 'The merry matanzie' it was a 'cushion dance'. The Opies' 1978 version of 'Best bed' was sung to a variant of 'Castles in the air'. A 1952 Dundee recording made by the Montgomeries had a cheekier tune, saying that wheat straw 'dirties aa yer shirtie'.

Hey, bonny lassie, will ye lay the cushion doon?
Will ye lay the cushion doon?
Wheat straw's dirty, dirties aa yer goon
Hey, bonny lassie, lay the cushion doon

*(Rodger nd)*

The next game holds a dreaming whisper of long ago times when ambassadors from foreign lands came seeking a bride for a prince:

We are three brethren come from Spain
All in French garlands
We are come to court your daughter Jean
And adieu to you, my darlings

My daughter Jean she is too young [etc.]
She cannot bide your flattering tongue [etc.]

Be she young or be she old [etc.]
It's for a bride she must be sold [etc.]

A bride a bride she shall not be [etc.]
Till she go through this world with me [etc.]

Come back, come back you courteous knights [etc.]
Clear up your spurs, and make them bright [etc.]

Smell my lilies, smell my roses [etc.]
Which of my maidens do you choose? [etc.]

Are all your daughters safe and sound? [etc.]
Are all your daughters safe and sound? [etc.]

In every pocket a thousand pounds [etc.]
On every finger a gay gold ring [etc.]

*(Chambers 1842)*

Chambers says the suitor 'is quite assured by the answer and marries the "daughter Jean"'. The Argyllshire version is used to find who is hiding a ball. It ends with a struggle and an insult about body piercing sung by the 'Mother':

The ball is ours, it's none of yours
Go to the garden and pluck your flowers
We have pins to pin our clothes
You have nails to nail your nose

*(Maclagan 1901)*

A hundred years later, the version collected by Ritchie (1965) retains the core of the story and the sweet little tune, plus a surprising coda; he says it was 'played in Bothwell Street (1938)':

*(Ritchie 1965)*

There came three Jews from the land of Spain
To call upon my sister Jane

My sister Jane is far too young
I cannnot bear her chattering tongue

Go away Corkscrew!
My name is not Corkscrew
I stamp my foot and away I go

Come back, come back, your coat's so green
And choose the fairest one you seen

The fairest one that I can see
Is bonnie wee Jean, will ye come to me?

No!
Ye dirty wee rat, ye'll no come oot
No come oot, no come oot
Ye dirty wee rat, ye'll no come oot
To help me wi aa ma washing

The same applies to you, sir
E-I-O sir

Now I've got the Prince of Wales
To help me with my washing

*(Ritchie 1965)*

The Castlemilk Pensioners (*Ma Maw Says* late 1980s) sang a version of this with vigour. In Loanhead around 1840 a game was played that suggests where the last three stanzas above came from, to be welded on to the old courting game:

Bonny may, will ye come oot? Will ye come oot, will ye come oot?
Bonny may, will ye come oot and help us wi oor dancing?
Out o my sicht, ye dirty slut, your faither was a tinkler
He made a pair o shoon for me, they didna last a winter

*(Rymour Club 1911)*

## Anthology: Courting, formation, dance, processional

### Courting

THE BONNIE BUNCH O ROSES
Up against the wall, the London ball
The London ball, the London ball
Up against the wall, the London ball
An a bonnie bunch o roses

Ah met ma laud in the bramble law [etc.]
Wi a bonnie bunch o roses

Ha ha ha, ye needna rin [etc.]
Wi a bonnie bunch o roses

Ma faither bocht a new top-coat [etc.]
An Jeannie tore the lining

Ha ha ha, ye needna rin [etc.]
For ye'll get yer licks in the mornin

*(School of Scottish Studies archive: Henderson, Leven, 1960,*
*recorded from the mother of singer Jean Redpath)*

In a 1952 Dundee version found by the Montgomeries, the father wore 'a rustic coat', the players went to the Banks of Aberfeldie, saw a lad who danced in a kilt and got a kiss and a gold ring.

In the 1950 Edinburgh film *The Singing Street* the girls sang 'She buckled up her skirt and away she went' and 'She met her lover on the way'.

HAVE YOU EVER?
Have you ever ever ever in your long legged life
Seen a long legged sailor with a long legged wife
No I've never never never in my long legged life
Seen a long legged sailor with a long legged wife

*(Ian Davison Card Index, Temple School)*

In Culbokie Primary School in 2006 this sailor was followed by shipmates who were short-legged, knock-kneed, and bow-legged.

I WROTE A LETTER
Sea shells cockle shells
Eevory ivory over
I wrote a letter to my love
And on the way I dropped it
I dropped it once I dropped it twice
I dropped it three times over
Over over over
In and out the clover

*(Ian Davison Card Index)*

JANET JO
I've come to court Janet jo
Janet jo, Janet jo
I've come to court Janet jo
How's she the day?

She's up the stair washin [etc.]
Ye canna see her the day

The suitor tries again, and is repulsed by her parents, who say she is bleaching, drying, then ironing clothes. At last

Janet jo's dead and gane [etc.]
She'll never come hame

*(Chambers 1842)*

This is 'the Edinburgh version', in which she sometimes revives. The Kirkcudbright-shire version was 'a dramatic entertainment amongst young rustics' in which the swain was rebuffed till he offered 'a peck o gowd'. Maclagan (1901) reports a lengthy version called 'Genesis' Ghost', in which the dressed corpse is being buried, but her ghost leaps up to catch a new Genesis. Duncan (Shuldham-Shaw et al. 2002, no. 1597) gives a stirring ninety-seven lines in which ailing Georgina dies, much effort is spent selecting dresses for the funeral and the mourner ends as a skeleton.

POOR MARY LIES A-WEEPIN
Mary lies a-weepin, a-weepin, a-weepin
Mary lies a-weepin on sighs summer day
On the grass go she shall be
Till the grass grows on the field

Stand up stand up, polly veelly veep
And show me the girl and the next two asleep

How do you marry? I'd marry for joy
First to a girl, and the next to a boy

*(Alan Lomax archive: Garrynamonie schoolchildren, South Uist)*

A rather garbled text from native Gaelic singers. Other published versions begin with 'What's poor Mary weeping for?' Sometimes she cries for her dead father, sometimes for lack of a sweetheart, sometimes for a lover at sea.

SALLY WATERS
Sally Sally Waters, sprinkling in a pan
Rise Sally, rise Sally, for a young man
Come choose from the east, come choose from the west
Come choose out the very one that you love the best

Now there's a couple married in joy
First a girl and then a boy
Now you're married you must obey
Every word your husband says
Take a kiss and walk away
And remember the promise you've made today

*(Gomme 1894: Gregor, Fochabers)*

Rev. W Gregor contributed to Gomme several more versions collected around the North-East that cut and paste verses, like the following:

Rise, Sally Walker, rise if you can
Rise, Sally Walker, follow your gudeman
Come choose to the east, come choose to the west
Come choose to the very one that you love best

Now they're married I wish them joy
Every year a girl or boy
Loving each other like sister and brother
And so they may be kissed together

Cheese and bread for gentlemen
And corn and hay for horses
A cup of tea for aa good wives
And bonnie lads and lassies

When are we to meet again?
And when are we to marry?
Raffles up, and raffles down, and raffles aa adancin
The bonniest lassie that ever I saw was (child in centre) dancin

*(Gomme 1894: Gregor, Aberdeen Training College)*

SANDY SEATON'S WOOING
O Sandy Seaton's gane to woo
Down by Kirkady Lea
And there he met wi a puir auld man
His guid-father to be

He led his daughter by the hand
His daughter ben brought he
'O, is not she the fairest lass
That's in great Christendye?'

'I winna marry wi ony lad
In aa the land o Fife
I winna leave my mammie yet
And I winna be his wife'

He's courted her and brocht her hame
His guidwife for to be
He's gi'en her jewels and gi'en her gold
And he's kissed her three times three

*(Moffat 1933)*

'This is an old Fifeshire singing-game. It seems to be a nursery derivative of "Kempy Kaye", an ancient ballad.'

TWO DUKES
Here are two dukes arriving
Arriving, arriving
Here are two dukes arriving
My ramsy tamsy telimsay

What is your good will, sir [etc.]
My will, sir, is to get married [etc.]
Take one of my fair daughters [etc.]

They are all so black and so browsy
They sit on the sides o Rousay
They have no chains about their necks
And they are all so black and so browsy

Good enough for you, sir [etc.]

Before I ride the cities so wide
I will take Miss (name of player) to be my bride

*(Shuldham-Shaw et al. 2002, no. 1567)*

Rousay is an Orkney island. In Campbeltown in 1956 the arrivals were 'Three gypsies', one of whom turns out to be the Prince of Wales – he got about!

In 1981 Glenrothes only one gypsy rides in, and his courting is strenuous:

A gypsy came a-riding
A-riding, a-riding
A gypsy came a-riding
Ipsy dipsy doo dah

What you riding here for? [etc.]
Came here to marry [etc.]

Who're you gonny marry? [etc.]
I'm gonny marry four-eyes [etc.]

Who the heck is four-eyes? [etc.]
Her first name is Caroline [etc.]

How you gonny get her? [etc.]
Climb through the keyhole [etc.]
Stick [or 'stuff'] it up with bubble gum [etc.]

Climb through the windows [etc.]
Lock all the windows [etc.]

Climb down the chimney [etc.]
Put a big fire there [etc.]

(Spoken) Then I'll blow your house down
(Spoken) Well, you can have her

*(School of Scottish Studies archive: Hendry, Glenrothes, 1981)*

THE WADDS
O it's hame, and it's hame, and it's hame, hame, hame
I think this night I maun gae hame
Ye had better light, and bide aa night
And I'll choose you a bonny ane

O wha will ye choose, an I wi you bide?

The fairest and rarest in aa the countryside

> I'll set her up on the bonny pear-tree
> It's straught and tall, and sae is she
> I wad wauk aa night her love to be
>
> I'll set her up i the bank dike
> She'll be rotten ere I be ripe
> The corbies her auld banes wadna pike
>
> I'll set her up on the high crab-tree
> It's sour and dour, and sae is she
> She may gang tae the mools unkissed by me
>
> She's for another, and no for me
> I thank you for your courtesie

This was chanted back and forth at the fireside by a group of lads and lasses. The boys think of going home, the girls offer them a named choice of female companion if they stay. The boys either accept, or make objections to the choice. Then the girls are in turn offered a named boy, and respond either:

> I'll put him on a riddle, and blaw him owre the sea
> Wha'll buy (Johnnie Paterson) for me?
> I'll put him on my big lum head
> And blaw him up wi pouther and lead

Or

> I'll set him on my table head
> And feed him up wi milk and bread

*(Chambers 1842)*

Greig–Duncan informant Miss Bell Robertson gave fifteen verses that she said were 'hopelessly entangled' elements of two versions. They begin

> Hey bonnie May, wi yer true lovers gay
> Will ye go to the green grass
> And tell me faur my bonnie lovie lies?
> And I'll gie ye thanks for your kindness

and continue with much repetition to threaten to set him in trees of thorn, rodden and rose, ending

I'll tak him in my arms twa
And lie doon atween him and the wa
It's him that will haud the caul awa
And gie ye much thanks for your kindness

*(Shuldham-Shaw et al. 2002, no. 1576)*

A wadd was a forfeit, to be redeemed with a kiss. It was a game for adolescents.

WHAT A LEMAN WILL YE GIE ME
What a leman will ye gie me gin I gie you a bride?
I'll gie ye A— B— to sit doon by your side
Wi the riddle and the girdle
And the gowd aboot his middle
Wi the siller shakin frae his heels
To mak the lasses like him

*(Shuldham-Shaw et al. 2002, no. 1587)*

A small gem, sharing elements with other game songs, but not identifiably a shard of any well-known game.

WHEN GRANDMAMA MET GRANDPAPA
When grandmama met grandpapa
They danced the minuet
The minuet was too slow
They danced another step

With a heel toe heel toe
Give it a kick, give it a kick, give it a kick
That's the way to do it

Bake that cake and turn around
That's the way they do it

Hands up, stick-em-up, drop down dead
That's the way they do it

*(Ian Davison Card Index: Temple School)*

*Formation, dance, processional*

A DROP-SEE
A drop-see a drop-see, a-dee a-doo a drop-see
I sent a letter to my love and by the way I lost it
I post it
I had a little dog, I sent for snuff
He broke the box, and skailed the snuff
He'll not bite you, nor you, but YOU

*(Rymour Club 1919: Duchess of Sutherland,
collected in Helmsdale and Portgower Schools)*


A GIRL FROM FRANCE
There came a girl from France
There came a girl from Spain
There came a girl from USA
And this is how she came

Knees up Mother Brown
Knees up Mother Brown
Knees up, knees up
Don't get the breeze up
Knees up Mother Brown

Hoppy on one shoe
Hoppy on one shoe
Hoppy hoppy, never stoppy
Hoppy on one shoe

Birly birly round [etc.]
Touchy touch the ground [etc.]

*(School of Scottish Studies archive:
Henderson, Campbeltown, 1956)*


In 1954 Edinburgh they sat on the ground rather than just touching it, and began
with

There came a girl from France
She didn't know how to dance
The only dance that she could do
Was Knees up Mother Brown

Hot peas and barley
Hot peas and barley O, barley O, barley O
Hot peas and barley O, sugary cakes and candy

*(McVicar Collection: St Robert's PS, Glasgow, 1997)*

How many miles to Babylon?
How many miles to Babylon?
Threescore and ten
Will we be there by candlelight?
Yes, and back again
Open your gates and let us go through
Not without a beck and a boo
There's a beck and there's a boo
Open your gates and let us go through

*(Chambers 1842)*

Two boys hold hands to make a barring gate. Others must make a gesture of respect and a bow to pass.

Chambers (1842) also describes a chasing game with these 'romantic' words:

King and queen of Cantelon
How many miles to Babylon?
Eight and eight, and other eight
Will I get there by candlelight?
If your horse be good and your spurs be bright
How mony men have ye?
Mae nor ye daur come and see

Mactaggart in 1824 proposed that Cantelon was a 'corruption of Caledon'.

In and out the dusty bluebells
In and out those dusty bluebells
In and out those dusty bluebells
In and out those dusty bluebells
I am the master

Tipper ipper apper on my shoulder [x3]
I am the master

Follow me my master says [x3]
I am the master

*(Ian Davison Card Index: Rottenrow School)*

*Tippety tappity on my shoulder*

One of the few singing games still in use in the twenty-first century.

> A PREEN
> I'll gie ye a preen to stick in your thoom
> To cairry a lady to London toon
> London toon's a braw braw place
> Aa covered ower wi gold and lace
> Hotch her up, hotch her doon
> Hotch her into London toon
>
> *(Rymour Club 1911: Calder Ironworks, 1850s)*

> ROUND APPLES
> Round apples, round apples, by night and by day
> The stars are a valley down yonder by day
> The stars – poor Annie with a knife in her hand
> You dare not touch her, or else she'll go mad
>
> Her cheeks were like roses, but now they're like snow
> Oh Annie, oh Annie, you're dying I know
> I'll wash her with milk, and I'll dry her with silk
> I'll write down her name with a gold pen and ink
>
> *(Maclagan 1901)*

'The stars' is surely meant to be 'There stands'. The Opies (1985) label the game Scots, and give several variants.

> SUNNY SIDE UP
> Keep the sunny side up, up
> And the other side too, too
> See the soldiers marching along
> And Paul McCartney singing a song
> Bend down and touch your toes
> Then you're an Eskimo
> Bend down and touch your knees
> Then you're a Japanese
> Bend down and touch your hands
> Then you're a Pakistan
> Bend down and touch your chin
> Then you're an Indian
> Keep the sunny side, keep the sunny side
> Keep the sunny side up
> Cha cha cha!
>
> *(Ian Davison Card Index: Temple School)*

Water wallflower
Water water wallflower
Growing up so high
We are all maidens
And we all must die
Except (Mary Morrison)
The fairest of us all
She can dance
And she can sing
And she can knock us all down
Fie fie fie and shame
Turn your back to the wall again

*(Ian Davison Card Index)*

In two Greig–Duncan versions the youngest of all can 'turn the sofa'. (Shuldham-Shaw et al. 2002, 1595 A & D) The Opies (1985) suggest this 'may bear phonetic relationship to "she can lick the sugar"', a phrase used in other versions.

Who's got the ball?
Alla balla alla balla
Who's got the ball?
I haven't got it
It isn't in my pocket
Alla balla alla balla
Who's got the ball

*(Ian Davison Card Index: Rottenrow School)*

# 7

# *Katie Bairdie had a zoo*

## Performance and narrative – animal life

> Poussie poussie baudrons, where hae ye been?
> I've been at London seeing the queen
>
> Poussie poussie baudrons, what got ye there?
> I got a guid fat mousikie rinning up a stair
>
> Poussie poussie baudrons, what did ye do wi't?
> I put it in my meal-poke to eat it to my bread

As ever, many lyrics I include here could almost equally well be included as activity songs and chants, and they have been so labelled by some collectors. Assemblers of monograph collections based on their recollections of childhood are particularly confident in their categorising. One distinguishing characteristic is length and richness of language: the skipping, ball and clapping pieces tend to be short, sharp and thin, since they are supporting an activity; those here are as much to be appreciated for their wit, clever wordplay, orraness and development of story.

One can slice and dice these texts so many ways. I have chosen to subdivide by topic – animal life, characters, confrontation/defiance, courting, family life, in school, and others – but you are welcome to disagree with where I place what.

As with the singing games, there is an ocean of such non-specific children's song and rhyme washing through their playgrounds, parties and uniformed activities. Mostly they eventually sink far out at sea, but a few are dredged up again by adults desperate to entertain a young charge, or are reclothed in the language and habit of the current times.

The well-worn rhymes imparted to children by adults are far more likely to retain the old form they were printed in by Mother Goose and others of her flock. You and I are likely to agree on the texts of the following: 'Hickery pickerty my black hen', 'Hot cross buns', 'Humpty Dumpty', 'Little Bo Peep', 'Little Jack Horner', 'Oh dear, what can the matter be?', 'Polly put the kettle on', 'Please to remember the 5th of November', 'See saw Margery Daw', 'The spider and the fly', 'Three blind mice' and 'Who killed Cock Robin'.

I have found none of the above dressed in distinctive Scots attire and printed and recorded collections of them and their copyright-free kin can be found in charity shops through the land, so I have no need to give the texts here.

Animals feature strongly in the rhymes adults share with small children, especially lambs, cats and dogs, but are less present in activity rhymes. Children's own rhymes bring a menagerie into the playground, particularly birds and monkeys.

> Katie Beardie had a coo
> Black and white about the mou
> Wasna that a dentie coo?
> Dance, Katie Beardie
>
> Katie Beardie had a hen
> Cackled but and cackled ben
> Wasna that a dentie hen?
> Dance, Katie Beardie
>
> Katie Beardie had a cock
> That could spin backin rock
> Wasna that a dentie cock?
> Dance, Katie Beardie
>
> Katie Beardie had a grice
> It could skate upon the ice
> Wasna that a dentie grice?
> Dance, Katie Beardie

This is the standard version, given by Robert Chambers (1842), but Ms Beardie or Bairdie, sometimes known as Dolly or Dally, had other animals:

> Katie Beardie had a cat
> That could eat baith moose and rat
> Wasna that a daintie cat?
> Dance, Katie Beardie

*(Rymour Club 1911)*

She seems also to have had another cat, of rather less athletic habits:

> Dally Bairdy had a cat
> That aye aboot the ingle sat
> She was sleekit plump an fat
> Canty Dally Bairdy

*(Shuldham-Shaw et al. 2002, no. 1657C)*

The change in name above adds a confusion: 'Dolly' is, I understand, short for 'Adolphus'. The following verse confirms the apparent sex change:

> Dolly Bairdie hid a wife
> She could use baith fork an knife
> Wisna she a dainty wife?
> Dance, Dolly Bairdie

(Shuldham-Shaw et al. 2002, no. 1657B)

The song 'Katie Bairdie' has indeed been around a long time. Mactaggart (1824) said 'In Galloway now slumbers a singular old song and dance, called "Dolly Beardy". After going through a world of trouble with great pleasure, I got a hint respecting the song, and here is the result of that'.

Mactaggart then expounded eight verses based upon the original, but only his third stanza draws upon the traditional words:

> Dolly Beardy had a cow
> Black and white about the mou
> She keeped her ay riftin fu
> Smock, Dolly Beardy

No, dictionaries have not helped me to be very sure what is going on in this verse. I think we are being told that the cow was so well fed a plentiful supply of methane resulted, and Mactaggart thought this a good thing. I could be wrong – it has happened before.

What sex was this person, and what was his/her name? Fraser (1975) has it both ways. After the usual farmyardful, she adds 'If more verses were needed for skipping, the following were added':

> Katie Bairdie hid a wean
> Wadna play when it cam on rain
> Wasna that a dentie wean?
> Dance, Katie Bairdie

> Katie Bairdie hid a coo
> It was yellow, black and blue
> Aa the monkeys i the Zoo
> Lauched at Katie Bairdie's coo

That last verse may have wandered in from 'Cockabendy'. The next version also breaks the old last line formula of 'Wisna that a dainty (coo)':

> Katie Bairdie had a coo
> It was yella black and blue
> Open the gates and let it through
> Dance, Katie Bairdie

*(Ian Davison Card Index: Rottenrow School)*

In a verse contributed to a 1991 exhibition in Glasgow's Scotland Street School Museum, a city kid who does not know what a 'coo' is has recycled the verse:

> Kitty Birdie had a canoe
> It was yellow, black and blue
> Open your legs and let it through
> Dance Kitty Birdie

Then the name goes haywire:

> Kitsy Katsy had a canoe
> It was yellow black and blue
> Open the gate and let her through
> So that's Kitsy Katsy

*(Ian Davison Card Index: Rottenrow School)*

> Jeannie Bairdie had a wean
> Somebudy hit it wi a stane
> The doactur said it wuz a shame
> Dance Jeannie Bairdie

*(Children's Singing Games: Webb, St James Girls Sch, Paisley, 1961)*

Still, people were fiddling with these verses a hundred years ago, too:

> Katie Bairdie had a soo
> It was reid, and black, and blue
> Ye needna gang wi peelins noo
> For Katie Bairdie's killed her soo

*(Rymour Club 1919)*

The way in which traditional children's songs can be hacked into tools of child-rearing and education by childcare professionals is ably demonstrated by some publications aimed at nurseries and playgroups. 'Katie Beardie' teaches her sheep to 'skip and leap' as a circus turn, along with cavorting frogs, mice and worms. Is this the sad end of Katie Bairdie? Surely not.

The ancient tale of courtship between a frog and a mouse has some versions so long and tongue-twisting they were surely sung to delighted children, rather than by them. Its history goes back to 1549, when, in *The Complaynt of Scotland*, one of the 'sueit melodius sangis' that the shepherds sing is 'The frog cam to the myl door'. Here, from an Aberdeenshire crofter at the start of the twentieth century, is the same title, and perhaps some of the same words. Some may detect remnants of Gaelic or some other old tongue in the refrain – others may doubt it.

> Froggie cam to the mill door
> Kye my dearie, kye me
> Saddled and bridled and shod afore
> Kye my dearie, kye me
> Kye my dearie kill a geerie
> Kye my dearie, kye me
> Wi my rum strum bumereedle
> Bullabulla rig dum
> Rig dum boomie meerie kye me
>
> When they were all at supper sat [etc.]
> In cam the kittlin and the cat [etc.]
>
> It's next cam in the sulky deuk [etc.]
> And she plucket Froggie out o the neuk [etc.]
>
> Wouldna that mak a hale heart sair [etc.]
> To see sic a company gathered wi care [etc.]
>
> And wadna that mak a hale heart crack [etc.]
> To see sic a company aa gone to wrack [etc.]
>
> *(Shuldham-Shaw et al. 2002, no. 1669B)*

The remarkable refrain lines were naturally pummelled by the oral process as they moved about the country. In Calder Ironworks in the 1860s they sang

> There was a moosie in a mill
> Kiltie keerie ca ye me
> And a froggie in a well
> Rigdum bummaleerie ca ye me
> Ca ye deemie, ca ye keemie
> Ca ye deemie, ca ye me
> Streem stram pummareedle, rally-bally rantan
> Rigdum bummaleerie ca ye me
>
> *(Rymour Club 1911)*

Chambers (1842) begins with an 1824 version which has what he terms 'the unmeaning burden and repetitions' of 'Cuddy alone, Cuddy alone', and 'Kickmaleerie, cowden down, Cuddy alone and I'. He tells us that in 1580 the Stationers' Company licensed 'a ballad of a most strange wedding of the frogge and the mouse', and he then gives a version 'copied from a small quarto manuscript of poems formerly in the possession of Sir Walter Scott, dated 1630' that begins

> Itt was ye frog in ye wall
> Humble doune, humble doune
> And ye mirrie mouse in ye mill
> Tweidle, tweidle, twino

and ends with 'Gib our cat' and 'Dick our drack' killing the new husband and wife:

> Ye ratt ran up ye wall
> A goodlie companie, ye devall goe with all

Chambers' 1842 version is kinder to the mouse:

> But Lady Mouse, baith jimp and sma
> Crept into a hole beneath the wa
> 'Squeak' quo she, 'I'm weel awa'

*Greig–Duncan* version 1669 A is child-sized and much simpler in language and refrain, ending

> The next to come in was a great big snake, ha ha, ha ha
> The next to come in was a great big snake
> He licked the sugar off the cake, ha ha

The Scottish origins of this song are well concealed in the American versions made popular by 'balladeer' Burl Ives and others, such as 'Froggie went a-courting' or 'Mr frog would a-wooing ride'. These can feature a banjo, the president, and in the thirty-five-verse epic in *American Ballads and Folk Songs* (Lomax 1934) there are nineteen guests – animals, birds and insects.

## Anthology: Animal life

THE ANIMALS WENT IN
The animals went in one by one
Some were deaf and some were dumb
Ee-i – ee-i – ee-i – o, Eldorado

The animals went in two by two
Some were black and some were blue [or] Some wore clogs and some
    wore shoes [etc.]

Some were big and some were wee [or] Some like you and some
    like me [etc.]

Some through the windy and some through the door [etc.]

Some were dead and some were alive [etc.]

Some with crutches and some with sticks [or] Some were poofs and
    some were pricks [etc.]

Some play hell and some play heaven [or] Some like men and some
    like women [etc.]

Some were early some were late [etc.]

Some with whisky some with wine [etc.]

If you don't know the story I'll tell you it again [or] Some with pencils,
    some with pens [etc.]

*(Ian Davison Card Index)*

AS I WENT O'ER THE BRIG O DEE
As I went o'er the Brig o Dee
I spied a dead horsie
I oned it, I twoed it, I threed it
I foured it, I fived it, I sixed it
I sevened it, I atc it

*(McVicar Collection; source not recorded)*

One child begins, the second comes in at 'twoed it', then they take number about. This gristly feast is variously located by Scots children.

BEETLE BEETLE
Beetle beetle go away – go away
I'm afraid you cannot stay – cannot stay
Remember what the Brown Owl said
No to beetle in a bed – in a bed

*(Ian Davison Card Index; tune: 'Tavern in the town')*

Seems a little raunchy for Brownies. In East Calder, 2007, they had a longer version in which 'Once a beetle went to camp / Went to bed without a lamp'.

### The cattie rade

The cattie rade to Passelet
To Passelet, to Passelet
The cattie rade to Passelet
Upon a harrow tine, O

'Twas on a weetie Wednesday
Wednesday, Wednesday
'Twas on a weetie Wednesday
I missed it aye sin-syne, O

*(Chambers 1842)*

### Cheetie pussie

Wee cheetie pussie o, rinnin through the hoosie o
The parritch pat fell aff the fire and burnt aa its feetie o

*(Rymour Club 1911: St Bernard's School, Edinburgh, 1909)*

### Clash-pyotie

Clash-pyotie clash-pyotie, sits on the tree
Dings doon aipples, one two three
One to the master, and one to the man
And one to the laddie that ca's the caravan
But nane to the clash-pyot, what will we gie
Gie to the clash-pyot that sits on the tree?
A barrowfu o muck, and a barrowfu o hay
And we'll cairry the clash-pyotie doon to the Bay

*(Rymour Club 1919: Annie Shirer, Mintlaw)*

In a Rymour Club 1911 version headed 'On a tale-bearer', the aipples go to the laidie and the laird. MacLennan (1909) gives the last one to 'the auld man that delves in the yaird'.

### Cleaverie, cleaverie

Cleaverie, cleaverie, sit i the sun
And let the weary herdies in
Aa weetie, aa wearie
Aa droukit, aa drearie

I haena gotten a bite the day
But a drap o cauld sowens
Sitting i the blind bole

By cam a cripple bird
And trailed its wing owre
I up wi ma rung
And hit it i the lug

Cheep cheep, quo the bird
Clock clock, quo the hen
Fient care I, quo the cock
Come na yon road again

*(Chambers 1842)*

This lyric was noted down seventy years before the following, fine, markedly different version given by Bell Robertson to Greig, but that does not make the Chambers version necessarily earlier, or the 'original'.

Sinne sinne set ye
Owre the hill o Benachie
And lat the peer herdie hame
Till's caul meal an bree

The black chicken an the grey
Has suppit amon't aa day
He up wi's club
And gae't o the lug

Pee peek, quo the chicken
Care care, quo the hen
Deil care, quo the cock
Ye sud a come to yer bed fin I bade ye

*(Shuldham-Shaw et al. 2002, no. 1636)*

The Montgomeries (1985) give an Aberdeenshire version in which the Hirdy Dirdy comes home hungry for his gruel, the hen says 'will-a-wins' and the cock says 'little maitter'.

## The craw's killed the pussie

The craw's killed the pussie oh
The craw's killed the pussie oh
The muckle cat sat doun and grat
In Willie's wee bit housie oh
The craw's killed the pussie oh
The craw's killed the pussie oh
An aye an aye the kitten cried
'Oh, wha'll bring me a mousie oh?'

*(Moffat 1933; tune:*
*'Green grow the rashes oh')*

## Happy birthday

Happy birthday to you
You live in the zoo
You look like a monkey
And you smell like one too

*(McVicar Collection: Moray, 2006)*

Happy birthday to you
You were born in the zoo
With the donkeys and the monkeys
And the kangaroos like you

*(Ian Davison Card Index)*

The original of the song parodied here was first published as recently as 1935. In 2007 in East Calder Primary I was given six variants.

## Hi gee-up ma cuddie

Hi gee-up ma cuddie
Ma cuddie is ower the dyke
An if ye touch ma cuddie
Ma cuddie will gie ye a bite

*(McVicar from personal recollection:*
*Dingwall, 1940s)*

Sometimes said as 'Jock my cuddy' and then mistaken by folksong collectors for a song about a fanged fellow called Jock McCuddy. In *County Folklore – Fife* (1912) this is said to be a riddle, the answer being 'a nettle'.

I HAD A LITTLE CHICKEN
I had a little chicken
It wouldn't lay an egg
I poured hot water all
Up and down its legs
I giggled, and giggled
And giggled all day
Cause hard-boiled eggs
Were all it would lay

*(Ian Davison Card Index)*


I KNOW A TEDDY BEAR
I know a teddy bear
Blue eyes and curly hair
Roly poly through the town
Knockin all the people down
I know a teddy bear

*(McVicar Collection: Glasgow, 1992;*
*tune: 'Let's all go down the strand')*

In Erskine in 1992 the bear had 'red eyes and spiky hair' and went 'cartwheeling through the malls, knocking down all the stalls', but this may have been Andrew Howie (P5) of Rashielea Primary's own adaptation.

I SEE THE GOUK
I see the gouk
But the gouk sees na me
Atween the berry buss
An the aipple tree

*(MacLennan 1909)*


JEAN
Jean Jean Jean
The cat's at the cream
Suppin wi her fore-feet
An glowerin wi her een

*(MacLennan 1909)*

KATE
Kate the spinner
Come doon to your dinner
An taste the leg of a frog
All you good people
Look owre the kirk steeple
An see the cat play wi the dog

*(MacLennan 1909)*

Kate the spinner is a spider.

THE LION AND THE UNICORN
The lion and the unicorn
Fighting for the crown
Up starts the little dog
And knocked them baith down

Some gat white bread
And some gat brown
But the lion beat the unicorn
Round about the town

*(Chambers 1842)*

The unicorn was a symbol of Scotland, the supporter of the Royal Arms before the Union.

MA WEE BROON HEN
I had a wee broon hen I liked it very well
An oh aboot ma wee hen a story I will tell
I sent it fur the messages away oot in the rain
An ma wee broon hen never came back again

I'll hae a funeral for ma wee hen
Ah'll hae a funeral for ladies and gentlemen
Ladies and gentlemen come ben for ma wee hen
For ma wee broon hen, it never came back again

*(Ian Davison Card Index)*

MY DOGGIE AND I

My doggie and I gaed doon to the well
My doggie fell in and he drooned himsel
He drooned himsel and naebody saw im
And fat will come o me, my doggie's awa

Ae wow-ow my doggie's deid
Bowf-bow-ow my doggie's deid
Sae weel I can spin at a spangi thread
But bowf-bow-ow my doggie's deid

*(Shuldham-Shaw et al. 2002, no. 1660)*

MY LILY-COCK

I had a wee cock, and I loved it well
I fed my cock on yonder hill
My cock, lily-cock, lily-cock, coo
Every one loves their cock, why should not I love my cock too?

I had a wee hen, and I loved it well
I fed my hen on yonder hill
My hen, chuckie, chuckie
My cock, lily-cock, lily-cock, coo
Every one loves their cock, why should not I love my cock too?

Other animals are added in turn, until the the last verse is

I had a wee pig, and I loved it well
I fed my pig on yonder hill
My pig, squeakie, squeakie
My cat, cheetie, cheetie
My dog, bouffie, bouffie
My sheep, maie, maie
My duck, wheetie, wheetie
My hen, chuckie, chuckie
My cock, lily-cock, lily-cock, coo
Every one loves their cock, why should not I love my cock too?

*(Chambers 1842)*

In the *Greig–Duncan Folk Song Collection* no. 1666B the henny says 'jim-a-jick', and the cockie cries 'leely gowkoo'. (Shuldham-Shaw et al. 2002)

My wee monkey
My wee monkey's dead
He's lying in its bed
He cut his throat
With a five pound note
My wee monkey's dead

*(Ian Davison Card Index)*

An orange cat
Once we had an orange cat
It sat upon the fender
Every time it burnt its tail
It said 'We'll no surrender'

*(Ian Davison Card Index: Cranhill School;*
*tune: 'Yankee Doodle')*

King Billy had an orange cat
It sat upon the fender
And every time the Pope passed by
It shouted 'No surrender'
Beads an beads an holy beads
Beads an holy waater
The priest fell doon the chapel stairs
An made an awfu clatter

*(McVicar Collection:*
*Bill Tulloch, Greenock, 1950s)*

The references are to Northern Ireland's Orangemen and one of their slogans.

Our cat's dead
Lingle, lingle, lang tang
Our cat's dead
What did she die wi?
Wi a sair head
Aa you that kent her
When she was alive
Come to her burial
Atween four and five

*(Chambers 1842)*

THE PARSON HAD A WITTY COO
The parson had a witty coo
And she was wondrous wise
The coo she danced a hornpipe
And gie the piper a penny
To play the same tune owre again
The corn rigs are bonny

*(Shuldham-Shaw et al. 2002, no. 1655B)*


PICKEN'S HEN
No a beast in aa the glen
Laid an egg like Picken's hen
Some witch-wife we dinna ken
Sent a whitterit frae its den
Sook'd the bluid o Picken's hen
Picken's hen's cauld and deid
Lyin on the midden heid

*(Rymour Club 1928: Dumfriesshire)*


POUSSIE BAUDRONS
Poussie poussie baudrons
Where hae ye been?
I've been at London
Seeing the queen

Poussie poussie baudrons
What got ye there?
I got a guid fat mousikie
Rinning up a stair

Poussie poussie baudrons
What did ye do wi't?
I put it in my meal-poke
To eat it to my bread

*(Chambers 1842)*


Categorised as a nonsense verse to sucklings, but a sensible enough story, with one more verse than the widely known 'Pussy cat pussy cat, where have you been?' In Argyllshire the tale lengthened again:

Pussy pussy paten, where hae ye been?
I hae been in London seeing the Queen
What got ye there? Sour milk and cream
Where's my share? In the black dog's tail
Where's the black dog? In the wood
Where's the wood? The fire burned it
Where's the fire? The sea drowned it
Where's the sea? The bull drunk it
Where's the bull? The butcher killed it
Where's the butcher?
Ten miles below my granny's door, eating two salt herrin
   and two raw potatoes

*(Maclagan 1901)*

PUSSIKER, PUSSIKER
Pussiker, pussiker, myawie, myawie
Far will ye get mait in the snyawie?
I'll gae doon tae the boggies, and worry the hoggies
And I'll get beenies to gnyawie, gnyawie

*(Shuldham-Shaw et al. 2002, no. 1674)*

The North-East diminutive – ie in full flight. 'Beenies' are bones.

ROBIN LAD
Guid-day now, bonnie Robin lad
How lang hae ye been here?
O I've been bird about this glen
For mair three thousand year

Singing father linkum linkum
Singing father linkum dear
O sic a bird as Robin is
Ne'er sat among the brier

I've biggit on yon bonnie bank
This mair three thousand year
And I wad mak my testament
Guidman, if you would hear

Now, in there cam my Lady Wren
Wi mony a sigh and groan
'O what care I for aa the lads
If my wee lad be gaun?'

Then Robin turned him round and said
E'en like a little king
'Go, pack ye frae my chamber-door
Ye little cuttie quean'

(Moffat 1933)

One yearns for an explanation of this deathbed rejection. Chambers' eleven-verse version has Robin die aged a more reasonable twenty years, and details his bequests. His neb for a hunting horn for the Duke of Hamilton, his neb feathers for a feather bed for the duchess, his right leg to mend the Tay Brig, his left for the Brig o Weir, his tail feathers for a flail, his breast feathers to bring a priest. At last Robin makes his testament

Upon a coll of hay
And by came a greedy gled
And snapt him aa away

(Chambers 1842)

SANNY COUTTS' LITTLE DOGGIES
Sanny Coutts' little doggies
Little doggies, little doggies
Sanny Coutts' little doggies
Licket Sanny's mou, man
Sanny ran aboot the stack
An aa's doggies at's back
An ilka doggie gied a bark
An Sanny ran awa, man

(Rymour Club 1928)

THE SOO'S TA'EN THE MEASLES
O what will we mak o the auld soo's heid?
It'll mak as guid a toaster as ever toasted breid
A toaster, a fryin pan, or ony mortal thing
O the soo's ta'en the measles and she's deid, puir thing

O what will we mak o the auld soo's lug?
It'll mak as guid a dish-clout as ever dichted mug
A dish-clout, a scourin-clout, or ony mortal thing
O the soo's ta'en the measles and she's deid, puir thing

O what will we mak o the auld soo's tail?
It'll mak as good a souple as ever hung a flail
A souple, a walkin-stick, or ony mortal thing
O the soo's ta'en the measles and she's deid, puir thing

(Rymour Club 1919: Crossmichael)

The informant 'mentions that other parts of the pig's anatomy were similarly disposed of'. An unusual version of a type of accumulative song widely popular throughout Britain. A Scots accumulative version of another titled 'Herrin's heid' is still popular.

TAM TAITS
'What ca they you?'
'They ca me Tam Taits!'
'What do ye?'
'Feed sheep and gaits!'

'Where feed they?'
'Down i' yon bog!'
'What eat they?'
'Gerse and fog!'

'What gie they?'
'Milk and whey!'
'Wha sups it?'
'Tam Taits and I!'

*(Chambers 1842)*

The *Greig–Duncan Folk Song Collection* version, no. 1634, ends 'Fa sups that? / Tam Tat and the cat'.

THREE CRAWS
Three craws sat upon a wa
Sat upon a wa, sat upon a wa aw aw aw
Three craws sat upon a wa
On a cold and frosty mornin

The first craw was greetin for its maw [etc.]

The second craw couldny flee at aa [etc.]

The third craw fell an broke its jaw [etc.]

The fourth craw wisnae there at aa [etc.]

*(McVicar from personal recollection: Glasgow, 1950s)*

Very popular still, with finger-waving actions and a screech on the top note.

THREE WEE MICE
Three wee mice skating on the ice
Singing 'Polly Wolly Doodle all the day'
The ice was thin and they all fell in
Singing 'Daddy, mammy, daddy, ah'm away'

*(McVicar Collection: Glasgow, 1992;*
*tune: 'Polly Wolly Doodle')*


THE TOD
'Eh', quo the tod, 'it's a braw licht nicht
The win's in the west an the mune shines bricht
The win's in the west an the mune shines bricht
An I'll awa tae the toun o

'I was doon amang yon shepherd's scroggs
I'd like tae been worrit by his dogs
But by my sooth I minded his hogs
The nicht I cam tae the toon o'

He's ta'en the grey goose by the green sleeve
'Eh, you auld witch, nae langer shall ye live
Your flesh it is tender, your bones I maun prieve
For that I cam tae the toun o'

Up gat the auld wife oot o her bed
An oot o the window she shot her auld head
'Eh gudeman, the grey goose is dead
An the tod's been in the toun o'

*(Buchan 1962)*


A WEE BIRD CAM
A wee bird cam tae oor ha door
Ah thocht it was a sparra
For it began tae whistle tae
The man they cry O'Hara

Ah threw the bird a thrupenny bit
Ah didny think ah hud yin
The wee bird widny pick it up
Because it wis a dud yin

*(Buchan 1962: Glasgow, 1950s)*

A wee bird cam tae ma wee door
I thocht it was a sparra
I lifted up its hairy leg
And spanked its wee terrara

*(Ian Davison Card Index: Anniesland School)*

The tune for both versions is 'Yankee Doodle'.

A WEE BIT MOUSIKIE
There was a wee bit mousikie
That lived in Gilberaty o
It couldna get a bite o cheese
For cheetie-poussie-cattie o

It said unto the cheesikie
'O fain wad I be at ye o
If it were na for the cruel paws
O cheetie-poussie-cattie o'

*(Chambers 1842)*

Moffat (1933) says the tune is 'Green grow the rashes o'.

WEE CHUCKIE BIRDIE
Wee chuckie birdie, toll lol lol
Laid an egg on the window sole
The window sole began to crack
An wee chuckie birdie roared and grat

*(Rymour Club 1928: Dumfriesshire)*

Still popular in 1950s Glasgow as 'Wee chookie burdie'.

WEE COCK SPARRA
A wee cock sparra sat in a tree
A wee cock sparra sat in a tree
A wee cock sparra sat in a tree
Chirpin awa as blythe as can be

Along cam a boy wi a bow an an arra (x3)
An he shouted 'Ah'll get ye, ye wee cock sparra'

Ra boy wi ra arra let fly at the sparra (x3)
But he hut a wee man who wiz wheelin a barra

Ra man wi ra barra cam ower wi the arra (x3)
He says 'Dae ye tak me fur a wee cock sparra?'

Ra man hit ra boy though he wisnae his farra (x3)
An ra boy stood an glowered, he wiz hurt tae ra marra

An aa this time the wee cock sparra (x3)
Wiz chirpin awa on the haft o the barra

*(As sung by Duncan Macrae in 1960s)*

Made famous in the 1960s by actor Duncan Macrae in a performance that parodied formal concert hall singing. I discuss the song in more detail in *One Singer One Song* (1990). Versions in standard English from the 1840s are given by the Opies (1951).

WHEN I WAS A WEE THING
When I was a wee thing
'Bout six or seven year auld
I had no worth a petticoat
To keep me frae the cauld

Then I went to Edinburgh
To bonnie burrows town
And there I coft a petticoat
A kirtle, and a gown

As I cam hame again
I thought I wad big a kirk
And aa the fowls o the air
Wad help me to work

The heron, wi her lang neb
She moupit me the stanes
The doo, wi her rough legs
She led me them hame

The gled he was a wily thief
He rackled up the waa
The pyat was a cursed thief
She dang down aa

The hare came hirpling owre the knowe
To ring the morning bell
The hurcheon she came after
And said she wad do't hersel

The herring was the high priest
The salmon was the clerk
The howlet read the order
They held a bonnie wark

*(Chambers 1842)*

The *Greig–Duncan Folk Song Collection* version, no. 1637, is also very attractive, with 'herring' replaced by 'Hymen' and 'salmon' by 'Choral', and last lines of 'An bonnie sang the mavis / An that's a merry wark'. (Shuldham-Shaw et al. 2002) The last lines of Moffat's version are 'The bull-finch played the organ / All in my bonnie kirk'. (1933)

# 8
# *The Queen and who else?*

## Performance and narrative – characters

Oh the sun shines bright on Charlie Chaplin
His boots are crackin for the want of blackin
And his wee baggy trousers they need mendin
Before they send him to the Dardanelles

What characters these rhymes introduce to us! Aiken Drum, Baldy Bane, Cripple Dick, Wee Maggie, Cowboy Joe, Jean MacColl, Mrs MacGuire, Old King Coul, Skinny Malinky Longlegs and Tibby Fowler. Some come from history or fable: Robert Burns, Captain Cook, Davie Crockett, Batman and Robin, Shirley Temple, Betty Grable, Salome, Tarzan, Tommy Morgan. Some from everyday life: doctor, prisoner, washerwoman, factor, minister, soldier.

Queens feature in quite a few rhymes, though they are not as important as grannies, of course:

Lady Queen Ann she sits in her stand
And a pair of green gloves upon her hand
As white as a lily, as fair as a swan
The fairest lady in aa the land

*(Chambers 1842)*

Queen, Queen Caroline
Dipped her hair in turpentine
Turpentine made it shine
Queen, Queen Caroline

*(Ritchie 1965)*

Queen Alexandra has lost her gold ring
Send for the king, lost her gold ring
Queen Alexandra has lost her gold ring
Guess who has found it

*(source not recorded)*

Mary Queen of Scots got her head chopped off
Head chopped off, head chopped off
Mary Queen of Scots got her head chopped off
Head chopped off

*(McVicar from personal recollection: Glasgow, 1950s)*

But the most popular, found in Hexham Workhouse, Soho, Devon, the Quantock Hills, and throughout the glens and deadends of Scotland, is

*(Transcription: McVicar, from singing of several informants)*

Queen Mary, Queen Mary my age is sixteen
My faither's a fermer in yonder green
He's plenty o money to dress me sae braw
But there's nae bonnie laddie will tak me awa

Each morning I rose and I looked in the glass
Says I tae mysel, what a handsome young lass
Put my hands to my sides and I gave a ha, ha
But there's nac bonnie laddie will tak me awa

*(Ian Davison Card Index: Rottenrow School)*

Davison comments 'another old song known everywhere'. Of course, English versions iron out the Scots, in particular the foreign-to-them-word 'braw'.

Often the song is acted out by small girls, who place their hands on their hips ('henches' in some versions of the song) to give their dainty laughs. The present day traditional singers Ray and Cilla Fisher sing a version in which 'what a handsome young lass' is replaced by 'with a shove ye might pass', but that might be just them.

The following third stanza was noted by Glasgow teacher, collector and songwriter Ian Davison in the 1970s. It feels very much like an immigrant or 'mak-ye-up'.

One morning a drover came in fae Carlisle
I drapped him a curtsey, he gied me a smile
Now my ain drover laddie I loo aboon aa
And there has come a laddie tae tak me awa

*(Ian Davison Card Index)*

The tune used in Golspie was sometimes 'The Campbells are coming' and sometimes 'Will ye gang tae Sheriffmuir'. Now, the above sweet and wistful little tune is employed in Scotland. The tune, like the text, has a strong character, but the two have not been linked together throughout their existence. In 1915 Anne G Gilchrist gave a very full account of the tune. She said 'The game-tune is a variant of a melody of unknown origin, which used to be known in Scotland as *The Band at a Distance*. (Mr Kidson thinks it may have been a part of some programme music). It used to be played on the piano as a *tour de force* by the young ladies of Edinburgh about [the 1830s], to represent the gradual approach and passing by into the distance of a military band.' In about 1840 a celebrated contralto, Madame Sainton-Dolby was visiting Scotland, and 'had the happy thought' of uniting the tune to Sir Walter Scott's stirring lyric *Bonny Dundee*.

Around 1855 a musician, Henri Hemy, noted the tune from the singing of little girls at play in the mining village of Stella, near Newcastle, and adapted it for use with a hymn text called 'Hail, Queen of Heaven, the Ocean Star'.

*(Gilchrist 1915; tune: 'Stella')*

So we begin with a piano piece around the 1830s that imitated the sound of a band approaching from far off, coming closer and becoming deafening, then receding again. The piano piece tune is much later applied to 'Bonny Dundee' in preference to the old tune to which Sir Walter set his words. In 1855 the tune is heard in use for play, probably for our 'Queen Mary' verses.

The story about the musician Henry Hemy is odd. The story of his applying the tune to the 'Hail, Queen of Heaven, the Ocean Star' text does not say what lyric was attached when he heard it, and he may have heard it already sung for 'Queen Mary', but oddly serendipitous indeed is his hearing it in a village named Stella, then applying it to a text about a stellar queen.

The usual two neat little verses sung in Scotland reach far back. The Opies (1985) observe that the text of the children's song derives from a fifteen-verse composition written at the end of the eighteenth century 'by a Thomas Scot of Falkirk in honour of, or rather at the expense of, the daughter of a local farmer named Russel or Russell'.

Mrs Margaret Gillespie sang fourteen stanzas to Rev JB Duncan in 1905, to a tune which is 'Whistle and I'll come tae ye my lad' in lines 1, 2 and 4, while line 3 resembles the third line of 'When I look to yon high hills'.

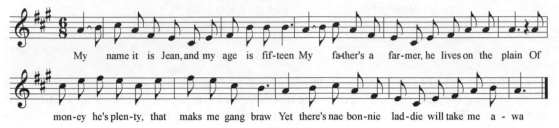

My name it is Jean, and my age is fif-teen My fa-ther's a far-mer, he lives on the plain Of mon-ey he's plen-ty, that maks me gang braw Yet there's nae bon-nie lad-die will take me a - wa

*(Shuldham-Shaw et al. 2002, no. 1373)*

Mrs Gillespie had learned the song from her step-grandmother Mrs Duncan of Craigculter. Here are her verses 1, 2 and 9:

> My name it is Jean, and my age is fifteen
> My father's a farmer, he lives on the plain
> Of money he's plenty, that mak's me gang braw
> Yet there's nae bonnie laddie will take me awa
>
> Each morning I rise and mak mysel clean
> Wi ruffles an ribbons an everything fine
> Wi the finest hair cushin hair curls an a
> Yet nae bonnie laddie will take me awa
>
> It's ten times a-day I look in the glass
> And I think wi mysel that I am a fine lass
> I gie a loud laugh and a louder guffaw
> Yet nae bonnie laddie will take me awa

*(Shuldham-Shaw et al. 2002, no. 1373)*

Fourteen verses neatly boiled down to three, with tunes borrowed from here and there from Scottish historical song. There's economy, and pragmatism too!

## Anthology: Characters

AIKEN DRUM
There cam a man to our town, to our town, to our town
There cam a man to our town and his name was Willy Wood
And he played upon a razor, a razor, a razor
And he played upon a razor, and his name was Willy Wood

His hat was made o the guid roast beef [etc.]
His coat was made o the haggis bag [etc.]
His buttons were made o the baubee baps [etc.]

But another man cam to the town, and they ca'd him Aiken Drum
And he ate up aa the guid roast beef [etc.]

*(Chambers 1842)*

This song is usually sung now with Aiken Drum the one being dressed, with no mention of Willy Wood. James Hogg quoted this epic puzzling song in 1821. The mysterious Aikendrum also appears in one of the ballads about the Sheriffmuir fight of 1715.

AN ANGEL SAID TO ME
An angel said to me
'Would you like a cup of tea?'
I said, 'No, no, I like cocoa
Better than tea'

*(Alan Lomax archive: Cedar Place children, Aberdeen;*
*tune: 'Down in the glen')*

BALDY BANE
What's your name? Baldy Bane
What's your other? Ask my mother
Where do you sleep? Among the sheep
Where do you lie? Among the kye
Where do you take your brose?
Up and down the cuddy's nose

*(Maclagan 1901)*

BARLINNIE
I wanna go home, I wanna go home
To ma ain wee hoose in Barlinnie
You don't need this, you don't need that
You only need a hammer and a chisel
When you get there they cut off your hair
They put it in a tin-tin-tinnie (and gie it tae the weans in the dinnie)

*(Ian Davison Card Index: Govan Adventure Playground;*
*tune: 'Polly Wolly Doodle')*

BEFORE WEE MAGGIE DIED
Before wee Maggie died, she took me by her side
She offered me a pair of ragged drawers
They were baggy at the knees, and fulla fulla fleas
And that was the end of Maggie's drawers

*(Ian Davison Card Index)*

BIG FAT WOMAN
There's a big fat woman
Twice the size of me
She's got hairs on her arms
Like the branches of a tree
She can sing and she can dance
And dae the Heiland Fling
The only thing she cannae dae
Is slim, slim, slim

*(Ian Davison Card Index)*

Mixed up ingredients from several songs given a modern twist.

BETTY BETTY
Betty Betty show us your leg
Show us your leg show us your leg
Betty Betty show us your leg
An inch above the knee

*(Ian Davison Card Index: Rottenrow School; tune: 'Fishers of men')*

Still sung to the bus driver on a school trip as 'Driver, driver show us your leg'.

BLOODY TOM
Who went round the house at night?
None but Bloody Tom
Who stole all my chickens away
All but this poor one?

*(Rymour Club 1911: Calder Ironworks, 1850s)*

CAPTAIN COOK
Captain Cook was eating soup
His wife was eating jelly
Captain Cook fell in the soup
And burnt his rubber belly

*(McVicar from personal recollection: Dingwall, 1950s)*

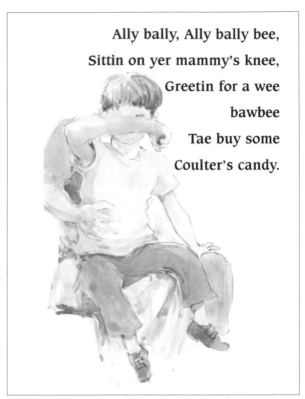

Ally bally, Ally bally bee,
Sittin on yer mammy's knee,
Greetin for a wee
bawbee
Tae buy some
Coulter's candy.

*Above.* Frontispiece of *Popular Rhymes of Scotland*, 1842, showing the 'Wee Bannock' story

*Right.* 'Coulter's candy', postcard published by Edinburgh City Libraries, 1990

'Bee baw babbitty' by Louis Mackay, 1909

'This is the way the ladies ride' by Louis Mackay, 1909

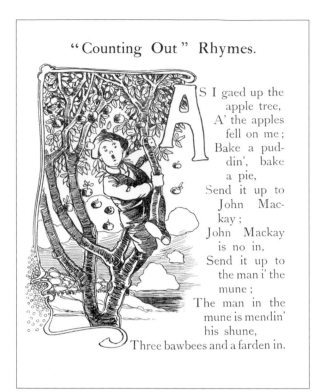

## "Counting Out" Rhymes.

AS I gaed up the apple tree,
A' the apples fell on me;
Bake a puddin', bake a pie,
Send it up to John Mackay;
John Mackay is no in,
Send it up to the man i' the mune;
The man in the mune is mendin' his shune,
Three bawbees and a farden in.

By Louis Mackay, from MacLennan's *Scottish Nursery Rhymes*, 1909

Frontispiece of Rymour Club volumes, 1911–1928

'Monday is my washing day' by Raymond Townsend, from *The Singing Street*, 1964

'Plainie clappie' by Raymond Townsend, from *The Singing Street*

'One two three a-leerie' by Raymond Townsend, from *Golden City*, 1965

'Skipping' by Raymond Townsend, from *Golden City*

*Above.* 'The roaring playground' by David
Brogan, from *Scotscape,* 1978

*Right.* 'Skipping down the years' by David
Brogan, from *Scotscape*

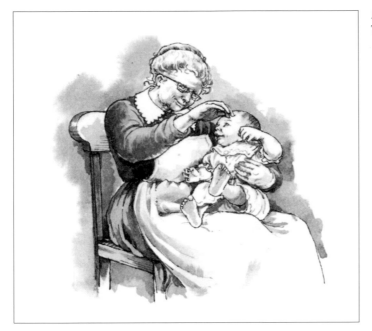

*Left.* 'Here's the broo o knowledge' by Shirley Tourret, from *Scotsgate*, 1982

*Right.* 'Hunt the stagie', from *The Traditional Games of England, Scotland and Ireland*, 1894

*Right.* 'Oranges and lemons', from *The Traditional Games of England, Scotland and Ireland*

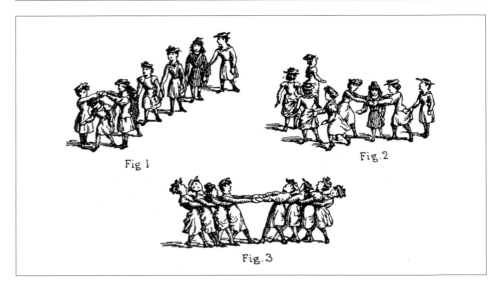

Fig. 1

Fig. 2

Fig. 3

*Right.* 'Poor and rich', from *The Traditional Games of England, Scotland and Ireland*

*Below.* 'The King of the Barbarie', from *The Traditional Games of England, Scotland and Ireland*

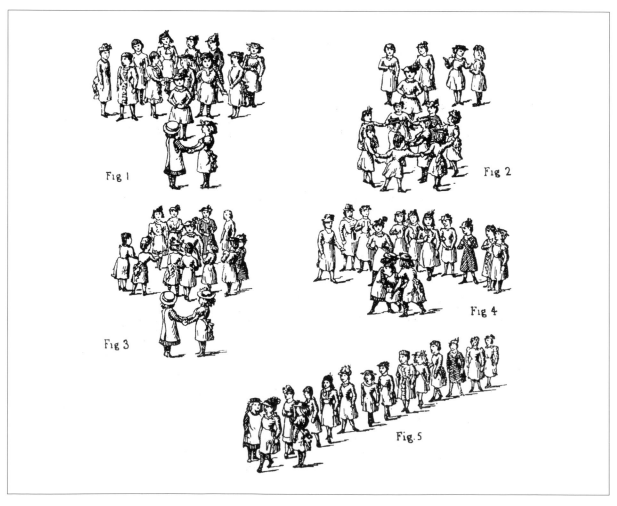

Davison's version features Captain Hook eating all the soup and bursting his belly.

CHARLIE CHAPLIN
Oh the sun shines bright on Charlie Chaplin
His boots are crackin for the want of blackin
And his wee baggy trousers they need mendin
Before they send him to the Dardanelles

*(Ian Davison Card Index: Rottenrow School; tune: 'Redwing')*

Another version ends with 'We'll need to send him to Alec Auld's' – surely a local outfitter.

CHARLIE CHAT
Charlie Chat he milk'd the cat
And Dorothy made the cheese
And Feathery Breeks sat at the door
And ca-ed awa the flees

*(Rymour Club 1911: Mintlaw)*

'In derision of the name Charlie'.

COBBLER
Cobbler cobbler mend my shoe
Have it done by half past two
Stitch it up and stitch it down
Now I owe you half a crown

*(Ian Davison Card Index: Bellahouston School)*

CRIPPLE DICK
Cripple Dick upon a stick and Sandy on a soo
Ride awa to Gallowa to buy a pund o oo

*(Rymour Club 1911: Rev. Wm. Findlay)*

'Said by a child a-straddle on a stick'.

COUNTRY GEORDIE
Country Geordie, Brig o Dee
Sups the brose an leaves the bree

*(Wilson 1993)*

A CUP OF TEA
Batman an Robin came to visit me
Took me tae the café tae buy a cup a tea
The tea was so delicious ah had another cup
An poor Cinderella had tae dae the washing up

*(McVicar Collection: Glasgow, 1993)*

A Strichen 1960 version featured the Yellow Rose of Texas, the Man from Laramie and Davie Crockett, all film titles.

DANCIN WI A MOONMAN
Dancin wi a moonman
Doon at the Barrowlands
Dancin wi a moonman
Tae McGregor and his band
When the lights are turned doon low
And they play the rock an roll
Oh it's smashin dancin wi a moo-oo-oo-oon man

*(McVicar from personal recollection:*
*Morris Blythman, Glasgow, 1950s; tune: 'Roamin in the gloamin')*

The Barrowlands is still a dancehall in Glasgow.

DAVIE CROCKETT
Born on a dustbin in Park Square
Davie Crockett did not care
He swept the lums for half a crown
The best chimney sweep in Campbeltown
Davie, Davie Crockett
King of the chimney sweeps

*(School of Scottish Studies archive: Henderson, Campbeltown, 1956)*

Born in a tenement at Partick Cross
Had a razor gang of which he was the boss
Carried a razor ten feet wide
With it he slashed all the cops
And threw them in the Clyde
Davie, Davie Crewcut
King of the razor gang

*(McVicar from personal recollection: Glasgow, 1950s)*

Two of many Davie Crockett parodies in the 1950s.

DOWN IN THE JUNGLE
Down in the jungle where nobody knows
There's a big mama washing her clothes
With a rubadub here, and a rubadub there
That's the way she washes her clothes
Tiddly aye tie a bokey
Tiddly aye tie bokey wokey wokey
That's the way she washes her clothes

*(McVicar Collection: Glasgow, 1991)*

ELLA BELLA
I went to a Chinese restaurant
To buy a loaf of bread
He wrapped it up in a five-pound note
And this is what he said:
'My name is Ella-Bella-Cheeky-Fella-
Chinese-Chopsticks-Indian-Feathers-
Woo-Woo-Pow!'

*(Ian Davison Card Index)*

ELVIS IN THE MORNING
Elvis in the morning
Cliff in the evening
Tommy at suppertime
Put them all together
And love them all the time
So rock rock rock everybody
Twist twist twist everybody
Listen to the TV show
Sugar in the morning

*(Ian Davison Card Index: John St School; tune: 'Sugar in the morning')*

Sung to the tune of a pop song from about 1954.

FOOLS
Katherine Nicolson is a fool
Send her to the ragged school
When she's dead, bile her head
Make it into gingerbread

*(School of Scottish Studies archive: Henderson, Edinburgh, 1954)*

FRANCIE AND JOSIE
Francie and Josie
Were sailing down the Clyde
Francie said tae Josie
Will you be my bonnie bride
Josie said 'Aye,
I'll love you till I die'
Sailing doon the Clyde wi Francie

*(Ian Davison Card Index: John St School;*
*tune: 'Roamin in the gloamin')*

Francie and Josie were two male music hall and TV comic characters.

GEORDIE KILORDIE
Geordie Kilordie, the laird o the Knap
Suppit his brose and swallowed the cap
He gaed to the byre and swallowed the coo
'Hey,' said Geordie, 'I'll surely do noo'

*(MacLennan 1909)*

Other versions name him Sawney Kail Cunnie, Sandy Golandy, or Andrew ca's
Andro.

GYPSY CAROLINE
Gypsy gypsy Caroline
Gypsy gypsy Caroline
Washed her hair in turpentine
Turpentine will make it shine

Gypsy gypsy Caroline
Gypsy gypsy Caroline
Washed her hair in VP wine
VP wine will make it shine

Gypsy gypsy Caroline
Gypsy gypsy living in a tent
Had no money to pay the rent
The rent man came and threw her out
And now she's living in the roundabout

*(Ian Davison Card Index: Rottenrow School)*

I'M SHIRLEY TEMPLE
I'm Shirley Temple, and I've got curly hair
Two big dimples, I wear my skirts to there
And I'm not able to do the Betty Grable
Cause I'm Shirley Temple, and I've got curly hair
I've got the legs like Ginger Rogers
I've got the figure like Marilyn Monroe
I've got the hair like Ginger Rogers
And a face like an elephant's toe

(Ian Davison Card Index)

Another version from Davison has

I got the hairy legs like Tarzan
I got the figure like Marilyn Monroe – Quite so
I got the hair like Ginger Rogers
And a face like an elephant's toe

(Ian Davison Card Index)

JEAN
Jean Jean from Aberdeen
Stole a penny from the queen
The queen was mad and Jean was glad
Jean Jean from Aberdeen

(Ian Davison Card Index: Rottenrow School)

JEAN MCCOLL
Jean McColl was pinching coal
Pinching coal pinching coal
Jean McColl was pinching coal
When the wagon caught her bending

(Ian Davison Card Index: Bellahouston School;
tune 'Mulberry bush')

JEAN PREEN
Jean Preen pickit oot the cat's e'en
Wi a needle and a preen
Gaein ower the double-dykes
Playin on the wind-pipes

(Rodger nd)

JIMMY PIMMY
Jimmy Pimmy, paper hat
Rade a mile upon a cat
When the cat begood to fling
'Hey', says Jimmy, 'haud her in'

*(MacLennan 1909)*

JINGLE BELLS
Jingle bells, Batman smells
Robin laid an egg
The batmobile lost a wheel
And the Joker went to bed

*(McVicar Collection: Erskine, 1992)*

Jingle bells, Batman smells
Robin flew away
Kojak lost his lollypop
And bought a Milky Way

*(Ian Davison Card Index)*

K-K-K-KATIE
(Oh) K-K-K-Katie she swallowed a ha'penny
And twopence worth of chips the night before
The night before that she swallowed a doormat
And now she's swallowed the key of the kitchen door

*(Ian Davison Card Index: Temple School)*

A parody of the popular 1950s song.

LEERIE
Leerie leerie, licht the lamps
Lang legs and crookit shanks
Tak a stick and brak his back
And send him to the market

*(Rymour Club 1911)*

To mock a lighter of gas street lamps.

MA WEE LAD
Ma wee lad's a sodger, he lives in Maryhill
Goes to the pub on a Saturday night and buys a half a gill
Goes to the kirk on Sunday, half an hour late
Pulls the buttons off his shirt and puts them in the plate

*(McVicar from personal recollection: Glasgow, 1950s)*

MATTHEW MARK
Matthew Mark Luke John
Haud the horse till I loup on
Haud it fast, and haud it sure
Till I get owre the misty muir

*(Chambers 1842)*

Matthew Mark Luke and John
Hold the horse till I get on
When I got on I couldna ride
I fell off and broke my side

*(Maclagan 1901)*

See Henderson (1992) for an article linking this to 'I'm a little orphan girl'.

MINISTER IN HIS PULPIT
A minister in his pulpit
He couldn't say his prayers
He giggled and he gaggled
Till he fell down the stairs
The stairs gave a crack
And he broke his humpie back
And all the congregation
Gave a quack, quack, quack

*(Rymour Club 1911)*

This rhyme is explained in other publications as a flock of ducks making a noise, rather than an account of an event in a church.

THE MONKEES
Hey hey we're the Monkees
Ma maw's a chimpanzee
Ma dad's a hairy gorilla
And he works for the BBC

*(Ian Davison Card Index; tune: theme for The Monkees TV show)*

MRS MCGUIRE
Mrs McGuire peed in the fire
The fire was too hot, she peed in the pot
The pot was too wide, she peed in the Clyde
And all the wee fishes went up her backside

*(McVicar Collection: Glasgow, 1992)*

Mrs McGuire peed in the fire
The fire was too hot so she peed in the pot
The pot was too round so she peed on the ground
The ground was too flat so she peed on the cat
And the cat ran away with a pee on its back

*(Ian Davison Card Index: East Milton School, East Kilbride)*

Wee Tammy Tyrie fell in the feirie
The feire wiz hot, he jamp ee pot
The pot wiz metal, he jamp ee kettle
The kettle wiz bress, he jamp ee press
The press wiz high, he jamp ee sky
The sky wiz blue, he jamp ee soo
The soo gae a roar, he jamp in the boar
The boar gae a loup
And wee Tammy Tyrie landit on eez doup

*(Rodger nd)*

The first version was quoted by Norman Buchan in the House of Commons during a debate on censorship.

MRS MACLEAN
Mrs Maclean had a wee wean
She didny know how tae nurse it
She gied it tae me, ah gied it some tea
And its bonny wee belly burstit

*(School of Scottish Studies archive:*
*Henderson, from Alec Ross, Glasgow, 1957)*

MRS MASON
Mrs Mason bought a rubber doll
She washed it she dried it
And then she let it fall
She sent for the doctor

The doctor couldn't come
Because he had a pimple
On his wee bare bum

*(Ian Davison Card Index: Rottenrow School)*

MRS MURRAY
Mrs Murray was in a hurry
To catch the electric train
She fell in the grass
And skinned her
Ask no questions tell no lies
Shut your mouth and you'll catch no flies

*(Ian Davison Card Index: Sir John Maxwell School)*

MRS RED
Mrs Red went to bed
In the morning she was dead
The policeman came and took her name
And told her never to die again

*(Ian Davison Card Index: Bellahouston School)*

MRS WHITE
Mrs White got a fright
In the middle of the night
Saw a ghost eating toast
Halfway up the lamppost

*(Ian Davison Card Index: Rottenrow School)*

THE NICHT O HALLOWEEN
This is the nicht o Halloween, aa the witches to be seen
Some o them black, and some o them green, some o them like a Turkey bean

*(Rymour Club 1911: Edinburgh)*

NOW THE WAR IS OVER
Now the war is over, Mussolini's dead
He wants to go to Heaven with a crown upon his head
The Lord says, 'No, he's got to stay below
All dressed up and nowhere to go'

*(Alan Lomax archive: Jennifer & Pat Cushnie, Aberdeen, 1951)*

Now the war is over, Vasoline is dead
He wants to go to heaven with a crown upon his head
But the Pope says, 'No, you'll have to stay below
There's only room for Elvis and his wee banjo'

*(McVicar Collection: Glasgow, 1992)*

In Jean Rodger's Forfar Churchill was the musician. Earlier again the Kaiser was the deceased:

As sure as I am leevin the Kaiser's deed
He thocht to gang to heeven with the crown upon his heed
But the Lord said, 'No, stap him doon below
An pour doon his thrapple a pint o molten leed'

*(Rymour Club Minute Book of 1913–1920, as a pencilled note
beside minutes of the meeting of 9/11/1918)*

OLD KING COUL
Old King Coul was a jolly old soul
And a jolly old soul was he
Old King Coul he had a brown bowl
And they brought him in fiddlers three
And every fiddler was a very good fiddler
And a very good fiddler was he

Fidell-didell, fidell-didell with the fiddlers three
And there's no a lass in Scotland
Compared to our sweet Marjorie

*(Herd 1776)*

Herd noted another four verses of this favourite, with pipers who blew ha-didell how-didell, harpers who plucked twingle-twangle, trumpeters who blasted twarra-rang, and drummers who beat rub-a-dub. Burns wrote to Johnson 'I have met with many different sets of the tune and words.' Sir Walter Scott theorised that this king was the father of the giant Finn MacCool. I would like to think of Coul as a native Scot, but his song was first noted in 1708 in England.

PETER PAN
Peter Pan drove a van
Over Wendy, now she's bendy

*(McVicar Collection: East Calder, 2007)*

A POOR LITTLE EWING
I'm only a poor little Ewing
JR's always picking on me
Sue Ellen's a drunk
And Lucy's a punk
And Bobby came out of the sea

*(Ian Davison Card Index)*

About the main characters in the popular 1980s TV show *Dallas*.

RAB HAA
Rab Haa, the Glasgow glutton
Ate his shirt and left a button
Rab Haa, the Glasgow glutton
Ate the steak and all the mutton

*(McVicar Collection: Erskine, 1992)*

RABBIE BURNS THE DIVER
Rob Tamson was a sporty lad
He bet a man a fiver
That he could loup Jamaica Bridge
Like Rabbie Burns the diver

The folk that stood aboot the bridge
Kicked up an awfu shindy
For he fell doon the funnel
O the Clutha Number Twenty

*(Buchan 1962)*

There was a man with the surname Burns, but not the first name Rabbie, who gave exhibition dives into the River Clyde in Glasgow. The Cluthas were pleasure paddle steamers.

ROMEO THE DARKIE
Romeo the darkie-o
Sells ice-cream-io
If you want a pokie-o
Go to Mr Romeo

*(Ian Davison Card Index: Rottenrow School; tune: variant of 'London Bridge')*

A racist reference, probably more usually about Romeo the tallie-o, i.e. Italian.

SAKY SAKY
Saky Saky Pirn-taes
The snaw's fa'en doun
And ilka lass wi kilted claes
Is rinnin thro the toun
Past the Cross and past the Kirk
And doun the Netherbow
Saky Saky Pirn-taes
I'm waitin on my jo

*(Moffat 1933)*

SALOME
Oh Salome, Salome
You should see Salome
Hands up there, skirts in the air
You should see Salome
Wing it swing it
You should see her swing it
Hands up there, skirts in the air
You should see her swing it
Her boyfriend, her boyfriend
You should see her boyfriend
Bowler hat, nose in the air
You should see her boyfriend

*(Ian Davison Card Index)*

SANTA CLAUS
Santa Claus came doon the lum
Wi toys for oor wee Minnie
He stole ma mammy's best fur coat
And noo he's in Barlinnie

*(Ian Davison Card Index: Balornock School; tune: 'Pop goes the weasel')*

A pigeon-toed urchin I should like to know more about.

SKINNY MALINKY
Skinny Malinky Longlegs
Big banana feet
Went tae the pictures
But couldnae find a seat
When the picture started
Skinny Malinky farted
Skinny Malinky Longlegs
Big banana feet

*umberella feet*

*(Ian Davison Card Index:*
*Rottenrow School)*

SOME SAY THE DEIL'S DEID
Some say the deil's deid
The deil's deid, the deil's deid
Some say the deil's deid
And buried in Kirkcaldy

Some say he'll rise again
Rise again, rise again
Some say he'll rise again
An dance the Hielan Laddie

*(Cheviot 1896)*

TARZAN
Tarzan in the jungle
Looking for Jane
Jane's in the toilet
Kissing John Wayne

*(Ian Davison Card Index)*

Tarzan in the jungle
Picking up grass
Along came an elephant
And kicked him up the

Tarzan in the jungle
Picking up sticks
Along came and elephant
And pulled doon his knicks

Tarzan in the jungle
Picking up stones
Along came an elephant
And broke all his bones

Tarzan in the jungle
Waiting for a train
Along came an elephant
And called him Baldy Bain

*(Ian Davison Card Index)*

TEXAS COWBOY JOE
I'm a Texas, Texas Cowboy Joe
I'm a Texas, Texas Cowboy Joe
And I come from the land that everyone knows
I can ride, I can shoot
I can do the hula-hoop
When the Indians come to town
There's a guy over there, he winks one eye
He says he loves me, but he's telling a lie
His hair don't curl, and his boots don't shine
He ain't got the money, so he won't be mine

All the girls wear red, white and blue
All the boys say 'I love you'
With a wiggle and a wriggle
When the Indians come to town
(In the land of Texas)

*(Ian Davison Card Index)*

THREE LITTLE ANGELS
Three little angels all dressed in white
Tried to get to heaven on the end of a kite
But the kite end was broken, down they all fell

They couldn't get to heaven so they all went to

Two little angels, all dressed in white [etc.]

One little angel, all dressed in white [etc.]

Three little devils all dressed in red
Tried to get to heaven on the end of a bed
But the bed end was broken, down they all fell
They couldn't get to heaven so they all went to

Two little devils [etc.]

One little devil [etc.]

Don't be mistaken, don't be misled
They couldn't get to heaven so they all went to bed

*(McVicar Collection: Erskine, 1992)*

A Brownie song. In East Calder Primary, 2007, they sang of a broken kite string and broken bed knob, and then of

Three little girl guides all dressed in blue
Tried to get to heaven on the seat of a loo
But the loo chain was broken [etc.]

THREE MEN THEY WENT A HUNTIN
Three men they went a huntin
Tae see what they could find
They came across a mountain
Something left behind
The Englishman said 'mountain'
The Scotsman he said 'nay'
Said Paddy, 'It's a dumplin
The currants have blown away'

Ay tiddly ay ty
Ay tiddle eh
Said Paddy, 'It's a dumplin
The currants have blown away'

Three men they went a huntin
Tae see what they could find
They came across a lamppost
Something left behind
The Englishman said 'lamppost'
The Scotsman he said 'nay'
Said Paddy, 'It's a policeman
His buttons have blown away' [etc.]

Three men they went a huntin
Tae see what they could find
They came across a monkey
Something left behind
The Englishman said 'monkey'
The Scotsman he said 'nay'
Said Paddy, 'It's yer auld man
Badly needin a shave' [etc.]

*(McVicar from personal recollection:*
*as sung by Ray Fisher, Glasgow, 1960)*

Tibbie Fowler
Tibbie Fowler in the glen
Stealt her mither's black hen
Be she black, or be she fite
Tibbie Fowler got the wyte
Be she rossen, be she raw
Tibbie Fowler ate her aa

*(Shuldham-Shaw et al. 2002, no. 1691A)*

Tom Thumb
Tom Thumb in a cellar
I-Spy Cinderella
Cinderella in a wood
I-Spy Robin Hood
Robin Hood up a tree
I-Spy the bumble-bee
Bumble-bee in a basin
I-spy Perry Mason
Perry Mason is a star
S-T-A-R

*(Ian Davison Card Index: Rottenrow School)*

TOMMY MORGAN
Tommy Morgan played the organ
And his father played the drum
And his sister had a blister
In the middle of her bum

*(Ian Davison Card Index: Rottenrow School)*

Morgan was a Glasgow music hall star.

WEE JOHNNIE'S JAURIE
Wee Johnnie's lost his jaurie
Wee Johnnie's lost his jaurie
Wee Johnnie's lost his jaurie
Doon by the Broomielaw

He drapped it doon a stank [etc.]

He went and got a clothespole [etc.]

He shoved it doon the stank [etc.]

But he couldnae reach it [etc.]

He went and got gunpowder [etc.]

He rammed it doon the stank [etc.]

He blew up half of Glasgow [etc.]

But still he didnae get it [etc.]

It was in his bloody pocket
It was in his bloody pocket
It was in his bloody pocket
It wisny lost at aa

*(McVicar from personal recollection: Glasgow, 1960s)*

WEE MAN FROM GOVAN
There was a wee man from Govan
He locked himself in the oven
The silly wee ass he turned on the gas
There was a wee man from Govan

*(Ian Davison Card Index: Sir John Maxwell School)*

WEE SANDY WAUGH
I hae a wee bit Hieland man
His name is Sandy Waugh
He sits upon a puddock-stool
And fine he sups his broth

Sing hey, my bonnie Hieland man
My Sandy trig and braw
Come prinkum prankum, dance wi me
A cock-a-leerie-law

There's herring in the silver Forth
And salmon in the Tay
There's puffins on the auld Bass
And there's bairns that greet aa day

*(Moffat 1933)*

Another cute song about people littler than children. The two verses seem to be from different voices.

WEE WILLIE WINKIE
Wee Willie Winkie, up an doon the toon
Tried to steal a croon, an then turned broon

*(McVicar Collection: East Calder, 2007)*

The original twenty-line poem, pronounced by Rev G Gilfillan to be 'the greatest nursery song in the world', was written by William Miller of Glasgow (1810–72).

WHEN I WAS A WEE THING
When I was a wee thing
Just like a little elf
Then aa the meat that e'er I gat
I laid upon the shelf
But when I gat a wifie
She wadna bide therein
Till I gat a hurl-barrow braw
To hurl her out and in

She wadna eat nae bacon
She wadna eat nae beef
She wadna eat nae lang-kail

For fyling o her teeth
But she wad eat the bonnie bird
That sits upon the tree
So gang doun the burn, Davie dear
And I shall follow thee

*(Moffat 1933)*

'More than a hundred and fifty years ago an Edinburgh Firm printed it as an ancient song.' The tune is a stripped down version of 'John Anderson my jo'. The final couplet is borrowed from another song, a lyric writer's device to suggest the suppression of a negative comment.

WHEN SUZIE WAS A BABY
When Suzie was a baby
A baby Suzie was
She went a goo goo
A goo goo goo

When Suzie was a toddler
She went a walk walk
A walk walk walk

When Suzie was a schoolgirl
She went a 'Please, miss, I can't do this'

When Suzie was a teenager
She went a 'Oo Ah, ah lost ma bra
Ah left ma knickers in ma boyfriend's car'

When Suzie was a mother
She went a 'Shoo shoo
Shoo shoo shoo'

When Suzie was a grannie
She went a 'Knit, knit
I lost my stitch'

When Suzie was a dead
A dead Suzie was
She went [silence]

*(School of Scottish Studies archive: Hendry, Glenrothes, 1981)*

Suzie's popularity continues, and mothers quote the 'boyfriend's car' verse to show the depravity of the twenty-first century, unaware the verse has been flaunted since the 1960s.

From Dalkeith in 1997 came

> When Suzie was a child, she went
> Miss, miss, I need a piss
>
> When Suzie was an adult, she went
> Smack smack, a smack smack smack
>
> When Suzie was a ghost
> She went whoo whoo, a whoo whoo whoo

WILLIAM TELL
Come away come away with William Tell
Come away to the land he loved so well
What a day what a day when the apple fell
For Tell and Switzerland
Come away come away with William Tell
To the land to the land where his trousers fell
Pull them up, pull them up, what an awful smell
For Tell and Switzerland

*(Ian Davison Card Index: Rottenrow School; tune: 'William Tell' theme)*

# 9

# *If you hit the one wee moll*

## Performance and narrative – confrontation and defiance

Last night there was a murder in the chip shop
A wee dug stole a haddy bone
A big dug tried tae take it aff him
So ah hit it wi a tattie scone

I have placed most of the threats and accounts of personal or gang violence and warfare in the Boy's Game section. Here I include those rhymes involving violence that girls tend to make use of, and more general tales of threatening behaviour, confrontations and insults.

A rhyme of family violence I first met when aged eight has led me on a merry dance of enquiry:

(Transcription: McVicar from personal recollection, Dingwall 1940s)

Today is Hogmanay, tomorrow's Hogmananny
And ah'm gaun up the brae, tae see ma Irish grannie
Ah'll take her tae a ball, ah'll take her tae a supper
And when ah get her there ah'll stick her nose in the butter
Singin ah ah ah ah ah, ah ah ah ah ah ah
Ah, ah ah ah ah, and that's the Gaelic chorus

*(McVicar from personal recollection: 1940s)*

I learned this song from my parents. My memory is that I got it from my father, William McVicar, who learned it in Kilbarchan, Renfrewshire, in the 1920s. But a few years ago my mother told me that both she and my father had contributed parts of it, but she could not remember who knew which parts. So it is partly from Kilbarchan, and partly from Plean near Stirling. The 'ah ah ah' sound is an imitation of the sound of a bagpipe in which the nose is pinched with the left thumb and forefinger, and the throat is beaten rhythmically with the flattened fingers of the right hand. My father also used this effect as a chorus for the song 'The massacre of ta Fhairson', a cod Gaelic lay written by the nineteenth-century poet WE Aytoun, which begins:

Fhairson swore a feud
Against the clan M'Tavish
Marched into their land
To murder and to rafish
For he did resolve
To extirpate the vipers
With four-and-twenty men
And five-and thirty pipers

Another cod Gaelic song to this tune has the chorus

Come a ree come a rye come a ro
Come a ree come a rye come a ro russ
Come a ree come a rye come a rach ee oh
And that's the Fenian chorus

Other lyrics that utilise this tune are 'Ah'm gaun awa on the train' and 'My boots are lined with silver'. When a second strain is added the tune becomes 'Courting in the kitchen'.

*(Transcription: McVicar, from singing of several informants; tune: 'Courting in the kitchen')*

Arranger Charles D'Esteve knew it as 'Bob and Joan'.

*(D'Esteve 1883; tune: 'Bob and Joan')*

When it is converted from major to minor mode it becomes the old Jacobite ballad 'Cam ye ower frae France', in which the second line of the last verse says 'Hey for Bobbing John, and his Highland quorum'. A link to 'Bob and Joan', and another Gaelic reference.

*(Transcription: McVicar, from singing of several informants; tune: 'Cam ye ower frae France?')*

Viewed as a whole the Hogmananny song is a satisfying performance piece, which I have taught to children in Russia and the USA and to thousands in Scotland. I also gave it to Artie Trezise and Cilla Fisher of the children's show *The Singing Kettle*, who recorded it commercially. Through this, my parents' assembly version of the song became known to thousands of Scots children, but there are many other versions about. Jean C Rodger recalled a Forfar version:

> The nicht's Hogmanay
> The morn's Hogmanay
> Far across the sea
> Tae see my Susannay
> Some fowks says I'm daft
> Some fowks says I'm crackit
> Offer me half-a-croon
> And see if I'll no tak it

> I took her tae a ball
> And took her tae a supper
> She fell ower the table
> And stuck her nib ee butter

*(Rodger nd)*

Lines five to eight seem interpolated from a 'music hall' song, one of those Daft Sandy songs about a village fool who is wise enough. The other lines, as you can see, are closely related to my father's song. So far, so good. I've not yet found another Hogmananny version, but no less exalted a personage than her Grace the Duchess of Sutherland herself has assisted me. She went collecting rhymes in the village schools in Helmsdale and Portgower, and one was the following:

> My uncle died a week ago, he left me all his riches
> A wooden leg, a feather bed, a pair of leather breeches
> A tobacco box without a lid, a jug without a handle
> A coffee pot without a spout, and half of a farthing candle
> I travelled east, I travelled west, I came to Alabama
> I fell in love with a nice young girl, her name was Susy Anna
> I took her to the ball one night, and also to the supper
> The table fell, and she fell too, and stuck her nose in the butter

*(Rymour Club 1919)*

Things get worse when James Ritchie (1964) gives us another Edinburgh version, from fifty years later than the Rymour Club one:

> Away down east, away down west
> Away down Alabama
> The only girl that I love best
> Her name is Susy Anna
>
> I took her to a ball one night
> And sat her down to supper
> The table fell and she fell too
> And stuck her nose in butter
>
> The butter, the butter
> The holy margarine
> Two black eyes and a jelly nose
> And the rest all painted green

'Please, sir, it was an accident, I never touched her, she did it to herself.' How believable is this? Someone pushed that girl. And what is this business about 'holy margarine'? Ritchie tries to help us. He considers the widespread (so to speak) use of margarine was a product of rationing during World War One. 'Margarine almost wholly took the place of butter. It was christened "Maggy Ann", or referred to sardonically as "the holy margarine".'

William and Norah Montgomerie also found a variant of the song, in Dundee in 1954. (*Tocher* 44) They recorded David Husband, aged ten, singing it. He had learned the song at the Rechabites meeting where they had singsongs on a stage. The Rechabites sound like a folk group who sang Jacobite songs very indistinctly, but they were in fact members of a teetotal benefit society, named for Rechab, who told his family they must avoid wine and live in tents. (*Jeremiah* 35, v.6–7) Para Handy's mate said 'I'm a Rechabite for six years, every time I'm in Gleska'. So when at home in Glasgow he was teetotal, but on the Vital Spark he took a dram or two.

I suppose they had hard drink at the ball, and Susy Anna fell over through getting intoxicated, so it serves her right. The following callous version was sung to me by an elderly gentleman in a Glenrothes Age Concern Centre in 2003:

*(Transcription: McVicar, from singing of informant; Glenrothes 2003)*

Three wee wives and three wee wives and three wee wives make nine
Says your wee wife tae my wee wife, 'Will ye lend me ma washin line?'
Says my wee wife to your wee wife, 'When will ah get it back?'
Says your wee wife to ma wee wife, 'Ah'll skelp yer humphy back'
Oh didn't we laugh, oh didn't we laugh tae skelp her humphy back
Didn't we laugh, oh didn't we laugh tae skelp her humphy back

I hunted east, I hunted west, I hunted Alabama
The only girl that I could find was bonny Susy Anna
I took her to the ball one night, set her down to supper
The table fell and she did yell and stuck her nose in the butter
Oh didn't we laugh, oh didn't we laugh tae see her nose in the butter
Didn't we laugh, oh didn't we laugh tae see her nose in the butter

The butter, the butter, the holy margarine
Twa black eyes and a jelly nose and her face aa paintit green
Her faither died twa weeks ago, left her aa his riches
A feather bed, a corky leg, and twa three broken crutches
Oh didn't we laugh, oh didn't we laugh tae see her broken crutches
Didn't we laugh, oh didn't we laugh tae see her broken crutches

*(McVicar Collection: Glenrothes, 2003)*

The tune used by David Husband and my Glenrothes informant was the same strain as 'Doh ray me, when ah wis wee'. It may be derived from an American song, either a true gospel rooflifter or maybe a parody used in black-face minstrel shows. The tune is the verse of 'Oh dem golden slippers', copyrighted 1879, except that the smooth original melody is now galvanised by a typically Scots octave leap at the end. But a novelty song about postal hire purchase, 'Dollar down and a dollar a week', was recorded in the 1930s by Chris Bouchillion, an early country star known as the 'Arkansas Woodchopper', using the 'Doh ray me' version of the air. I have also heard that air in use after rugby matches in Mombasa, Kenya, to a lyric that begins 'If I was the marrying kind of a man, which thank the Lord I'm not, sir'.

As is often the case with children's songs, there seems to have been a frankly rude and bawdy version of the margarine stanza, recalled from childhood by the famed Stewart traveller family of Blairgowrie:

I took my love to the station for to see the train
I lifted up her petticoats and I saw her Mary Jane
Her Mary Jane was hairy, fit for any king
Twa black eyes and a Roman nose and the rest aa painted green

*(MacColl & Seeger 1986)*

The non-rhyme between lines three and four is puzzling, line three was surely something like 'as fine as any queen'. I thought the resemblance of the word 'Mary Jane' to 'margarine' coincidental until I found, on a 1940 acetate disc in the Appalachian archives of East Tennessee State University, a variant sung by Jim Garland in which the protagonist is riding in the parlour car of a train, and sees a girl's 'magazine', which the song describes as the 'mother lode'. The lyric is a close version of the Stewarts verse, but so frankly bawdy I have tucked it away in the 'rude' section.

I have not yet identified any phrase that could be considered as the original phrase parodied as 'The butter, the butter, the holy margarine'. A part of some liturgy is one possibility, or perhaps a reference to Saint Margaret of Scotland, 'the Holy Margaret'.

Nor have I been able to find any trace of the word Hogmananny, other than in my father's song. As a child I assumed that the word was regular old Scots for 1 January, but the Scots dictionaries know it not. There is a rhyme which begins 'This is the nicht o Halloween, an the morn's Hallowday'. (Rodger nd) Shetland poet TA Robertson recalled that 'on the 12th January (New Year's Eve by the old style calendar) [. . .] in each house that we visited we sang the *New Year Song*, which we called *Da Huggeranonie Sang* [. . .] I never heard the word Hogmanay used in Shetland. People always spoke about Newr Even.' (Robertson 1991)

Chambers (1842) says that some 'old ballads allude to the hallow (or holy) days of Yule'. So maybe Hogmananny parodies Hallowday?

Or maybe it comes from further afield. In *Golspie, Contributions on its Folklore* (1897), Edward Nicholson is confident that the term 'Hogmanay' is French, from the word 'Aguillenneu' noted in 1472, and the 'late form Aguillanneuf'. He includes in his 'proof' of derivation two patois forms of the word from Normandy – 'Hoquinano' and 'Hoguinané', plus 'Oguinané' from Guernsey. Indeed, the *Concise Scots Dictionary* (1985) says 'Northern French dialect hoguinane, Old French aguillanneuf, a gift given on New Year's Eve, the word shouted in asking for this'. Is my parents' word 'Hogmananny', like the word 'aleerie', a little survival word from times long gone, frozen within a children's song? Could be.

Those violent little wives put me in mind of some other female tearaways celebrated in Scots children's song:

I went by the sweet-ie works, ma hert be-gun tae beat   Saw aa the her-ry pie wal-kin doon the street   Wi their

flash-y, dash-y pet-ti-coats,   flash-y, dash-y shawls Their five an tan-ner gut-ty boots, oh we're big gal-lus molls

*(Tocher 36/7 1982)*

Oh, yir ma wee gallus bloke nae mair
Oh, yir ma wee gallus bloke nae mair
Wi yir bell-blue strides an yer bunnet tae the side
Oh, yir ma wee gallus bloke nae mair

When I went by the sweetie works, ma hert begun tae beat
Saw aa the herry pie walkin doon the street
Wi their flashy, dashy petticoats, flashy, dashy shawls
Their five an tanner gutty boots, oh we're big gallus molls

*(School of Scottish Studies archive: Henderson Peel St, Glasgow; also Tocher 36–7)*

This was collected by Hamish Henderson from trade union leader Josh Shaw in Glasgow in 1957. The following verse was I believe composed by either singer Josh MacRae or teacher/songwriter Morris Blythman:

As I came by the dancin, I began tae think
Will all the lassies stand and talk aboot oor Jeanie's mink
Or will they hae a na'er wi me aboot ma past
But just as I came up to them they walked away right fast

When the song was picked up by adult Folk Revival performers the original singer's syncopated delay before 'ma wee gallus bloke' was ironed out, and the lyrics softened by 'herry pie' being changed to 'factory lassies'. Hamish Henderson asked famed Aberdonian singer Jeannie Robertson if she knew this song. She recalled the following, to a different tune:

For we are three wee Glesga molls, we kin let you see
An if you hit the one wee moll, ye'll hae tae hit the three
Flashy dashy petticoats, flashy dashy shawls
Twelve an a tanner's worth o boots, an we're the gallus molls

*(School of Scottish Studies archive: Henderson, Aberdeen, 1960)*

A year later Father Damien Webb recorded a tattered remnant of the lyric from Mosspark School Juniors, with a tune closer to Jeannie Robertson's than Josh Shaw's.

Oh, we are three wee gal-lus girls sail-ing on the sea And if you pick the fair-est one, the fair-est one shall be Oh, rash-a tash-a pet-ti-coat, rash-a tash-a tee Rash-a tash-a pet-ti-coat, the fair-est one shall be

*(Transcription: McVicar; from Webb 1983)*

Oh, we are three wee gallus girls sailing on the sea
And if you pick the fairest one, the fairest one shall be
Oh, rasha tasha petticoat, rasha tasha tee
Rasha tasha petticoat, the fairest one shall be

*(Children's Singing Games: Webb, Moss Park PS, Glasgow, 1961)*

## Anthology: Confrontation and defiance

AH WISH AH HUD
Ah wish ah hud a penny
Tae buy a penny gun
Ah'd pit it on ma shouder
An ah'd mak the bobby run

*(McVicar Collection: Moray, 2006)*

AN AWFY HAMMERIN
Aw maw I got an awfy hammerin
Who fae? wee Geordie Cameron
Whit fur? Because I wouldnae marry him
I'll tell the polis in the morning

*(Ian Davison Card Index: Rottenrow School)*

ARCHIBALD
Archibald bald bald
King of the jews jews jews
Bought his wife wife wife
A pair of shoes shoes shoes

When the shoes shoes shoes
Began to wear wear wear
Archibald bald bald
Began to swear swear swear

When the swear swear swear
Began to stop stop stop
Archibald bald bald
Bought a shop shop shop

When the shop shop shop
Began to sell sell sell
Archibald bald bald
He bought a bell bell bell

When the bell bell bell
Began to ring ring ring
Archibald bald bald
Began to sing sing sing
Doh, ray, me, fah, soh, lah, te, doh

*(Ian Davison Card Index: Rottenrow School)*

Elsewhere in Glasgow they sang that when he bought a bell he went to hell. In Edinburgh in 1945 they said that he sang 'Doh ray me fah soh lah te doh. Who stole my wife I do not know.' Elsewhere he was Scottie Malottie or Archie-ball-ball-ball. Earlier it was Nebuchadnezzar who was thus maligned. Ritchie in *Golden City* points out that in Amos II, v6 'They sold . . . the poor for a pair of shoes.'

ARE YOU GOING TO GOLF
Are you going to golf, sir?
No, sir
Why, sir?
Because I've got a cold, sir
Where did you get the cold, sir?
Up at the North Pole, sir
What were you doing there, sir?
Catching polar bears, sir
How many did you catch, sir?
One, sir, two, sir
Three, sir, four, sir
Five, sir, six, sir
Seven, sir, eight, sir
Nine, sir, ten, sir

*(School of Scottish Studies archive: Henderson, Craigmillar, 1954)*

BARLINNIE

There is a wee hoose ca'd Barlinnie haw haw
Where ye drink yer tea frae a tinny haw haw
The warders are there tae shave aff yer hair
In that lovely wee hoose ca'd Barlinnie

*(Ian Davison Card Index: John St School)*

Barlinnie is a large prison in Glasgow. The verse is a version of 'The big mansion hoose ca'd Barlinnie Hotel'. For longer versions see Campbell (1964) and Seeger and MacColl (1960).

THE BOYS BRIGADE

The Boys Brigade they are afraid
To stick their nose in marmalade

*(Ian Davison Card Index: Rottenrow School)*

EH'LL TELL THE BOABBIE

Eh'll tell the boabbie
Eh'll tell the boabbie
Eh'll tell the boabbie
If ye lay a hand on me

Thirty days in the tripe shop [etc.]
If ye lay a hand on me

As sung by singer Aileen Carr. Dundee pronunciation.

EVERYWHERE WE GO

Everywhere we go
People always ask us
Who we are
And where we come frae
And we tell them
We come frae Scotland
Bonny bonny Scotland
And if they canny hear us
We shout a little louder

*(McVicar Collection: Glasgow, 1992)*

Each line sung out, then repeated. Then the whole song sung twice more, getting louder/higher. Last time round the final line becomes 'They must be DEEF!' A school or place name usually replaces 'Scotland'.

Here comes the factor
Here comes the factor, the factor, the factor
Here comes the factor
Tae gaither in the rent
Catch him by the waistcoat, the waistcoat, the waistcoat
Tell him he's a nanny-goat
And throw him doon the stair

*(Ian Davison Card Index: Bellahouston School;*
*tune: 'The keel row')*

Another Glasgow version is:

Who shaved the barber, the barber, the barber?
Who shaved the barber
The barber shaved himself
Who put on his waistcoat, his waistcoat, his waistcoat
Who put on his waistcoat
He put it on himself
Catch him by the waistcoat
The jaicket, the overcoat
Tell him he's a billygoat
And throw him doon the stairs

*(Sinclair 1986)*

I place my hand
I place my hand upon your head
Now a thousand bugs are dead

*(Ian Davison Card Index)*

I ring I ring
I ring I ring a pinky
If I tell a lee
I'll gang tae the bad place
Whenever I dee
White pan, black pan
Burn me tae death
Tak a muckle gully
An cut ma breath
Ten miles below the earth

*(Hendry & Stephen 1978)*

I WANT MA BUTTER
I want ma butter, ma sugar, ma tea
Waiting at the Maypole door
I don't want to get the flu
Staunin in a queue
I want ma butter, ma sugar, ma tea

*(Ian Davison Card Index)*

Might this recall wartime rationing?

LAST NIGHT
Last night there was a murder in the chip shop
A wee dug stole a haddy bone
A big dug tried tae take it aff him
So ah hit it wi a tattie scone

Ah went roon tae see ma Aunty Sarah
Bit ma Aunty Sarah wisnae in
So I keeked through a hole in the windae
And ah shouted 'Aunty Sarah, are ye in?'

Her false teeth were lyin on the table
Her curly wig wis lyin on the bed
An ah nearly split ma sides wi laughin
When ah saw her screwing aff her wudden leg

*(McVicar from personal recollection: Glasgow, 1950s)*

On occasion the big dug shouted 'haufers'.

LITTLE FATTIE
Little fattie policeman don't blame me
Blame that boy behind that tree
He stole sugar he stole tea
Policeman policeman don't blame me

*(Ian Davison Card Index: Rottenrow School)*

MURDER MURDER
Murder murder polis, three stair up
The wumman in the middle flat hit me wi a cup
Ma heid's aa achin, ma lip's aa cut
Murder murder polis, three stair up

*(McVicar from personal recollection: Glasgow, 1950s)*

Line three is sometimes 'The cup was fu o jelly, it ran doon ma belly'. (Davison Card Index)

MY BARBIE DOLL
Here lies my Barbie doll
Pretty pink and dead
My horrid little brother's
Just blown off her head

*(McVicar Collection: Moray, 2006)*

NAE CHAP-CHAPSIES
Mary Ellen I'm no playin
Cos there's nae chap-chapsies
In this game
You get chapsies I get nane
So Mary Ellen I'm no playin

*(Ian Davison Card Index: Rottenrow School)*

A complaint about interpretation of game rules.

THE NIGHT WAS DARK
The night was dark, the war was over
Battlefields were covered in blood
There I spied a wounded soldier
Lying dying saying these words

God bless my home in bonny Scotland
God bless my wife and only child
God bless the men who died for Scotland
Holding up the Union Jack

*(Ian Davison Card Index)*

Though the tale suggests a lugubrious recitation for guising, it was recorded in 1951 Edinburgh by Alan Lomax in use for vigorous skipping.

ONE FINE DAY
One fine day in the middle of the night
Two dead men got up to fight
One blind man to see fair play
Another dumb man to shout hurray
Up came a nanny goat and knocked them through a nine-inch wall
Into a dry ditch that drowned them all

*(Rodger nd)*

THE QUARTERMASTER'S STORE
There was gravy, gravy
That sunk the German navy, in the store, in the store
There was gravy, gravy
That sunk the German navy
In the quartermaster's store
My eyes are dim I cannot see
I have not brought my specs with me
I have not brought my specs with me

*(Ian Davison Card Index)*

An army song of long pedigree. The following alternative chorus was also in use:

My hands are sore, I cannot fight
I got the teacher's strap last night

*(McVicar from personal recollection: Dingwall, 1940s)*

RIDE AWA TO ABERDEEN
Ride awa to Aberdeen and buy white breid
But lang ere she cam back again, the carlin she was deid
He up wi his muckle club, and gied her in the heid
Fie, carlin, rise again and eat white breid

*(Rymour Club 1919)*

Stated to be an 'old Edinburgh rhyme', but Greig got an Aberdeenshire version (Shuldham-Shaw et al. 2002, no. 1690).

ROSES ARE RED
Roses are red
Violets are blue
A face like yours
Belongs in the zoo

*(Ian Davison Card Index: Bellahouston School)*

SOUTH OF THE BORDER
South of the border down Germany way
There is a nasty bloke we'd love tae choke who dreams today
Of being the ruler of half the earth
We should have drowned him the day of his birth

*(Ian Davison Card Index: Bellahouston School;*
*tune: 'South of the Border')*

Another relic of World War Two.

> THE SWANEE RIVER
> Way down upon the Swanee River
> Where I fell in with a splash
> Along came an alligator singing
> Britannia, Britannia, ma maw's making jam
> Chinese sausages and Belfast ham
>
> *(Ian Davison Card Index)*

A jovial joining of two popular song elements: the first three lines would be sung to 'Swanee River', the last two to 'Rule Britannia'. In Kenya in 1964 rugby players tagged on to the end of a bawdy narrative song the following:

> Rule Britannia, marmalade and jam
> Five Chinese crackers up your —
> Bang bang bang bang bang
>
> *(McVicar from personal recollection: Mombasa, 1964)*

> TELL TALE TIT
> Tell tale tit
> Your knickers will split
> Your dad's in the dustbin
> Eating fish and chips
>
> *(McVicar Collection: Dalkeith HS, 1997)*

A more modern version of 'Tell tale tit, your tongue shall be split'.

> THERE IS A HAPPY LAND
> There is a happy land, doon in Duke Street jail
> Where aa the prisoners stand tied tae a nail
> Ham-and-eggs we never see, dirty water fur yer tea
> There we live in misery. God save the Queen
>
> *(McVicar from personal recollection: Glasgow, 1950s)*

Or 'That's the way they treated me doon in the jail'. (Davison Card Index)

> THERE SHE GOES
> There she goes, there she goes
> Peerie heels and pointie toes
> Look at her feet, she thinks she's neat
> Black stockins an dirty feet
>
> *(Margaret et al. 1990s: West Lothian)*

TOMMY HAD A GUN
Tommy had a gun and the gun was loaded
Tommy pulled the trigger and the gun exploded
No more Tommy no more gun
No more damage to be done

*(Ian Davison Card Index: Rottenrow School)*

TOMMY THISTLE
Tommy Thistle blew a whistle
On a Sunday morning
The policeman came and took Tommy's name
And Tommy bowed good-morning.

*(Ian Davison Card Index: Rottenrow School)*

UNDER THE OLD APPLE TREE
Under the old apple tree
An apple said to me
Apple pudding apple pie
Have you ever told a lie – NO
Yes you have, you stole your mother's teapot lid
What colour was it – GOLD
No it wasn't it was silver
That's another lie you told

*(Ian Davison Card Index: Bellahouston School)*

This was sung to a 'variation of "Knees up Mother Brown", with second half of song spoken'.

VOTE VOTE VOTE
Vote vote vote for Mr Churchill
Who's that knocking at the door
If it's Hitler and his wife
Take a poker and a knife
And we won't see Hitler any more
Shut the door

*(Ian Davison Card Index: Bellahouston School)*

Vote vote vote for Campbell Stephen
Vote vote vote for aa his men
And we'll buy a penny gun
And we'll make the Germans run
And we'll never see the Germans any more

*(Hanley 1958)*

Hanley's last line cries out to end in 'again', but then would not fit the tune. Hanley comments that 'It looks pretty silly now since Campbell Stephen was a pacifist all his life.'

> Whau'll buy me
> Whau'll buy me Jockey-be-laund?
> Wat an he dees ata me haund?
>
> De back sall bear da seddle-baund
> Troo moss and mire, troo barn and byre
> Owre stocks and stanes, an deed men's banes
> An au sall lie upo dy back and anes
> If do lets me janty Jockey edder dee or fa

*(Saxby 1932: Shetland)*

All but line 2 were said very quickly by someone holding a 'lowan taund' or burning peat. If he finished before the flame went out the other child had to take it and repeat the rhyme, seeking to be rid of it before the flame went out. Whoever was holding the peat when the flame went out paid the forfeit. 'Chiefly played at the time of the Beltan Foy'. Another version is in *Tocher* 28.

# 10
## *I'll gie tae you a yalla hairy muff*

### Performance and narrative – courting

> One o'clock, the gun went off
> I cannot stay no longer
> If I do my ma will say
> I play with the boys up yonder
>
> My stockings red, my garters blue
> My shoes all bound with silver
> A red red rose upon my breast
> And a gold ring on my finger

The concept of 'innocent childhood' is severely dunted by the preoccupation with emotional relationships between the sexes that the rhymes show. Between the complaints of unwed mothers in lullabies and the frank bawdry of my last section, there is in the lyrics here and in my singing games section a clanjamfrie of sentimental wishing, knowing comment and fossilised remnants of the social manners of other days.

'Down in yonder meadow' is a fine example of the collector's dictum that even if you recognise several opening lines you should never say 'I already know that one.' The following first six lines occur very generally in versions, but then it can split in many ways.

> Down in yonder meadow where the green grass grows
> There (Lucy Locket) bleaches her clothes
> She sang, she sang, she sang so sweet
> She sang of (Tommy Piper) across the street
> He hugged her, he kissed her, he took her on his knee
> And said 'Dear (Lucy) I hope we will agree'

*(Fraser 1975)*

In Dreghorn in 1886 they sang

> He hugged her, he kissed her, he bought her a gown
> A gown, a gown, a guinea-gold gown
> He bought her a hat with a feather at the back
> A pea-brown cherry on a pea-brown hat
> She went down to the draper's at the corner of the street
> To buy a pair of blankets and a pair of sheets
> And half-a-yard of moleskin
> To mend (Willie's) breeks

*(Fraser 1975)*

In Argyllshire before 1901 there was dumpling tasting in the game, followed by

> Up in the highway they heard a great noise
> What was't but Mary lost her wedding-ring
> Some say gold and some say brass
> Some say go up the street, kiss your bonnie lass

*(Maclagan 1901)*

In 1913 a simplified version was printed:

> Agree, agree, I hope you will agree
> A pair of blankets, and three pair of sheets
> Five pair of moleskins to mend Johnnie's breeks

*(Rymour Club 1919)*

And in Central Scotland in the 1960s they still sang

> Agree, agree, I hope you will agree
> For tomorrow is our wedding day and I must go
> Mary made a dumpling, she made it awfy nice
> She cut it up in quarters and gave us all a slice
> Saying 'Taste it, taste it, don't say no
> For tomorrow is our wedding day and I must go'

*(Ian Davison Card Index)*

In Edinburgh in 1951 the song went off at a tangent, and in came some sickly sweet confectionery followed by a taxicab:

> Down in the valley where the green grass grows
> Where Mary Gray she grows like a rose
> She grows, she grows, she grows so sweet
> That she calls for her lover at the end of the street

Sweetheart, sweetheart, will you marry me?
Yes love, yes love, half-past three
Iced-cakes, spiced-cakes all for tea
And we'll have a wedding at half-past three

Pom, pom, here comes the taxicab
Pom, pom, here comes the taxicab
Pom, pom, here comes the taxicab
Ready for the wedding at half-past three

*(Alan Lomax archive: Norton Park schoolchildren, Edinburgh)*

At the end of the nineteenth century in Glasgow another sheering off and reattachment to the song was used for a game, sometimes in a ring and sometimes in a row:

He kissed her, he courted her, he put her into bed
And sent for the doctor before she was dead
Oh, said the doctor, what's ado here?
Oh, said Willie, I wanted a glass o beer

*(Shuldham-Shaw et al. 2002, no. 1575B)*

In 1960 Jean Redpath, one of Scotland's most famous folk singers, took Hamish Henderson to meet her mother in Leven. Mrs Redpath sang him the following song that unites a verse of 'Down in yonder meadow' with a verse that tells quite a different story, of a death attended by the undertaker in his tall black silk hat reminiscent of the shape of a piece of sweet liquorice:

Down in the meadow where the green grass grows
There Jeannie Redpath bleaches her clothes
She sang and she sang and she sang so sweet
She sang her true love across the street

He kissed her, he cuddled her, he put her tae bed
He sent for the doctor before she was dead
In came the doctor and out went the cat
And in came the man wi the sugarelly hat

*(School of Scottish Studies archive: Henderson, Leven, 1960)*

The intermingling of courtship and death is also reported by Maclagan from nineteenth-century Argyllshire under the fine title of 'Tarra ding ding ding dido – green peas and mutton pies':

Down to the knees in blood, up to the knees in water
My boots are lined with gold, my stockings lined with silver
A red rose on my breast, a gold ring on my finger,
Tarra ding ding ding, tarra ding ding ding dido

Down to the knees in blood, up to the knees in water
My boots are lined with gold, my stockings lined with silver
I for the pots and pans, I for the man that made them
Tarra ding ding ding, tarra ding ding ding dido

Green peas, mutton pies, tell me where my Maggie lies
I'll be there before she dies, green peas, mutton pies
Three pair of blankets and four pair of sheets
One yard of cotton to mend my Johnny's breeks

Green peas, mutton pies, tell me where my Johnny lies
I'll be there before he dies and cuddle in his bosom
Baby in the cradle, playing with the keys
Maggie in the pea park, picking up the peas

*(Maclagan 1901)*

The two-part title suggests that the first two verses were sung to one tune and the third and fourth to 'Green sleeves and pudding pies', which we met earlier, in Chapter 6. From New Pitsligo in about 1875 came an agglomeration of three verses, each with a different narrative element and involving two sex changes:

Green peas, mutton pies
Tell me where my true love lies
I'll be there before she dies
Green peas, mutton pies

I'll hae on a fite goon
Festened at the back
Silk an satin at my side
An ribbons in my hat

Weary, weary waitin on her
I can wait no longer on her
Three times I've whistled on her
Lassie, are ye comin?

*(Buchan Observer 16 April 1929)*

The North-East has been credited with punching well above its weight with the fine versions of old ballads that Greig and Duncan found, and the North-East versions of children's ballads are also often the richest. In 1951 Alan Lomax recorded from Mr and Mrs John Mearns this superior version of a duet that the Opies (1985) consider a 'singing game':

> I'll gie tae you a pennyworth o preens
> Tae fasten up your flounces and ither bonny things
> If you'll walk, if you'll talk
> If you'll walk wi me
>
> I'll no hae your pennyworth o preens
> Tae fasten up my flounces and ither bonny things
> And I'll no, and I'll no
> And I'll no walk wi you
>
> I'll gie tae you a yalla hairy muff
> Tae keep your handies warm when the wither's cauld and rough [etc.]
>
> I'll no hae your yalla hairie muff
> Tae keep my handies warm when the weather's cauld and rough [etc.]
>
> I'll gie tae you a cosy armchair
> Tae rest yoursel in when your beens are auld and sair [etc.]
>
> I'll no hae your cosy armchair
> Tae rest mysel in when ma beens are auld and sair [etc.]
>
> I'll gie tae you the keys o my hert
> And frae you I'll never never part
> If you'll walk, if you'll talk
> If you'll walk wi me
>
> O but I'll tak the keys o your hert
> And frae you I'll never never part
> And I'll walk, and I'll talk
> And I'll walk wi you

Chambers (1842) printed it as part of a 'Fireside Nursery Story', in rich Scots, with 'an owre proud leddy' meeting up 'wi Auld Nick himsel' when he's hid his 'cloven feetie out a sight', an he 'begins at coortin' her:

I'll gie you a pennyworth o preens
That's aye the way that love begins
If you'll walk with me, leddy, leddy
If you'll walk with me, leddy

I'll no hae your pennyworth o preens
That's no the way that love begins
And I'll no walk with you, with you
And I'll no walk with you

O Johnie, o Johnie, what can the matter be
That I love this leddy, and she loves na me?
And for her sake I must die, must die
And for her sake I must die

For the tune to this see Moffat (1933). The Deil offers her 'a bonnie silver box, with seven silver hinges and seven silver locks', then a bonnie silver box with golden hinges and locks, then a pair of shoon, 'the tane made in Sodom, the tother in Rome' – one wonders if the manufacturing origin is an intended clue to his devilish nature? And at last 'the hale o Bristol town, with coaches rolling up and down'. This does the trick and he flies off with her. Again, I wonder why Bristol town is more attractive than say Aberdeen – was it known then for heavy sinning?

In Glasgow the pins were dispensed with:

Oh, I'll gie you a dress o red
Aa stitched roon wi a silver thread
If you will marry, arry arry arry
If you will marry me

Oh, I'll no tak your dress o red
Aa stitched roon wi a silver thread
An I'll no marry, arry arry arry
An I'll no marry you

*(Buchan 1962)*

Next he offers her a 'silver spoon tae feed the wean in the afternoon' – some singers had this as 'to beat the wean', or less alarmingly and more poetically 'to beat the waves in the afternoon'. He then offers her 'the keys o my chest, an aa the money that I possess'. She grabs at this, whereat he exclaims in triumph

Oh ma Goad, ye're helluva funny
Ye dinna love me but ye love my money
An I'll no marry, arry arry arry
An I'll no marry you

Sometimes one or other is so disgusted they announce 'an I'll no marry at aa'.

In 1846 Halliwell printed a version of the song in his *Nursery Rhymes of England* as 'The keys of Canterbury'. This became a staple of the drawing room duets repertoire, in the days that those and such as those put on the stuffed white shirt and collar stud or the off the shoulder gown to entertain by the piano of an evening.

Madam, I will give to you the keys of Canterbury
And all the bells of London town to ring and make you merry
If you will be my darling, my joy and my dear
If you will go a walking with me anywhere

The offers reduce somewhat. Next he offers a little ivory comb, a pair of cork boots, then the winning bid of the keys to his heart. Why did none of them start with that?

In the seaport of Cromarty before 1900 the song was part of an 'elaborate and interesting' old marriage ceremony between fisher folk, in which the woman took up the creel to bear it through the parish and sell her new husband's catch, 'relieving the man of the burden and taking it up for him'.

Donald A MacKenzie tells us that 'a favourite marriage song was sung by the best man or the best maid':

Hi'll gie to thee ha penny's worth ho preens
To tack up thy flounces hor hony hother things
Hif thoo'll walk, hif thoo'll walk, hif thoo'll walk with me honywhere

But hi'll no tak yer penny's worth ho preens
To tack up my flounces hor hony hother things
Hi'll not walk wi thee honywhere

Hi'll gie to thee a braw new dress
To sit hupon the cerpet, or to walk hupon the gress
Hif thoo'll walk, etc.

*(Rymour Club 1928)*

This verson is in the dialect of the fisher folk who lived on the 'sea edge' of the town. Cromarty then had a population of about one thousand two hundred. The landward people of what was termed 'the toon', spoke a different dialect: 'Braid Scots with Highland accent'.

Pins were used as currency and gaming pieces by children in the days when a penny was a substantial piece of currency. One use was to insert a pin within a book's pages. If a 'scrap', a small coloured picture, was in that opening the contestant won it, if not the pin was forfeited. Another occupation involved the construction of a 'peep show', which cost a pin to view. Maclagan (1901) describes a version of the peep show that used flowers – the 'pappy' or poppy show. It was announced ready for viewing:

> A pin to see a pappy show
> A pin to see a die
> A pin to see a wee man
> Running up the sky

## Anthology: Courting

Ah'm gaun awa
Ah'm gaun awa in the train
And you're no comin wi me
Ah've got a lad o my ain
His name is Kiltie Jamie

He wears a tartan kilt
He wears it in the fashion
And every time he turns roond
I canna keep frae laughin

*(McVicar from personal recollection:*
*Glasgow, 1950s)*

A big ship
A big ship was leaving Bombay today
Back from those isles of Man so they say
There stood (Jeanie) with tears in her eyes
Along came the captain with two big black eyes
Saying darling oh darling be mine
I'll send you a sweet valentine valentine
He turned round and kissed me
I ducked and he missed me
A big ship was leaving Bombay today

*(Ian Davison Card Index: Rottenrow School;*
*tune: 'Bless them all')*

BRAW NEWS
Braw news is come to town
Braw news is carried
Braw news is come to town
(Mary Foster's) married

First she gat the frying pan
Syne she gat the ladle
Syne she gat the young man
Dancing on the table

Or else:

Here is a lass with a golden ring
Golden ring, golden ring
Here is a lass with a golden ring
So early in the morning

Gentle Johnie kissed her
Three times blessed her
Sent her a slice o bread and butter
In a silver saucer

Who shall we send it to
Send it to, send it to
Who shall we send it to?
To (Mrs Ritchie's) daughter

Or the following:

Braw news is come to town
Braw news is carried
Braw news is come to town
(Sandy Dickson's) married

First he gat the kail-pat
Syne he gat the ladle
Syne he gat a dainty wean
And syne he gat a cradle

*(Chambers 1842)*

The above seven stanzas are given by Chambers as three separate rhymes. Elements of these verses get intermingled into other published versions.

BROKEN-HEARTED I WANDER
Broken-hearted I wander
At the loss of my brother
He's a jolly jolly fellow
At the battle he was slain

He had a silver sixpence
And he broke it in twae
And he gave me the half o't
Before he went away

If I were an angel
I would fly to the skies
And far beyond the mountains
Where my dear brother lies

*(Rymour Club 1911)*

'The air is evidently an adaptation of "Hallelujah to the Lamb"' (Rymour Club 1911). It was sung by girls at Gorgie Public School in west Edinburgh, and was also known in Aberdeenshire, Glasgow and Inverallochy at the beginning of the twentieth century.

Broken hearted I wander
At the loss of my beloved
He's a jolly, jolly soldier
And to battle he must go

He wrote me a letter
In the month of November
And he told me not to worry
As he was coming home

Sweet home, marrow bone
Treacle scone, ice-cream cone
Uncle John

*(Alan Lomax archive:*
*Peggy MacGillivray, Edinburgh)*

The odd rhythmic coda indicates that this version was used for skipping. The song derives from a long Irish ballad, 'The bonny light horseman'.

CHINKY CHINA
I come from chinky China
My home's across the sea
I wash my clothes in China
For two and six a week
Oh Mary Mary Mary
You ought to be ashamed
To marry marry marry
A man without a hame

*(Ian Davison Card Index: Rottenrow School)*

DOON AT BARRALAND
It happened doon at Barraland
He asked me for a dance
Ah knew he was a flyman
But ah had tae take ma chance

His shoes were neatly polished
His hair was neatly combed
And when the dance was over
He asked tae see me home

He promised me a satin dress
He promised me a ring
He promised me a cradle
Tae rock ma baby in

Ah never seen the satin dress
Ah never seen the ring
Ah never seen the cradle
Tae rock ma baby in

Oh listen aa you herries
Take this advice fae me
Never let a flyman
An inch above yer knee

But when ma wean is older
Ah'll take it by the hand
And teach it aa the jiggin
Up in the Barraland

*(Ian Davison Card Index: Rottenrow School; tune: 'Putting on the style')*

FRASER, FRASER
Fraser, Fraser, do you love me?
Fraser, Fraser, do you care?
Fraser, will you marry me
In my underwear?

*(Ian Davison Card Index)*


THE HEART OF TEXAS
Down in the heart of Texas with a banjo on my knee
I came from the heart of Texas with a banjo on my knee
Oh dear Louise, I hope you'll marry me
I came from the heart of Texas with a banjo on my knee
Oh no, oh yes, it's amanarita

*(McVicar Collection:*
*St Robert's PS, Glasgow, 1997)*


HEY YOU MONKEES
Hey you Monkees singing on TV
Send me Davy till half past three
If you can't spare Davy Micky will do
If you can't spare Micky send the other two

*(Ian Davison Card Index)*


I ONCE HAD A BOY
I once had a boy, a bonny sailor boy
A boy you could call your own
He ran away and left me, I dinna ken where
But he left me to wander all alone

One day as I walked by the riverside
Somebody caught my eye
It was that boy, that bonny sailor boy
Wi another young girl by his side

He gave me a look of his bonny blue eyes
And a shake of his lily-white hand
But I walked right by and I never cast an eye
For I hate to be jilted by a boy, by a boy

*(Alan Lomax archive:*
*Peggy MacGillivray, Edinburgh)*

I'VE A LADDIE
I've a laddie in America
I've another in Dundee ay ee ay ee
I've another in Australia
And that's the one who's goin tae marry me ay ee ay ee

First he took me tae the dancin
Then he took me tae my tea
Then he ran away and left me
Wi three bonny bairnies on my knee

One was sittin by the fireside
Another was sittin on my knee
Another was sittin by the doorway
Singin 'Daddie, daddie, please come back tae me'

*(McVicar from personal recollection:*
*Glasgow, 1950s)*

LITTLE DUTCH GIRL
I am a pretty little Dutch girl
As pretty as can be be be
And all the boys in cabaret
Go crazy after me me me

My boyfriend's name is Tony
He comes from Californy
He's got ten-inch toes
A two-inch nose
And this is how my story goes

One day as I was walking
I heard my boyfriend talking
To a sweet little girl with a strawberry curl
And this is what he said to her

I L-O-V-E love you
I K-I-S-S kiss you
And we'll go walking in the
D-A-R-K P-A-R-K, dark park

*(Ian Davison Card Index:*
*Bellahouston School)*

LONDON CASTLE
As I gaed up by London Castle
Ten o'clock on a summer's night
There ah spied a bonny lassie
Washin her face in the candlelight

She had boots of patent leather
And her stockings lined with silk
Ma dar aye the red red rosie
Halliloo for Jeannie oh

Jeannie I shall wear your ribbons
Jeannie I shall wear them braw
Jeannie I shall wear your ribbons
Till your laddie gangs awa

*(School of Scottish Studies archive: Henderson, Leven, 1960)*

From the mother of Scots singer Jean Redpath. The first verse relates to the song 'Spanish lady', the rest is rather confused and confusing.

MY GIRL'S A CORKER
My girl's a corker, she's a New Yorker
I do most anything to keep her in store
She's got a head of hair, just like a grizzly bear
That's where all my money goes

Roompa roompa roompa pa
Roompa pa, roompa pa
Roompa roompa roompa pa
Roompa roompa pa [etc.]

She's got a pair of eyes, just like two custard pies [etc.]

She's got a great big nose, just like a farmer's hose [etc.]

*(Alan Lomax archive: Cedar Place children, Aberdeen)*

In Erskine in 1992 they sang

She's got a pair of legs
Just like some scrambled eggs
I'll do most anything to keep her away

The Opies (1985) tell us that this is a parody of an American popular song of 1895.

ONE O'CLOCK, THE GUN WENT OFF
One o'clock, the gun went off
I cannot stay no longer
If I do my ma will say
I play with the boys up yonder

My stockings red, my garters blue
My boots all bound with silver
A red red rose upon my breast
And a gold ring on my finger

Heigh ho for Lizzie o
My bonnie Lizzie o
If I had but one to choose
I'd choose my bonnie Lizzie o

*(Rymour Club 1911: Gorgie Public School, west Edinburgh)*

The school was just about in earshot of Edinburgh Castle's famous one o'clock gun in the days before petrol engines began to roar. In Liverpool the first line was 'Off off off to the butcher's shop'. (Shaw 1970)

ROSEMARY ANN
I'll tell my mammy on Rosemary Ann
She's out walking with a fine young man
High heel shoes and a feather in her hat
What would you do with a sister like that

*(Ian Davison Card Index: Bellahouston School)*

# *11*
# *Swing yer grannie aff the wa*

## Performance and narrative – family life

> The wife put on the wee pan
> To boil the bairn's meatie o
> Out fell a cinder
> And burnt aa its feetie o
> Hap and row, hap and row
> Hap and row the feetie o't
> I never kent I had a bairn
> Until I heard the greetie o't

The everyday small calamities of the home are here, along with warnings to girls against marriage and much about mothers but very few fathers; there is not an uncle in sight although aunties get a good look in. But the family star is grannie:

*(Transcription: McVicar from personal recollection, Glasgow 1950s)*

> Oh ye canny shove yer grannie aff a bus
> No ye canny shove yer grannie aff a bus
> Ye canny shove yer grannie
> Cause she's yer mammy's mammy
> Ye canny shove yer grannie aff a bus

Ye can shove yer other grannie aff a bus
Ye can shove yer other grannie aff a bus
Ye can shove yer other grannie
Cause she's jist yer daddy's mammy
Shove yer other grannie aff a bus

*(McVicar from personal recollection: Glasgow, 1950s)*

What sense are we to make of this song? The modern urban Scots child is reared and taught within a matriarchal society. Perhaps this song is designed to teach kids about matrilineal lines of authority? Respect your mother's mother, or else. However, many maternal grandmothers have been known to assert that their son-in-law's family are at best a doubtful lot and more probably have prison records a mile long that they are successfully concealing from said grandmother's family – the men, that is. The women are a shower of bampots who swally wee white pills to cheer or calm them and pop into the short-term ward of their local loonie bin as regularly as they are thrown out of their local off licence. These maternal grandmothers' daughters married beneath them and that's a fact.

Here is another lyric that indicates the trouble grannie can create:

Me and my Grannie and a great lot mair
Kicket up a row gaun hame frae the fair
By cam the watchman and cried 'Wha's there?'
'Me and my Grannie and a great lot mair'

*(Rymour Club 1919)*

In Glasgow in the 1950s the gang 'Kicked up a rammy on the wash hoose stair' and were challenged by a polis. Grannie can also get herself into individual trouble:

My grannie went doon tae the cellar
A leak in the gas for to see
She lit a match so she'd see better
Oh bring back my grannie tae me

*(McVicar Collection: Glasgow, 1992)*

A grannie's life is indeed a hazardous one:

Grannie in the kitchen
Daein some stitchin
In come a bogey
And chases grannie out

*(McVicar Collection: Glasgow 1992)*

But she still has the right to the comforts of a cup of tea and a warm bed:

> Old Grannie Cockalie
> Come tae bed and cuddle me
> I'll gie ye a cup o tea
> Tae keep yer belly warrum

> *(McVicar from personal recollection: source unrecorded, 1994)*

The 'Old Grannie Cockalie' tune is 'Will ye gang tae Sheriffmuir'. Is the 'Canny shove yer grannie' tune Scots? Of course not; it is 'She'll be coming round the mountain when she comes', a Western number I first heard carolled on our little Broadcaster radio when singing cowboy Big Bill Campbell and his Rocky Mountain Boys were on the Scottish Home Service in about 1948.

The words are a little repetitious:

> She'll be coming round the mountain when she comes
> She'll be coming round the mountain when she comes
> She'll be coming round the mountain, coming round the mountain
> She'll be coming round the mountain when she comes

Hard to see why it made such an impact. The second verse informs that 'She'll be riding six white horses when she comes'. Clearly she is a circus performer of the old school, used to going round in circles, which is why she comes round the mountain rather than down the road. Big Bill's Boys performed before my astonished gaze in Dingwall Town Hall in the late 1940s, woolly chaps wearing woolly chaps and Stetsons. The creator of the band's name perhaps had little direct acquaintance with the USA – since one thing in short supply up the Rocky Mountains is cowboys, on account of the absence of flat bits to keep the cows on – although I recently learned that Big Bill himself was indeed from the US of A. Or was it Canada? There are other Scottish grannie songs to American tunes:

> Swing yer maw, swing yer paw, honey, oh honey
> Swing yer maw, swing yer paw, honey baby
> Swing yer maw, swing yer paw, swing yer grannie off the wa
> Honey, oh baby mine
> We're going to the barn dance tonight

> *(McVicar Collection: Margaret Stirling, Livingston, 2002)*

Perhaps the rest of the Rocky Mountain Boys hailed from the Wild West of Govan – like the most famed Scots cowboy of all, Lobey Dosser, who rode a two-legged horse called Fideldo or Elfie for short, and whose arch enemy was the dastardly Rank Bajin (which transliterates to Really Bad One). You'll have guessed that Lobey was a cartoon character, created by Bud O'Neill for a Glasgow newspaper many years ago, and more recently immortalised in bronze in Glasgow's West End opposite a pub popular with journalists.

Glasgow is full of cowboys and country and western music – some treat the role with rather deadly intent, wearing black stetsons and competing in quick-draw competitions. Others believe they live a wild and outwith-the-law life, especially when they have overimbibed. A city centre drunk hailing a taxi to convey him home to a distant tough housing estate will still say 'Take me tae the Ponderosa'.

> If you see a big fat wumman
> Standin on the corner bummin
> That's ma grannie
> Grannie, grannie
> Ah'd walk a million feet
> Just tae meet ma – grannie

*(McVicar from personal recollection: source not recorded, Glasgow, 1960s)*

This in part parodies another American tune, 'Mammie', made famous by Al Jolson. One can still now and then encounter in Glasgow's Argyle Street a blacked-up Jolson imitator lipsynching to a tape and collecting money by the bucketful. I have met verses used both in Scotland and America to the 'Canny shove yer grannie' tune that laud the female grandparent, but I suspect they are late accretions, probably adult softenings of the original message.

Oh, we'll all go round to see her after school. HULLO, GRANNIE [etc.]

Or

She'll feed us mince and tatties when we go. YUM, YUM [etc.]

Or

Ma grannie wears an awfy woolly vest. SCRATCH, SCRATCH [etc.]

My personal theory is that someone put American tune and Scots words together after ruminating upon that old Glesca maxim 'Never shove yer grannie when she's shavin'.

Lyrics to the tune seem tied to females. An enquiry on the Internet for American versions found no old verses on the pushing about of US grandparents, but an informant naming herself 'Dulcimer' said about 'She'll be coming round the mountain' 'I heard the song is about Ma Jones going to promote union organisation in the coal mining camps in the Appalachians. I think she also organised in cities. At first the railroads, who also owned the mines or vice versa, let her ride, often for free because she was an old lady. But when she became so popular, they refused her passage. So she had to sometimes find other means – horses – to get into the camps – must have been some travel on those mountain roads.' Great story. I don't believe a word of it, Dulcimer.

American poet and song collector Carl Sandburg (1927) says 'Coming round the mountain' was 'made by mountaineers' out of 'an old-time negro spiritual "When the chariot comes"', but these song-making mountaineers came from Ma Jones's stomping ground, the Appalachians, not the Rockies that Big Bill Campbell's boys were named for.

In the chariot song it is the chariot that is female – modes of transport tend to be, don't they – and King Jesus who drives her. Sandburg's chariot verses do not mention the horses, let alone their number or colour, but surely there were six of them.

But none of this addresses what is for me the core problem: the most enthusiastic singers of 'Ye canny shove yer grannie' I meet are pensioners, grannies themselves – why do they not object? Half of them must after all be 'daddy's mammy'. Perhaps they welcome the song as an astringent antidote to the sickly taste of the maudlin ballad 'Ma grannie's heilan hame' and its like.

Perhaps when they sing they are thinking back to childhood days and childhood values, when the idea of cheeking your elders was a fantasy to be played out in song rather than a realistic option, as it was for the children who delighted in telling me that after I taught them the song 'Today is Hogmanay', in which grannie gets her nose stuck into butter, they went home and sang it to their grannie. And blamed me.

## Anthology: Family life

> AYE, YE'LL GO
> Aye, ye'll go, aye, ye'll go
> Whether ye want tae or no
> Ye'll go and ye'll get it, and never regret it
> Ye'll go, aye, ye'll go, aye, ye'll go
>
> Aye, ye'll go, aye, ye'll go
> Whether ye want tae or no
> Wee dirty nappies and wee greeting weans
> Sign in the book and yer life's no the same
>
> *(Ian Davison Card Index; tune: 'Bless them all')*

A 'bottling song', sung when a rowdy group escorted along the street a female workmate who was about to be married, carrying a chanty and salt, demanding a kiss and a coin in the chanty from every passing male.

BONNY WEE BARRA
Ma Auntie Jean frae Greenock came
Alang wi ma Auntie Lizzie
They gave me a penny tae buy some rock
But ah met wi Wee O'Hara
He said 'Gie me a sook o yer rock
And ah'll gie ye a hurl in ma barra'
Oh, the bonny wee barra's mine
It doesny belang tae O'Hara
Cause the fly wee bloke, he stuck tae ma rock
And ah'm gaunny stick tae his barra

*(McVicar from personal recollection: Glasgow, 1950s;*
*tune for first six lines: 'Yankee Doodle', for last four: 'British Grenadiers')*

THE DAY I WENT TO SEA
When I was one I sucked my thumb
The day I went to sea
I jumped upon a pirate's ship
And the captain said to me
'We're going this way, that way
Forward and back way
Over the deep blue sea
A bottle of rum to fill my tum
And that's the life for me'

When I was two I tied my shoe [etc.]

When I was three I skelpt my knee [etc.]

When I was four I shut the door [etc.]

When I was five I did a dive [etc.]

When I was six I did the splits [etc.]

When I was seven I went to heaven [etc.]

When I was eight I shut the gate [etc.]

When I was nine I broke my spine [etc.]

When I was ten I started again [etc.]

*(McVicar Collection: Glasgow, 1992)*

In Erskine in 1992 they sang 'A jar of honey will fill ma tummy'.

DOES YER MAW DRINK WINE?
Does yer maw drink wine?
Does she dae it aa the time?
Does she get a funny feeling
When her heid goes through the ceiling?
Does yer maw drink wine?

Does yer maw drink beer?
Does she drink it aa the year? [etc.]

Does yer maw drink gin?
Does she drink it frae a tin? [etc.]

Does yer maw drink whisky?
Does it have her feeling frisky? [etc.]

*(Ian Davison Card Index)*

DON'T GO DOWN THE MINE
A miner was leaving his home for the mine
When he heard his little boy cry
He went to his bedside to see what was wrong
'Daddy, oh daddy, don't go down the mine

Don't go down the mine, dad
Dreams will always come true
Daddy, oh daddy, it'll break my heart
If anything happened to you'

*(Ian Davison Card Index)*

A chip off a longer song. Davison says it was 'Sung with great feeling by children of all ages'.

HAP AND ROWE
The wife put on the wee pan
To boil the bairn's meatie o
Out fell a cinder
And burnt aa its feetie o
Hap and row, hap and row
Hap and row the feetie o't
I never kent I had a bairn
Until I heard the greetie o't

Sandy's mother she came in
When she heard the greetie o't
She took the mutch frae her head
And rowed about the feetie o't

*(Chambers 1842)*

The four line 'Hap and rowe' chorus is also used in an adult Scots song about the unexpected birth, to the tune 'The reel of Stumpie'.

HALLOWEEN, A NICHT AT EEN
Halloween, a nicht at een, a canle and a custock
Doon Dons has got a wean, they ca it Bessie Aitken
Some ca't a kittlin, some ca't a cat
Some ca't a wee wean wi a straw hat

It gaed to its grannie's, to seek a wee bit breid
The grannie took the ladle and brak it owre its head
Oh, says the mither o't, my wean's deid
O, says the faither o't, never you heed

Gang oot by the back door, in by the tither
Through amang the green kail, you'll sune get anither

*(Rymour Club 1911: 1850s, Calder Ironworks, near Glasgow)*

A rhyme for All Hallows Eve. Oddly, there is no version of this rhyme in the book titled *Nicht at Eenie* (Shelmerdine & Greirson 1932).

I HAD THE GERMAN MEASLES
I had the German measles
I had them very bad
They threw me in an ambulance
And took me in a cab

The cab was very bumpy
I nearly fell out
And when I got to the hospital
I heard a baby shout

Mammy, daddy, take me home
I've been here a week or two
Here comes Doctor Alistair
Slidin down the bannister

Halfway down he ripped his pants
Now he's doin the cha cha dance
Cha cha cha cha cha cha cha
Cha cha cha cha cha cha cha

*(McVicar Collection: Glasgow, 1992)*

The Opies (1985) consider this a clapping game song, but it seems to me to be an amusement piece.

I LOST MY WIFE ON SETTERDAY NICHT
I lost my wife on Setterday nicht
And cudna tell far to find her
Up in the mune, sellin shune
A penny the piece, they're aa dune
I lost my wife on Setterday nicht
And didna ken far to find her
Ahint the pump I garred her jump
Tally ho the grinder

*(Rymour Club 1911: Forfarshire)*

I ONCE HAD A DEAR OLD MOTHER
I once had a dear old mother
She was all the world to me
And when I was in trouble
She sat me on her knee

One night as I was sleeping
Upon my feather bed
An angel came from heaven
And told me mum was dead

I woke up in the morning
To see if it was true
Yes mum had gone to heaven
Up in the sky so blue

So children obey your parents
And do as you are told
For when you lose a mother
You lose a heart of gold

*(Ian Davison Card Index: Rottenrow School)*

Davison says that this 'classic tearjerker is known to almost every girl in Glasgow', with a standard spoken introduction of 'There once was a song about a dear old mother, and this is how it goes.'

I WANT TO GO HOME
Oh I want to go home
Oh I want to go home
I'm nae gonnie stay in the orphanage no more
The place where the matrons are always indoor
Take me over the sea
The matron'll never catch me
Oh my, I think I shall die
If you don't take me home

*(Haynes 1973)*

IF YOU SEE A BIG FAT WUMMIN
If you should see a big fat wummin
Standin at the corner bummin
That's ma mammy
If you should see her wearin glasses
Smilin at each one that passes
That's ma mammy

*(Sinclair 1986;*
*tune: Al Jolson's 'Mammy')*

I'M A LITTLE ORPHAN GIRL
I'm a little orphan girl
My mother she is dead
My father is a drunkard
And won't buy me my bread

I sit upon the windowsill
To hear the organ play
And think of my dear mother
Who's dead and far away

Ding-dong, my castle bell
Farewell to my mother
Bury me in the old churchyard
Beside my eldest brother

My coffin shall be white
Six little angels by my side
Two to sing and two to pray
And two to carry my soul away

*(Alan Lomax archive: Peggy MacGillivray, Edinburgh)*

'Castle bell' should be 'passing bell'. American folklorist Alan Lomax transcribed the line 'And won't buy me my bread' as 'And goes right in my bed'! This song, like 'The night was dark', reads like a guiser recitation, but is a bouncing 'two rope' skipping song.
   In her autobiographical account of orphanage life Haynes says they sang

I am a little orphanage girl
My mother she is dead
My father he is far away
And cannot buy me bread

*(Haynes 1973)*

See *Alias MacAlias* (Henderson 1992) for an article about this song and the 'White Paternoster'.

MA MAMMY SAYS TAE ME
Ma mammy says tae me
Wid ye like a cup o tea?
Ah says no no ah like cocoa
Down in the glen
She took me by the hand
All the way tae Barrowland
Ah says no no ah like cocoa
Down in the glen

*(Sinclair 1986; tune: 'Down in the glen')*

MA MAW SAYS
Ma maw says ah've tae go
Wi ma daddie's dinner oh
Champit tatties, chewin steak
An a wee bit currant cake

Ah came tae a river and ah couldnae get across
Ah paid five bob for a scabby auld horse
Ah jumped on its back, its bones gave a crack
And ah played ma fiddle till the boat came back

The boat came back, we aa jumped in
The boat capsized and we aa fell in
Singin don't be weary, aye be cheery
Don't be weary cause we're aa gaun hame

*(Ma Maw Says late 1980s)*


MA MAW'S A MILLIONAIRE
Ma maw's a millionaire
Blue eyes and curly hair
Walkin doon Buchanan Street
Wi her big banana feet
Ma maw's a millionaire

Sittin among the Eskimos
Playin the game of dominoes [etc.]

*(McVicar Collection:*
*Erskine, 1992)*

Or


Sittin among the Eskimos
Showin them how tae wash their toes [etc.]

*(McVicar Collection:*
*Glasgow, 1991)*

Or


Sittin among the Eskimos
Puttin her finger up her nose [etc.]

*(Ian Davison Card Index)*

Or


Stots my faither off the wa
Like a wee cahoutchie ba [etc.]

*(McVicar Collection: singer Alastair MacDonald, Glasgow, 1950s;*
*tune: 'Let's all go down the Strand')*

MOTHER MOTHER
Mother mother I am ill
Send for the doctor up the hill
Up the hill is too far
We will have a motorcar
A motorcar is too dear
We will have a pint of beer
A pint of beer is too strong
We will try a treacle scone
A treacle scone is too tough
We will have an ounce of snuff
An ounce of snuff makes you sneeze
We will have a pound of cheese
A pound of cheese makes you sick
Run for the doctor, quick quick quick

*(Rodger nd)*

MY MUMMY IS A BAKER
My mummy is a baker
Yummy yummy, yummy yummy
My father is a dustman
Pong pongie, pong pongie
My sister is a show off
How'd yeh like it, how'd yeh like it
My brother is a cowboy
Bang bang, you're dead
Fifty bullets in the head
Turn around, touch the ground
Singing ai yi yippee yippee yi
Apple pie
Singing ai yi yippee yippee yi
Apple pie
Singing ai yi yippee yippee
Dancing like a hippy
Singing ai yi yippee yippee yi
Apple pie

*(McVicar Collection: Applegrove PS, Moray, 2006)*

MY GRANDMA AND YOUR GRANDMA
My grandma and your grandma
Were sitting by the fire
My grandma said to your grandma

'I'm going to set your flag on fire'
Singin ah oh
Singin ah oh darlin
Ma grandma

*(McVicar Collection: Erskine, 1992)*

MY MUM'S CHINESE
My mum's Chinese
My dad's Japanese
Look what happened to me
My mum's Chinese
My dad's Japanese
Look I skint my knee

*(McVicar Collection: Erskine, 1992)*

MY SON JOHN
Diddle diddle dumpling, my son John
Went to bed with his trousers on
One shoe off and the other shoe on
Diddle diddle dumpling, my son John

*(McVicar from personal recollection: Dingwall, 1940s)*

MY WIFE AND I
My wife and I lived all alone
In a little wooden house
We call our own
She likes whisky I like rum
And we both like Wrigley's Spearmint gum
Ha ha ha hee hee hee
We both like the Addams Family

*(Ian Davison Card Index: John Street School)*

OH MOTHER MOTHER
Oh mother mother what a cold I've got
Drinking tea and coffee hot
Wrap me up in a nice big shawl
And take me to the doctor
Doctor doctor shall I die?
No my darling you shan't die
Take this medicine twice a day
And that will cure your cold away

*(Ritchie 1965)*

*Greig–Duncan* no. 1613 has 'Take me to the doctor's shop', which would make line four above more regular.

ROON AN ROON THE HOUSE
Roon an roon the house, tryin tae catch a flea
Mix it up wi butter and tak it ti ma tea
Ah didny want it ah gied it tae ma chum
Ma chum didny want it so he flung it up the lum
The lum gave a crack the hoose gave a shak
And doon came ma grannie in her wee cutty sark

*(School of Scottish Studies archive:*
*(Headlee) Williamson, from Betsy Whyte, Montrose, 1976)*

TEN IN THE BED
Please remember to tie a knot in your pyjamas
Single beds are only meant for
1, 2, 3, 4, 5, 6, 7, 8
Nine in the bed and the little one said
'Roll over, roll over'
So they all rolled over and one fell out
And banged his head and began to shout

Please remember to tie a knot in your pyjamas
Single beds are only meant for
1, 2, 3, 4, 5, 6, 7
Eight in the bed and the little one said
'Roll over, roll over' [etc.]

*(School of Scottish Studies archive:*
*Hendry, Glenrothes, 1981)*

You can tell what comes next. This looks like a cheery 'Brownie' elaboration of the usual 'There were ten in the bed and the little one said'. Elsewhere in Glenrothes 'suspenders' replaced 'pyjamas'.

THIS HOUSE IS AWFY SMELLY
This house is awfy smelly
Patricia's making jelly
They canny afford a telly
The Addams Family

*(Ian Davison Card Index:*
*John St School)*

TOMMY RISE

Tommy rise and kindle the fire
Turn the gas a wee bit higher
Go and tell your aunt Maria
Baby's got the toothache

Or

To fry my ham and eggs

*(Ian Davison Card Index: Rottenrow School;*
*tune: 'Men of Harlech')*

WHEN I WAS IN THE GARDEN

When I was in the garden
I found a penny farthin
I took it to my mother
To buy a baby brother
My brother was a sailor
He sailed the seven seas
And all the fish that he could catch
Was one two three a-larry
My brother's name is Harry
If you think it's necessary
Look it up in the dictionary

*(Ian Davison Card Index:*
*Rottenrow School)*

WHEN I WAS ANE

When I was ane I was in my skin
When I was twa I ran awa
When I was three I could climb a tree
When I was four they dang me o'er
When I was five I didna thrive
When I was sax I got my cracks
When I was seven I could count eleven
When I was aught I was laid straught
When I was nine I could write a line
When I was ten I could mend a pen
When I was eleven I gaed to the weaving
When I was twall I was brosy Wull

*(Chambers 1842)*

WHEN I WAS SINGLE
When ah was single ah used to comb ma hair
Noo ah'm married ah huvny the time tae spare
It's a life a life a weary weary life
Yer better tae be single than tae be a married wife

When ah was single I used a powder puff
Noo ah'm married ah canny afford the stuff [etc.]

One says 'Mammie, help me intae ma pram'
Anither says 'Mammie, gie's a piece and jam' [etc.]

One says 'Mammie, help me intae ma bed'
Anither says 'Mammie, scratch ma wudden leg' [etc]

*(McVicar from personal recollection: Glasgow, 1950s)*

Davison found additional verses.

Wan shouts 'Mammy, help me dae ma sums!'
The ither shouts, 'Mammy, help me scratch ma bum!'

'Mammy, take me for a walk'
'Mammy, help me wi ma sock'

'Mammy, sit me on yer knee'
'Mammy, let me climb the tree'

*(Ian Davison Card Index: Bellahouston and Rottenrow Schools)*

Glasgow advice to the put upon wife. English versions of this song are more po-faced:

When I was young I lived in a hall
But now that I'm married I've no home at all
Oh what a life what a weary weary life
Better be a maid than a poor man's wife
Better be a maid all the days of your life
Better to be a maid than a poor man's wife

*(Williams & Lloyd 1959)*

THE WORLD MUST BE COMING TO AN END
We sent her for eggs oh aye oh aye
We sent her for eggs oh aye oh aye
We sent her for eggs and she fell and broke her legs
Oh the world must be coming to an end oh aye

We sent her for cheese and she fell and skint her knees [etc.]

We sent her for butter and she dropped it in the gutter [etc.]

We sent her for jam and she brought back ham [etc.]

We sent her for breid and she drapped doon deid [etc.]

*(McVicar from personal recollection: Glasgow, 1950s)*

In Edinburgh Ritchie (1964) found a starting verse that provides a context: 'I married me a wife / And she's the plague o my life'. It ends more dramatically:

I bought her a coffin
And she fell through the bottom [etc.]

I buried her in durt
And she jumped oot her shurt [etc.]

# 12
# *The baldy heided master*

## Performance and narrative – in school

> Ye dae sixteen sums and what dae ye get?
> Fifteen wrang and six of the belt
> Teacher don't ye call me cause I can't come
> Ah'm stuck tae ma seat wi bubbly-gum

Much of the collecting of children's song in the field has been done by teachers, and kids well understand the need for self-censorship when in the classroom. When they don't, teachers are alert to the image of their school and the need for a presentation of proper behaviour standards – and all that. It is therefore of little note that lyrics that are rude – about teachers, school, or about sexual and bodily function – seldom appear in the literature. In my days collecting in Glasgow in early 1992 I innocently asked one class for lyrics about school life. Every head in the class snapped round to see the strong-voiced teacher's reaction to my query. She nodded indulgently – they were off home turf and were permitted to use demotic language and concepts, for this was a literature setting, so standards might be relaxed for once. I got a few of the milder lyrics. But not this one:

> On top of Old Smokey, all covered with sand
> I shot my poor teacher with an elastic band
>
> I shot her with pleasure, I shot her with pride
> I couldn't have missed her, she's forty foot wide
>
> I went to her funeral, I went to her grave
> Some people threw flowers, I threw a grenade
>
> *(McVicar Collection: Glasgow, 1991)*

This is the 'standard' text, but one 1991 Glasgow child gave me a verse I've not met elsewhere:

A million wee pieces went up in the sky
And that was the first time my teacher could fly

Another child, in Erskine, 1992, said

I opened her grave, saw she wasn't quite dead
I got a bazooka, and blew off her head

The original song, 'Old Smokey', a sad love lyric with simple open words and tune, entered Scottish schools I suppose in the 1940s when 'cowboy songs' were the rage, though I doubt if one in a thousand of the children who carolled versions could have put a finger on the globe to show where Old Smokey stands.

As ever, the kids change the lyric:

On top of old Snowy, on top of the snow
I shot my poor teacher, five minutes ago

*(McVicar Collection: Glasgow, 1991)*

On top of Mount Snowdon, all covered with snow
I shot my poor teacher, with a bow and arrow

*(McVicar from personal recollection, source not recorded)*

And more violence comes squelching in:

On top of old Smokey, all covered in blood
There lives a poor vampire, stuck in the mud

An axe through his belly, a knife through his head
I came to the conclusion, the poor soul was dead

*(Ian Davison Card Index: Blairdardie PS)*

Of far greater age, known throughout Scotland and sung to the staccato tune also used for this book's title lyric, is

Ma wee school's a braw wee school
It's made wi brick an plaster
The only thing that's wrang wi it
Is the baldie heided master

He gangs tae the pub on Saturday night
He gangs tae the kirk on Sunday
He prays tae God tae gie him strength
Tae ba'er the weans on Monday

*(School of Scottish Studies archive: Hendry, Glenrothes, 1981)*

A school's name is sometimes inserted in the first line, and second line becomes 'The best wee school in (Glesca)'. The last line also changes. 'Ba'er' or 'batter' was more often 'belt', but with the abolition of corporal punishment by 1991 in Glasgow I found 'To murder the weans on Monday' or even the ever so polite 'To correct the sums on Monday'.

The easie-osie bounce of American song and dance tunes makes them ideal for children's song. The 'Coming round the mountain' tune was pressed into service not just in consideration of grannydom, but for complaint about strict educators:

> Oh it's murder mighty murder in the hoose
> When the cat he does the rhumba wi the moose
> If ye hit him wi a poker
> He'll dae the Carioca
> It's murder mighty murder in the hoose
>
> It's murder mighty murder in the school
> When the teacher hits ye wi a widden rule
> If ye canny dae yer grammer
> She hits ye wi a hammer
> It's murder mighty murder in the school
>
> If ye canny dae yer spellin
> She'll melt ye wi a mellon [etc.]
>
> It's murder mighty murder in the jail
> Where they feed ye breid and watter frae a pail
> If ye ask them for a tinnie
> They'll send ye tae Barlinnie
> It's murder mighty murder in the jail

*(McVicar from personal recollection: Glasgow, 1950s)*

The word 'grammar' is one unknown to Scots primary school children – they understand the concept fine, but that word has slipped out of teaching vocabulary. So it becomes 'If you don't do your drama, she'll hit ye wi a hammer'.

The folk entymology (as explained by adult folk singers) of 'mellon' is a mason's mallet, a variant of 'mell' or 'maul', but this is not supported by the authoritative dictionaries of English or Scots I have consulted, so maybe all along the kids have visualised an assault with a large fruit.

The formula of this song proved irresistible when I was making new songs out of old with children. Here are a few of many dozens that have come from classes:

If you don't do your art, she'll pull your head apart
If you don't mind your language, she'll eat you in a sandwich
If you don't read your book, she'll sell you to a crook
If you don't read your novel, she'll make you really grovel
If you don't do your math, she'll drown you in a bath

## Anthology: In school, other topics

*School*

THE BELL THE BELL
The bell the bell the B-I-L
Tell the teacher I'm no well
If you're late shut the gate
And don't come back till half-past eight

*(Ian Davison Card Index:*
*Rottenrow School)*

COME TO OUR SCHOOL
Come to our school come to our school
For a life of misery
There's a notice in the playground
Saying 'Welcome unto thee'
Don't believe it don't believe it
It's a load of bloody lies
If it wasn't for the teachers
It would be a paradise
Build a bonfire build a bonfire
Put the teachers on the top
Put the jannie in the middle
And burn the bloody lot

*(McVicar Collection:*
*Whitburn, 1997)*

GLORY GLORY
Glory glory halleluiah
Teacher hit me wi a ruler
The ruler broke in two
And she hit me wi her shoe
And I went greetin hame

Glory glory halleluiah
Teacher hit me wi a ruler
I hit her on the seater
With a 45 repeater
And I've never saw the teacher any more

*(Ian Davison Card Index)*

Glory glory halleluiah
The teacher hit me wi a ruler
Ah punched her in the belly
And she wobbled like a jelly
And she never came back to school

Glory glory halleluiah
The teacher hit me wi a ruler
The ruler broke in two
And she hit me with her shoe
And I went greetin hame

*(Ian Davison Card Index)*

Hi ho
Hi ho, hi ho, it's off to school we go
Wi a bucket and a spade and a hand grenade
Hi ho, hi ho

Hi ho, hi ho, it's off to school we go
It's yap yap yap, and we get the strap
Hi ho, hi ho

*(Ian Davison Card Index:*
*East Milton School, East Kilbride)*

In Beechwood
They say that in Beechwood the food is mighty fine
A pea fell off the table and killed a pal of mine
Oh I don't want to be a Beechwood Bird
Gee boys, I wanna go home
(To see ma mammy)

Gee boys, I wanna go home

They say that in Beechwood the fags are mighty fine
You ask for twenty Regal, they gie ye five Woodbine [etc.]

They say that in Beechwood the booze is mighty fine
You ask for Eldorado, they gie ye turpentine [etc.]

They say that in Beechwood the beds are mighty fine
You jump on a pillow and nearly break your spine [etc.]

*(Ian Davison Card Index)*

An 'Army Life' version of this song was recorded by American singer Huddie Leadbetter.

IT'S RAINING
It's raining it's pouring
The teachers are boring
We'll bash their heads and off to beds
And finish them off in the morning

*(McVicar Collection: Moray, 2006)*

LATE AGAIN
Ali Baba and the forty thieves
Went to school with dirty knees
The teacher said you'll catch disease
Ali Baba and the forty thieves

*(Ian Davison Card Index: Rottenrow School)*

Bill and Ben flowerpot men
Went to school at half-past ten
The teacher says you're late again
Bill and Ben flowerpot men

*(Ian Davison Card Index: Rottenrow School)*

Robin Hood and his merry men
Went to school at half-past ten
Teacher said you're late again
Robin Hood and his merry men

*(Ian Davison Card Index)*

Master Foster
Master Foster very good man
Sweeps his college now and than
After that he takes a dance
Up from London down to France
With a black bonnet and a white snout
Stand ye there for ye are out

*(Chambers 1842)*

More recently the teacher 'teaches the pupils when he can'. In another 1842 version the rod is wielded:

Doctor Faustus was a good man
He whipped his scholars now and then
When he whipped them he made them dance
Out of Scotland into France
Out of France into Spain
And then he whipped them back again

Mine eyes
Mine eyes have seen the glory
Of the burning of the school
We have tortured every teacher
We have broken every rule
Down with education and up with liberation
The school is burning down

*(McVicar Collection: Glasgow 1991)*

Seems to be another American import.

My teacher's barmy
My teacher's barmy
She wears a tammy
She joined the army
When she was 1, 2, 3, 4, 5 [etc.]

*(Ian Davison Card Index: Temple School)*

Off to school
Off to school off to school
Pass your 'quali' and that's the rule
You silly wee ass you couldnae pass
Now John Smith is the bottom of the class

*(Ian Davison Card Index: Rottenrow School)*

OOR TEACHER
Oor teacher's a smasher
A face like a tattie masher
A nose like a pickled onion
And eyes like green peas

*(Ian Davison Card Index; tune: 'The ash grove')*

PINKSTON DRIVE
From the hills of Pinkston Drive
To the shores of Bubble-gum Bay
We will fight the caretaker
With stink bombs mud and clay
We will fight him for the glory
We will fight him round the bend
We will fight him for the fun
We will fight him to the end

*(Ian Davison Card Index)*

The mention of a caretaker rather than a jannie shows this to be a recent import from down south or across the pond.

SCHOOL DINNERS
School dinners, school dinners
Concrete chips, concrete chips
Dinner's on the wall, dinner's on the wall
I hate school, I hate school

*(Ian Davison Card Index)*

SIXTEEN SUMS
Ye dae sixteen sums and what dae ye get?
Fifteen wrang and six of the belt
Teacher don't ye call me cause I can't come
Ah'm stuck tae ma seat wi bubbly-gum
If ye go to school dinners better leave them aside
A lot of kids didn't and a lot of kids died
The meat's made of iron the totties of steel
And if that doesny get ye then the pudding will

see p 224

*(Ian Davison Card Index;*
*tune: 'Sixteen tons')*

### Stop the Bus

Stop the bus ah need a wee wee
Stop the bus ah need a wee wee
Stop the bus ah need a wee wee
A wee wee drink o juice

Or

A wee wee cup o tea

(School of Scottish Studies archive:<br>
Hendry, Glenrothes, 1981)

Or

And the driver needs one too

(McVicar Collection: East Calder, 2007)

### Teacher teacher

No more English no more French
No more sitting on the old school bench
Teacher teacher I declare
I can see your underwear
Is it black? Is it white?
Oh my god it's dynamite

(McVicar Collection: Dalkeith HS, 1997)

Known in every school

Teacher teacher let me in
Ma feet's cauld ma shin's thin
If ye dinna let me in
Ah'll no come back this aifternin

(Children's Singing Games:<br>
Webb, Noblehill Jun Sch, 1960)

Webb found it used for skipping.

### Under the bramble bushes

Under the bramble bushes
Down by the sea
True love for you my darling
True love for me

When we get married
We'll have a family
A boy for you a girl for me
How many fishes are in the sea?

Eleven and twelve makes twenty-three
That's the end of chapter three
Twelve and twelve makes twenty-four
Push your teacher out the door

If she says 'Don't do that'
Hit her on the head with a baseball bat
Row row row your boat
Gently down the stream
Push the teacher overboard
And listen to her scream
AAAAHHHH

*(McVicar Collection: Glasgow, 1996)*

'A girl for you, a boy for me' can be followed by 'That's the way it's got to be' or 'That's the end of Chapter Three'. The boat lines perhaps derive from a version of

Rock rock rock your boat
Gently down the stream
If you see a crocodile
Don't forget to scream

*(McVicar Collection: Moray, 2006)*

WE BREAK UP
We break up we break down
We don't care if the school falls down
No more English no more French
No more sitting on the old school bench

If your teacher interferes
Knock her down and box her ears
If that does not serve her right
Blow her up with dynamite

*(McVicar Collection: Glasgow, 1991)*

In Moray in 2006 they included

> Kick the teachers, kick the chairs
> Kick the schoolboys down the stairs

## Other topics

> As I GAED UP THE APPLE TREE
> As I gaed up the apple tree
> Aa the apples fell on me
> Bake a puddin bake a pie
> Send it up to John MacKay
> John MacKay is no in
> Send it up to the man i the mune
> The man in the mune is mendin his shune
> Three bawbees and a farden in

*(MacLennan 1909)*

Rodger (nd) has 'Tuppence the pair and they're aa dune'.

> As I WENT UP A STAIR
> As I went up a stair
> I met a bobby there
> Wi his whiskers tied tae the railing
> He asked me ma name
> I said leave me alane
> My name's Treacle Toffee in the Hielands

*(Ian Davison Card Index:*
*Bellahouston School; tune 'Loch Lomond')*

THE CAMP IN THE COUNTRY
We're off to the camp in the country, hooray hooray
We're off to the camp in the country, hooray hooray
Apple jam for supper, ham and eggs for tea
Roly poly doon yer belly hip hip hip hooray

*(McVicar from personal recollection: Glasgow, 1950s;*
*tune: 'My wife's gone to the country')*

> COME UP AND SEE MA GARRET
> Come up and see ma garret
> Come up and see it noo
> Come up and see ma garret

For it's aa furnished new
A broken cup-an-saucer
A chair wi oot a leg
A humphy-backit dresser
And a bandy-leggit bed

*(Ian Davison Card Index)*

Earlier, in Rodger's Forfar they sang

It has a chair athoot a boddom
A stuil athoot a leg
A humfy-backit dresser
And a bowsy-leggit bed

*(Rodger nd)*

DON'T BE A FOOL
Don't be a fool stick to the rule
Listen to the message and just act cool
It ain't no joke so don't sniff coke
Don't drink alcohol and please don't smoke

*(Ian Davison Card Index)*

FAR ARE YE GAEIN?
Far are ye gaein? Across the gutter
Fat for? A pund o butter
Far's yer money? In my pocket
Far's yer pocket? Clean forgot it

*(Rodger nd)*

From the days when a pocket was a separate thing, pinned on to the apron.

FOUND A PEANUT
Found a peanut found a peanut
Found a peanut just now
Found a peanut found a peanut
Just now just now

Going to eat it [etc.]

Got a pain [etc.]

Ring the doctor [etc.]

'Pendicitis [etc.]

Rip her open [etc.]

No more peanuts [etc.]

Couldnae find it [etc.]

Went to heaven [etc.]

Didnae like it [etc.]

Went below [etc.]

Saw ye's aa there [etc.]

*(Ian Davison Card Index: Bellahouston School;*
*tune: 'Clementine')*


GREEN WHITE AND BLUE
Green [or red] white and blue
The cat's got the flu
The dog's got the chickenpox
And so have you

*(Ian Davison Card Index: Rottenrow School;*
*tune: 'Knees up Mother Brown')*


IN MI WEE RID MOTOR CAR
In mi wee rid motor car
I can gang for miles
Up and doon the garden
Through the lobby whiles
Mony a bigger motor
Gangs ta toons afar
But nane can gang where a kin gang
In mi wee rid car

*(McVicar Collection:*
*Dalkeith HS, 1997)*

The neatness of line, and the unusual spelling given by the young informant, suggest a poet's hand. Whose?

LAST NIGHT
Last night as I lay on my pillow
Last night as I lay on my bed
I stuck my feet out of the window
In the morning the neighbours were dead

*(Ian Davison Card Index)*

LET YOUR WHISKERS GROW
Let your whiskers grow
Let your whiskers grow
What's the use of trying?
Pull them out by the roots
Make laces for your boots
And look at all the money you'll be saving

*(Ian Davison Card Index)*

THE MORN'S THE MARKET
The morn's the market and I'll be there
Kissin my lad and gettin my fair
The cocks'll be crawin and the hen'll be layin
For the morn's the merry merry Market Day

*(Rodger nd)*

Sleepy Dukie sits i the neukie
Canna win oot to play
The drums 'ill beat an the pipes 'ill play
The cocks 'ill craw and the hens 'ill lay
An the morn's the merry merry market day

*(MacLennan 1909)*

Ree-a-ree a ranigate the pipers i' the Canigate
The drow is in the air
The cock craws the hen lays
The nicht afore the fair

*(Rymour Club 1911)*

'The child who repeated this [last] rhyme oftenest got the biggest fairing [a present for being there] at the Dunbar Fair.' (Rymour Club 1911)

MY SHIP'S HOME
My ship's home from China
With a cargo of tea
All laden with presents for you and me
She brought me one fan
Just think of my bliss
I fan myself daily like this like this

*(Ian Davison Card Index:*
*Temple School)*

NAEBODY LIKES ME
Naebody likes me everybody hates me
Think I'll go and eat worms
Big fat juicy ones wee thin skooshy ones
See how they wriggle and squirm
Cut off their heads squeeze out the juice
And throw the skins away
Nobody knows how I survive
On worms three times a day

*(Ian Davison Card Index:*
*Sir John Maxwell School)*

ON TOP OF SPAGHETTI
On top of spaghetti
All covered in cheese
I lost my poor meatball
When somebody sneezed
It rolled off the table
And onto the floor
Then my poor meatball
Rolled out of the door

It rolled in the garden
And under a bush
And then my poor meatball
Was nothing but moosh

*(McVicar Collection:*
*Erskine, 1992)*

Or

It rolled off the doorstep and onto the mat
Along came my father and the meatball went splat
It went up to heaven on the Meatball Express
And my poor spaghetti was one meatball less

*(Ian Davison Card Index)*

ONCE UPON A TIME
Once upon a time
When the pigs spoke rhyme
And the monkeys chewed tobacco
And the hens took snuff
To make them tough
And ducks went quack quack quack-oh

*(Rodger nd)*

Rodger says 'The old, old stories had beautiful beginnings'. The first three lines appeared in 1965 Top Twenty hit 'The clapping song'.

A PARTY ON THE HILL
There's a party on the hill
Would you like to come
(yes/no)
With your own cream face
And your own cream bun
(Can't afford it)
Who is your true love?
(name)
(name) will be there
With her knickers on her hair
Singing aye aye ippy ippy out

*(McVicar Collection: Dalkeith HS, 1997)*

Or 'With your knickers in the air'.

PEASE BROSE
Pease brose and barley-o barley-o barley-o
Pease brose and barley-o
Sugary cakes and candy

*(Ian Davison Card Index)*

PUIR WEE RAGGED LADDIE
Puir wee ragged laddie runnin doon the street
Greetin fur his mammy in his wee bare feet
Greetin wi the cauld shiverin wi the rain
Puir wee ragged laddie he's a drunken cairter's wean

*(Ian Davison Card Index:*
*Rottenrow School)*

SEE SEE MY BEST FRIEND
See see my best friend
I cannot play with you
My dolly's got the flu
Chicken pops and measles too
Swing on my drainpipe
Slide down my cellar door
And we'll be jolly friends
For ever more

*(McVicar Collection:*
*Glasgow, 1991)*

See see my playmate
I cannot play with you
My dolly's got the flu
So I flushed her down the loo
But now I'm older
I do not play with dolls
I play with B-O-Y-S
B-O-Y-S, boys, wow

*(McVicar Collection:*
*Dalkeith HS, 1997)*

See see my playmate
Come out and play with me
We'll bring our dollies
And climb the apple tree
Slide down my rainbow
Into my sailing ship
We'll be friends for ever more
1, 2, 3, 4 . . .

*(McVicar Collection:*
*Dalkeith, 1997)*

See see oh play me
Come out and play with me
And bring your dollies too
Ah oo ah oo ah oo
Slide down the drainpipe
And through the sailor's door
And we'll be jolly friends
Forever more, shut that door

*(McVicar Collection:*
*Bankton PS, 2007)*

Knowing, and romanticised, versions of a song very widely known. 'Cellar' becomes 'sailor'.

THREE CHEERS FOR THE RED WHITE AND BLUE
Three cheers for the red white and blue
It sticks to your nose like glue
You laugh and you laugh
And you canna get it aff
Three cheers for the red white and blue

*(Rodger nd)*

THREE WEE SAUSAGES
Three wee sausages
Frying in a pan
One popped out
And the other said 'Scram'

*(Ian Davison Card Index)*

UP IN THE MOUNTAIN SO HIGH
Up in the mountain so high
Just below the beautiful sky
And down in the floating stream
You can see the sunshine beam

*(McVicar Collection: Glasgow, 1993)*

A lofty offering from the informant who also gave me 'Tam Tam the Midgie Man'.

A WEE CREAM COOKIE
A wee cream cookie
For me and the bookie
I wouldnae gie ye a penny for
A wee cream cookie

*(Ian Davison Card Index:*
*Rottenrow School)*


WHEN I WAS YOUNG
When I was young I had no sense
I thought I'd go to sea
I stepped upon a Chinaman's ship
And the Chinaman said to me
Up skalla doon skalla
Back skalla roon skalla
That's what the Chinaman said to me

*(Sinclair 1986)*


WHERE ARE YOU GOING
Where are you going Mrs McGinty?
I'm going to see Brother John
And who's Brother John Mrs McGinty?
The man that keeps the pawn

*(Ian Davison Card Index:*
*Bellahouston School)*


WHETHER WOULD YOU RAITHER
Whether would you raither
Or raither would you whether
A soo's snoot stewed
Or a stewed soo's snoot?

*(Rodger nd)*

# 13
## *Only a boy's game*

### Gangs, violence and football

> Tam Tam the midgie man
> Lives in a midgie motor
> Running along the dyke
> And skelpt his head a stoter

While the girls hold and use rhymes and songs for skipping and co-operative social activities, the boys prefer those that deal with football and other aggressive matters and glory in bodily fundamentals.

Rev. William Findlay gives this example of organised violence, titling it 'The cobblin grace', cob here meaning to beat or strike. 'When one of a company of boys breaks wind, those next to him grasp his ears, and say this grace while the others uncover [take their caps off respectfully] and repeat it after them':

> Aa ye married men tween threescore and ten
> That dinna attend this cobblin 'll be cobbled owre again
> Wi the rug wi the pug wi the weel pu'd lug
> That dog o Andro Morrison's he sits afore the pu'pit
> Neeb neeb nabblin at his cods
> He'll aither gar me lauch or stick the preachin
> But ye can hund him up the lang lane or doon by Nellie Morrison's
> Dinna miss a stroke but kill him if ye can
> For he eatit aa Johnnie McFushie-ca'its peys
> No only that he pished amon the strae
> Which was a great sin
> Ye hunder, ye dunder, ye great goose horn
> Here a tift there a tift amang the laird's corn
> An X and an E and an auld aipple tree
> Whistle Jock and ye'll get free

*(Rymour Club 1911)*

Or, from the same source

> Call-a-cob, maraline
> Cast a barrel in a string
> A them at winna come to this call-a-cob
> Shall be weel call-a-cobbled owre again
> Wi the rug and the tug and the gray grace horn
> Here a tug, there, amang the laird's corn
> Whistle and I'll let gae

*(Rymour Club 1911)*

There is much could be unpacked from these rich lyrics – sources to find, language to translate, topics to isolate and consider, comparisons to draw with the rigmaroles I give earlier. However, I will just point out the threats of potential violence, to be defused by the simple act of whistling. Davison points out how blood-curdling gang threats are chanted by 'nice wee boys'. Everyone who observes boys interacting at a bus stop while they wait will have seen physical challenges that pretend to offer conflict but seem to be friendly energetic hugging – though sometimes the mood will change.

A boys' game of actual ritualised violence from Argyllshire a hundred years ago follows. The Opies did not find it still in use, so they did not include it in *The Singing Game* (1985). The group begins sitting round the fire with 'their feet well to the front. One of them has a stick with which he beats time on the floor, repeating'

> My father gives me meat
> My mother gives me clothes
> To sit about the fireside
> And nap folk's toes

The holder of the stick selects a victim, who is then assaulted cumulatively by the others in their allotted characters of Hammer, Poker, Red-Coal etc.

> We'll beat him into horse-nails
> Horse-nails horse-nails
> We'll beat him into horse-nails
> Tum a rio, tum a rad io

Poker's cue is 'We'll poke him in the ribs', Red-Coal's cue is, 'We'll bake him into scones' and at the end everyone joins in on 'Lay on him every man'. (Maclagan 1901)

The first four lines were also chanted in Aberdeenshire, by 'a child with a stick and stooping like an old person ... in a weird way hobbling after its playmates'.

(Shuldham-Shaw et al. 2002, no. 1620) The 'Tum a rio' refrain of the Argyllshire game ties it to another account of a systematised thumping boy's game that 'was very popular in the [Edinburgh] Canongate' in the 1840s. A chosen boy bends over to thole his 'table' or back being hammered by many fists in turn, to a tune that is known variously as 'My Johnny's grey breeks', 'The rose tree', or 'Come a ree ro come a raddie o':

And it's bak - in Bet - sy Bell, cum a ree o, cum a rad - die o And it's

bak - in Bet - sy Bell, cum a ree o, cuma rad - die o

*(Rymour Club 1911)*

> And it's bakin Betsy Bell, cum a ree o, cum a raddie o
> And it's bakin Betsy Bell, cum a ree o, cum a raddie o
> And it's on wi the hammer and the block
> And it's on wi the studdy and the stock
> And it's on wi the kettle and the pan
> Then it's on wi the poker and the tangs
> Then it's on wi the waterin can
> And it's on wi the red cowl man

*(Rymour Club 1911)*

Having withstood the onslaught, without crying, the table's place is taken by the alarmingly named Red Cowl Man.

The gang names brandished in the chants of threat that I include in the anthology section show which areas of Glasgow Davison I collected in. I expect the same could be gathered in any Scottish city where there are contested borders, but collectors of such stuff are few. The chants link to daubed slogans that delineate territories. A particularly succinct rhyming linking of a well-known Glasgow TV rental firm and a Shettleston gang graced the back of John Lewis's Argyle Street store for several years – RADIO RENTAL, FLEET ARE MENTAL.

There is one gang song found throughout the land and espoused by girls as well as boys. I first met it in Kilchattan Bay on the Isle of Bute, the nearest primary school being in Rothesay. A nine year old came up on her bike, asked 'Are you the man that is interested in songs?' and sang me the following to a droning little tune:

We are the Rothesay girls
We wear our hair in curls
We wear our dungarees
Below our sexy knees

My daddy was surprised
Tae see ma belly rise
My mammy jumped for joy
Tae see a baby boy

*(McVicar Collection: Bute, 1994)*

We are the bovver girls
We wear our hair in curls
We wear our dungarees
To just below our knees

We wear our fathers' suits
We wear our brothers' ties
And if we want a guy
We simply wink one eye

The boy next door
He had me on the floor
My mother was surprised
To see my belly rise

My father jumped with joy
To see a baby boy
We are the bovver girls
From Scurvy-Land

*(Ian Davison Card Index)*

The Woodburn girls wore their mothers' skirts rather than their brothers' ties, and their last two lines were

Ma brother hit the roof
It was a baby poof

*(McVicar Collection: Dalkeith, 1997)*

I gathered the next one in 2006 in Moray from a nine-year-old traveller girl, who said she intends to be a country and western star when she grows up and has already written some of her songs:

We are the gypsy girls
We got our hairs in curls
We got our dangarees upon our sexy knees
We wear our bras so tight
Show we can fight
We are the gypsy girls

*(McVicar Collection: Moray, 2006)*

In Bankton PS, Livingston, in 2007 the 'Bankton girls' ended with 'Bababa boosh-kaka, bababa booshkaka'.

We are the Scurvy boys
We make a lot of noise
We wear our trousers to our knees
We never smoke or drink
That's what our mothers think
We are the Temple Scurvy boys

*(Ian Davison Card Index)*

We are the Rab boys
We make a lot of noise
We wear our trousers to our knees, to our knees
What do our parents say
When we go out to play
We are the super Rab boys

*(McVicar Collection: St Robert's PS, Glasgow 1991)*

There are also the songs of religious intolerance:

Take a tramcar take a trolley
Take a bus to George's Square
There you'll see a famous Orangeman
Sitting on his big white mare
He is William Prince of Orange
And no Fenian can deny
That he slew the Fenian army
On the twelfth day of July

*(Ian Davison Card Index)*

Often versions of only the first four lines are known. In 1900s rural Argyllshire they knew not of tramcars, so they took a trumpet to Glasgow Cross, seeking a statue not known there:

If you want to see King William
Take your trumpet to the Cross
There you'll see a noble lady
Riding on a big black horse

Riddle doodle, deedle daddle
Riding on a big black horse

*(Maclagan 1901)*

The above was part of a game called 'Row chow, row chow, row chow tobacco o', involving couples first rolling downhill locked 'firmly together', then whirling round singing 'Hook and eye and oggrie dead', and ending with the 'King William' verse as they pulled each other back and forward.

Every class I ask has football rhymes, with neat rudeness and interchangeable team names. The fierce tribal loyalties involved mean that dissent and challenge are close to the surface. My sympathies are always with the class rebel, who rejects not just the nationally known Glasgow teams but also the local side, naming some far away heroes. But personally I support no football or other sporting team whatever, and side with Glasgow writer Cliff Hanley who tells of being challenged on his religious allegiance, being asked if he was 'A Billy or a Dan or an auld tin can?' His neutral response was 'an auld tin can because there was no known procedure for that'.

I would discuss the influence of adults' football terrace songs here, but I was always part of the silent majority who did not care who kicked whom yesterday. I have not supported a specific football team since 1955, when I was a schoolboy in Dingwall, Ross-shire. While I was always a peaceable soul, my rougher classmates enjoyed issuing an invitation to a fight, sometimes using football club allegiance as a pretext, but sometimes this song:

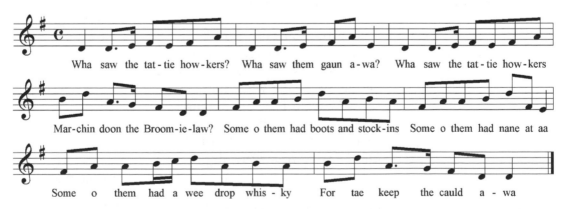

Wha saw the tat-tie how-kers? Wha saw them gaun a-wa? Wha saw the tat-tie how-kers
Mar-chin doon the Broom-ie-law? Some o them had boots and stock-ins Some o them had nane at aa
Some o them had a wee drop whis-ky For tae keep the cauld a-wa

*(Transcription: McVicar from personal recollection, Dingwall 1950s)*

Wha saw the tattie howkers?
Wha saw them gaun awa?
Wha saw the tattie howkers
Marchin doon the Broomielaw?

Some o them had boots and stockins
Some o them had nane at aa
Some o them had a wee drop whisky
For tae keep the cauld awa

*(McVicar from personal recollection: Dingwall, 1950s)*

Every year children from the less achieving schools of the cities got the Tattie Holidays, two extra weeks off school during which they were taken by train to the country to lift the potato harvest on our local farms. To add to the injustice of us going to school while they did not, these smooth-talking city lads (aged twelve to fourteen at most) used their urban guiles to chat up our small-town girls, and their ex-boyfriends took this very ill. Pitched battles occasionally ensued, the 'tattie howkers' lighting the fuse.

When I sang the 'Tattie howkers' at home, my father said 'We used to sing different words. We sang "Wha saw the 42nd gaun awa?"' He explained that the 42nd were Scottish soldiers – the 42nd Highland Regiment. They were marching down to the Glasgow dockside at the Broomielaw to board a ship that would carry them to foreign lands, there to protect us at home. The 42nd, the Black Watch, our oldest Scottish regiment, was formed by recruiting loyal Highlanders, uniforming them in a dark tartan and setting them to keep the Highlands at peace.

In more recent years I have often encountered the song, but usually with slightly varying words – an indication that it is passed on orally rather than through the fixing medium of print. In some versions of the song the soldiers carry 'champit tatties', 'beef an tatties' or 'barley bannocks' instead of whisky. In one version they wear 'white kerseckies' rather than 'boots an stockins'. Another has 'kilts an sporrans', 'rusty rifles' and 'picks an shovels'. (McVicar Collection: Bill Tulloch, Greenock, 1998)

In a little songbook of the early 1960s, *Carlton Folk Songs*, is a version that has them sporting 'braw Glengarries', and a footnote says 'The location was altered to suit whichever Town or Place where the ditty was sung. In Glasgow it was Broomielaw, in Perth it was Thimbleraw etc.'

Often, a child needs a longer song for some skipping or ball-bouncing purpose and a compendium song is made:

Nellie McSwiggan got tossed oot the jiggin
For liftin her leg too high
All of a sudden a big black puddin
Came flyin through the air

> Oh wha saw the kilties comin
> Wha saw them gang awa
> Wha saw the kilties comin
> Sailin doon the Broomielaw
> Some o them had tartan troosers
> Some o them had nane at a
> Some o them had tartan troosers
> Sailin doon the Broomielaw

*(Sinclair 1986)*

The first four lines are in a different metre from the rest. Such marked changes in metre are occasionally found in children's song performance, but when I first met the lines above I suspected they were conjoined through printing error and should be separated by some leading space – an empty line. Then I found the Opies (1985) giving a 1954 Glasgow version. Their first stanza tune is in 6/8 time, but instead of the 'Blaze away' Souza march that 'Nellie McSwiggen' is usually sung to, it is a fragment of 'The Campbells are coming'. Their second tune is the usual 4/4 time one. Consulting *Nicht At Eenie* produces another little puzzle about this song:

> Fa saw the Forty-Second
> Fa saw them gang awa?
> Fa saw the Forty-Second
> Gaein tae the wapenshaw?
> Some o them gat chappit tatties
> Some o them gat nane ava
> Some o them gat barley bannocks
> Gaein tae the wapenshaw
>
> Fa saw the Forty-Second
> Fa saw them gang awa?
> Fa saw the Forty-Second
> Marchin doon the Broomielaw?
> Some o them had tartan troosers
> Some o them had nane ava
> Some o them had green umbrellas
> Marchin doon the Broomielaw

*(Shelmerdine & Greirson 1932)*

The mention of the 'wapenshaw' would at first glance seem to be an anachronistic insertion of an ancient term denoting a mustering and showing of weapons by the men of a burgh or district. However, the *Scottish National Dictionary* gives a modern usage of 'a rifle-shooting competition organised by the Volunteer Corps and later by the Territorial Army or by private rifle clubs'. The 42nd Regiment as a unit of the British Army, would not I think undertake such an exercise as a shooting competition, so the word may still be an insertion by an inventive hand, or may point to some other volunteer unit being the 'original' subject of this version of the song.

Before *Nicht At Eenie*, Robert Ford in 1903 gave a neat account that suggests a topic development from cotton spinners to the 42nd Regiment and then to tattie howkers. He wrote 'Since about the time of the Crimean War – and more immediately after then than now – the children of Glasgow have shouted in the streets

> Saw ye the Forty-Second?
> Saw ye them gaun awa?
> Saw ye the Forty-Second
> Marching to the Broomielaw?
>
> Some o them had boots and stockins
> Some o them had nane ava
> Some o them had tartan plaidies
> Marching to the Broomielaw

'At an earlier period than the Crimean War, the children of Glasgow had:

> Wha saw the Cotton-spinners?
> Wha saw them gaun awa?
> Wha saw the Cotton-spinners
> Sailing frae the Broomielaw?
>
> Some of them had boots and stockins
> Some o them had nane ava
> Some o them had umbrellas
> For to keep the rain awa

*(Ford 1903)*

Who were these cotton spinners? Explaining the content of another song altogether, Roy Palmer (1979) says 'The Glasgow cotton spinners, of whom there were about a thousand, went on strike in April, 1837 . . . Five officials of the spinners union were brought to trial . . . There was such an outcry about the case the convicted spinners were not sent overseas, but kept in the hulks at Woolwich. They were pardoned in 1840.'

As usual, there are more suspect versions of the 42nd song. File 'March42' in the Digital Tradition database on the World Wide Web, accessed through the *Mudcat Café* webpage at www.mudcat.org, gives a number of the variants of 'Wha Saw the 42nd' I have already quoted, then the following:

Note: the version I heard is

> March past, the forty-second
> March past, the forty-twa
> March past, the barearsed bastards
> Comin from Ashanti war
>
> Some o them hae Hielan bonnets
> Some o them hae nane at a
> Some hae kilts an others hae na
> They be Hielan laddies raw

The contributor goes on to say 'I have no idea where I heard it, though. RG'

I myself have encountered a text similar to this variant some years ago, sung by the father of a fiddle-playing amigo Willie Beaton, but his version commented that the soldiers were not Highlanders at all but Glasgow laddies. From its rejection of the strong matrix favoured by all other variants, and its rather overly literary flavour, I suspect this strand of text to be the creation of an adult 'improver' – or else it might be the rude version that often accompanies a popular 'non-rude' song. The Ashanti War of 1873–74 was waged by the British against peoples of modern-day Ghana.

And the Internet produced another gem. In Colorado circa 1968 a girl scout troop sang

> Warsaw the forty-second
> Warsaw gone to war
> Warsaw the forty-second
> Marching through the brambles raw
>
> Zoomde men got boots and stockings
> Zoomde men got nain a taa
> Zoomde men got boots and stockings
> Marching through the brambles raw

(www.mudcat.org, 17/8/200, communication from C Dye)

Scots dialect has here turned into something about Poland in 1942 during the Second World War, with soldiers from Holland passing through. They 'sang it as an eight part round, holding the 'raw's for eight counts to make the bagpipe drone under the melody'.

The usual tune of 'Wha saw' songs is best known as 'Wha wouldna fight for Charlie'. James Hogg gives this song in *The Jacobite Relics of Scotland* and says in the song notes 'Likewise a Buchan song, sent to me by Mr John Wallace. The air has the same name, but in the South is called "Will ye go and marry Katie?"'

The only sharing between the 'Wha saw' songs and 'Wha wouldna fight for Charlie' other than the tune is that the first word of the first three lines of each stanza is 'Wha' in all cases:

> Wha wad na fight for Charlie?
> Wha wad na draw the sword?
> Wha wad na up and rally
> At the royal prince's word?

*(Anonymous, nd, 1850s)*

## Anthology: Gangs, violence and insult, football

*Gangs, violence and insult*

BAKER BAKER
Baker baker bake a pie, and send it up to Rory Mackay
Rory Mackay loot a fart, baker baker catch that

*(Rymour Club 1911: Bruce J Home)*

BARNEY
I hate you, you hate me
Let's shove Barney up a tree
With a baseball bat and a four by four
No more purple dinosaur

*(McVicar Collection: Bankton PS, 2007)*

BIRDS GO TWEET
Birds go tweet tweet
Cows go moo
Pigs go oink oink
How about you?

*(McVicar Collection: Bankton PS, 2007)*

BOMB THEM ALL
Bomb them all bomb them all
The Italians and Germans and all
Though they are bombing our cities and streets
Our army and navy will never retreat
For old Churchill will see to them all
That Hitler is put to the wall
And Goebbels and Goering will soon be a-roaring
So cheer up my lads bomb them all

*(Ian Davison Card Index: John St Schoo; tune: 'Bless Them All')*

BUDDY BOYS
Buddy Boys, Buddy Boys
Bovver boots and corduroys
Celtic Boys, Celtic Boys
Play with the Tonka Tonka toys

*(Ian Davison Card Index)*

CHOOKERHILL BRIGADE
We are the Chookerhill Brigade
And you don't need to be afraid
For we'll slaughter Wine Alley
For Chookerhill Valley
We are the Chookerhill Brigade

*(Ian Davison Card Index: Govan Adventure Playground;*
*tune 'Popeye the sailor man')*

THE CHUNKIE BOYS
We are some of the Chunkie Boys
We are some of the lads
We know our manners and how to wield our spanners
We are some of the boys

When we are passing through the Gallowgate
Doors and windows open wide
You can hear the people cry the Chunkie boys are passing by
We are some of the boys

*(Campbell 1964)*

COME FOLLOW ME
Come follow me, where skinheads grow on trees
In an English aggro garden
Bovver-boots and braces, smashing people's faces
That's what the skinheads do to you

*(Ian Davison Card Index; tune 'English country garden')*

DEDRIDGE YOUTH TEAM
A B C, 1 2 3
We're the Dedridge DYT
With a baseball bat and a snooker cue
We are going to hammer you

*(McVicar Collection: Bankton PS, Livingston, 2007)*

DOWN AT THE PREGO
Down at the Prego on a Saturday night
The Tiney Winey got into a fight
Out came the razors quick as a flash
And the cry was Tiney Winey YA BASS

*(Ian Davison Card Index: Govan Adventure Playground;*
*tune: 'Down in the jungle')*

Davison notes that 'the Tiney Winey are a crowd of nice harmless boys age 6–9'.

DOWN IN THE BODAY
Down in the Boday a boy and a blade
Mental Bonnar was his name
Many Spur tried and many Spur died
They were buried together by the Brigton Team
10, 20, 30, 40, 50 no more
The bloody old Nunny rode out the score
Many Spur tried and many Spur died
They were buried together by the Brigton side

*(Ian Davison Card Index: Rottenrow School;*
*tune: variation of 'The old 97')*

HAVE YOU EVER
Have you ever been in Govan?
That's where most of the fighting is done
It was there that a young KP rebel
Was shot by an old Govan gun
As he lay on the Langlands Road dying
He turned to our leader and said
'Will you bury me under the Winey?
When I'm finished with fighting and I'm dead?'

*(Ian Davison Card Index)*

HULLO, HULLO
Hullo, hullo, we are the Derry Boys
Hullo, hullo, we are the Derry Boys
We're up to our knees in Fenian blood
Surrender or you die
For we are the Brigton Derry Boys

*(Ian Davison Card Index;*
*tune: 'Marching through Georgia')*

I ONCE KNEW A BORSTAL BOY
I once knew a Borstal boy
He sure broke my heart
He told me a story
About his sweetheart

She committed a murder
And he took the blame
Two years in Borstal
Is a very long time

The jury said 'Stand up
And dry away your tears
We're sending you to Borstal
For the time of two years'

He counted the moonbeams
He counted the stars
He counted a million
Of these Borstal bars

He received a letter
From old Glasgow town
To tell him his sweetheart
Had just let him down

So listen you fellas
And listen to me
Two years in a Borstal
Is no place to be

*(Ian Davison Card Index)*

I WAS WALKING
I was walking in the morning
I was walking in the night
In the afternoon I was in a fight
I hit him in the stomach
I hit him in the face
Then I got walloped with his heavy case

*(McVicar Collection: Glasgow, 1991)*

I WENT TO A PARTY
I went to a party on Saturday night
The Shafton were there and they started a fight
I pulled out my razor as quick as a flash
And shouted 'Young Scurvy Ya Bass!'
I lifted my boot and he fell to the floor
He rolled in agony howled in pain
I lifted my boot and I walloped him again

*(Ian Davison Card Index)*

IF YOU'RE TIRED
If you're tired and weary
If you're off your beat
You'll get your – head kicked in
If you walk down James Street
If you go into the Mermaid
You will hear a famous noise
'Get out you Fenian bastard!
We're the Brigton Derry Boys!'

*(Ian Davison Card Index: Ruchazie School;*
*tune: 'Let him go let him tarry')*

Davison says 'A song of the Brigton Derry Boys based in the Mermaid pub at Bridgeton Cross.'

KILTY KILTY
Kilty kilty cauld erse, couldna play a drum
His father took the bellises and blew him up the lum

*(Rymour Club 1911)*

Said 'To a Highlander'.

THE MIGHTY P4
With a hey and a ho and away we go
Off to Glasgow we shall go
With a bottle and a brick and a hockey stick
We are the mighty P4

*(McVicar Collection: Bankhead, 1992)*

THE NUNNY
Well the Nunny won the battle at Bridgeton Cross
Bridgeton Cross, Bridgeton Cross
Well the Nunny won the battle at Bridgeton Cross
And the Spur came tumbling down

*(Ian Davison Card Index: Rottenrow School;*
*tune: 'Joshua fit de battle of Jericho')*

The Nunny and the Spur are two gangs.

PUNCH AND JUDY
Punch and Judy had a fight
Punch gave Judy a knock in the eye
Said Punch to Judy will you have any more?
Said Judy to Punch my eye is too sore

*(McVicar Collection: Glasgow, 1991)*

RED COAT
Sodger sodger red-coat followin the drum
Fire in the mountains run boys run
Up wi your pistol doon wi your gun
Tak a knife and cut your throat and that's weel done

*(Rymour Club 1911:*
*Calder Ironworks, 1860s)*

If a soldier came within sight, the boys shouted this in chorus.

RED NECK
Rabbit wi the red neck red neck red neck
Rabbit wi the red neck follow ye the drum
Fire on the mountains the mountains the mountains
Fire on the mountains run boys run

*(Chambers 1842)*

Shouted by 'juvenile bands' when they saw the annual burning of heather on the hill.

SPIDERMAN
Spiderman, Spiderman
Had a face like a frying pan
Is he tough? Is he heck
Touch this man and he'll break your neck
Come on, here comes the frying pan

*(McVicar Collection: Moray, 2006)*

THE SPUR
We are the Spur
The London Road Spur
We know our manners
We spend our tanners on
Two loose tips
Spur ya bass

*(Ian Davison Card Index: Rottenrow School)*

STAUNIN AT THE CORNER
Staunin at the corner swinging my chain
Along came Whitelaw and asked me my name
Ah kicked him in the balls and kicked his head
Now that bastard's lying there dead

*(Ian Davison Card Index)*

TAILORIE TAILORIE TARTAN
Tailorie tailorie tartan, gaed up the lum fartin
Aa the tailors in the toon couldna shoo a garten

*(Rymour Club 1911: Rev. Wm Findlay)*

Said 'in derision of tailors'.

TAKE A TRIP DOON TAE BRIGTON
Take a trip doon tae Brigton
Go without delay
That's where the Derry Boys
Are standing today
We chased the San Toi
Up the Gallowgate
And we are the Brigton Derry Boys

*(Ian Davison Card Index)*

Tam Tam the midgie man
Tam Tam the midgie man
Lives in a midgie motor
Running along the dyke
And skelpt his head a stoter

*(McVicar Collection: Glasgow, 1993)*

There's naething i Hielants
There's naething i Hielants but green kale and leeks
And lang-leggit Hielantmen wantin the breeks
Wantin the breeks, and without hose or shoon
They'll aa get the breeks when Jamie comes home

*(Rymour Club 1911:*
*Kirriemuir district, recollected by the ex-mayor of Leeds)*

Tiny Winey Brigade
We're the Tiny Winey Brigade
And there's no need to be afraid
For we'll slaughter Wine Alley
And Chookerhill Valley
We're the Tiny Winey Brigade

*(Ian Davison Card Index: Bellahouston School)*

'Wine Alley' was the byname for a notorious Glasgow estate.

The Toi
Hoi hoi we're the Toi
Inky winky bitchy
My bum's itchy

*(Ian Davison Card Index: Rottenrow School)*

Davison notes 'Common in Toi-land.'

Tommy Fraser
Tommy Fraser bought a razor
Now he's in the razor gang
Slashed a copper good and proper
Now he's in Barlinnie Jail

*(Ian Davison Card Index:*
*Govan Adventure Playground)*

*Football*

ABERDEEN ABERDEEN
Aberdeen Aberdeen
Canny keep their knickers clean
Aberdeen Aberdeen
Canny kick a jelly bean

*(McVicar Collection: Dalkeith HS, 1997)*


Aberdeen, what a team
Canny kick a jelly bean
Rangers canny kick a ball
Celtic are the best of all

*(McVicar Collection: St Robert's PS, Glasgow, 1997)*


Aberdeen Aberdeen
Canny kick a jelly bean
Celtic won a rubber duck
Rangers won the Scottish Cup

*(McVicar Collection: Glasgow, 1993)*


AFTER THE MATCH WAS OVER
After the match was over
After the game was through
Hitler got up in a temper
And over the field he flew
He passed the ball to Churchill
Churchill scored a goal
And that was a goal for the British
And the Germans are up the pole

*(Ian Davison Card Index: John Street School;*
*tune: 'After the ball')*


THE BALL'S IN THE CENTRE
The ball's in the centre
The ball's in the net
The poor wee Celtic
Lying in the net

Come away Rangers
Never be afraid
Show the dirty Celtic
How the game is played

*(Ian Davison Card Index: Bellahouston School)*

A BIG BUS WAS LEAVING
A big bus was leaving from Hampden Park
The Rangers had just won the cup, the cup
The Celtic were greetin because they were beaten
A big bus was leaving from Hampden Park

*(Ian Davison Card Index: Rottenrow School;*
*tune: 'Bless them all')*

CELTIC
Celtic Celtic that's the team for me
Celtic Celtic I hope you will agree
It's the finest team in Scotland
I hope you will agree
They never gave up till they won the cup
A Scottish victory

*(Ian Davison Card Index: Rottenrow School)*

Celtic went up the greasy pole
The greasy pole the greasy pole
Celtic went up the greasy pole
And couldny get down to score a goal

*(Ian Davison Card Index: Rottenrow School)*

CHEER UP JIM JEFFRIES
Cheer up Jim Jeffries
Oh what can it mean
To a sad jam tart
And a crap football team

*(McVicar Collection: Dalkeith HS, 1997)*

DOWN THE LINE
Down the line the train came puffing
Rangers three Celtic nothing

*(McVicar Collection: Dalkeith HS, 1997*

FOREVER AND EVER
Forever and ever we'll follow the Jags
The Partick Thistle the Harry Wraggs
For we made a promise that we will fulfil
To bring the Scottish Cup back to Maryhill

*(Ian Davison Card Index)*

A GRAND OLD TEAM
And it's a grand old team to play for
And it's a grand old team tae say
And if you know yer history
It's enough tae make yer heart go oh, oh, oh, oh
We don't care what the animals say
What the hell do we care
For we only know that there's gonna be a show
And the grand old Celtic will be there
Sellin bananas half price

*(McVicar Collection: St Robert's PS, Glasgow, 1997)*

HAIL, HAIL
Hail, hail the Celts are here
What the hell do we care?
What the hell do we care?

*(McVicar Collection: St Robert's PS, Glasgow, 1997)*

HAMPDEN IN THE SUN
Oh Hampden in the sun
Celtic seven Rangers one
All the people shout and scream
Cause they want a revival scene
Willie Fernie did a dance
And he gave the Gers no chance
He brought the ball in from the flag
And stuck it in the onion bag

*(Ian Davison Card Index)*

HIBS FOR EVER
Hibs for ever
Chuck them in the river
Pull them out and make them shout
Hearts are better

*(McVicar Collection: Dalkeith HS, 1997)*

Elsewhere in the same class the teams were Celtic and Rangers, Hearts and Rangers, etc.

I WENT TAE A MATCH
I went tae a match for the Rangers tae see
And two dirty Fenians came on after me
I told the conductor to stop at the Cross
And I showed them King Billy upon his white horse

*(Ian Davison Card Index;*
*tune: 'The old orange flute')*


IF YOU WANT TO GO TO HEAVEN
If you want to go to heaven when you die
You must wear a Celtic scarf and tie
You must wear a Celtic bonnet
With '— King Billy' on it
If you want to go to heaven when you die

*(Ian Davison Card Index)*


I'M THE ONLY CATHOLIC
I'm the only Catholic in the Rangers team
Isn't it a scream the Rangers team
Isn't it a miracle? Isn't it a dream?
I'm the only Catholic in the Rangers team

*(Ian Davison Card Index)*


ONLY ONE RAVIOLI
There's only one Ravioli
He eats cheese and macaroni
He's got no hair but we don't care
Walking in a winter wonderland

*(McVicar Collection:*
*Dalkeith HS, 1997)*


The informant said this was 'a football one'.

RANGERS
The famous Glasgow Rangers took a holiday to Rome
A holiday to Rome a holiday to Rome
The famous Glasgow Rangers took a holiday to Rome
To see what Pope Paul would say

He said go home you huns go home you huns
Go home you huns go home
Go home you huns go home you huns
We'll do it on our own

*(Ian Davison Card Index: Bellahouston School;*
*tunes: first four lines 'John Brown's body',*
*rest 'Auld lang syne')*


Rangers Rangers, na na na Rangers
I could walk a mile without a smile
To Rangers

*(McVicar Collection:*
*Glasgow, 1991)*


SANDY IN ROYAL BLUE
Sandy Sandy, Sandy in Royal Blue
We're all crazy, over the likes of you
You look so neat with the ball at your feet
And scoring a goal or two

*(Ian Davison Card Index)*


SKINNY PASSED TO FATTIE
My old man's a dustman he wears a dustman's hat
He bought two thousand tickets to see a football match
Skinny passed to Fattie and Fattie passed it back
Skinny put a rocket shot and knocked the goalie flat
Where was the goalie when the ball went in the net
Halfway up the goal post with his trousers round his neck
Singing oompah oompah, stick it up your joomper
Rule Britannia, marmalade and jam
We threw sausages at our old man
They put him on a stretcher, they put him on a bed
They rubbed his belly with five pound jelly but the poor
   old soul was dead

*(McVicar Collection:*
*Culbokie PS, 2006)*


The head teacher had taught this to the whole school.

SUPER
Supercalligobalistic
Rangers are atrocious

*(McVicar Collection: Moray, 2006)*

The typesetter of this book points out that this derives from a headline in the *Sun* newspaper in 2000, reporting on a defeat of Celtic, not Rangers, by Caley Thistle.

THERE WAS A YOUNG MAN
There was a young man named Danny
Who went to the match with his granny
When Celtic got beat, she started to greet
So he gave her a drink of his 'lanny'

*(Ian Davison Card Index)*

WE ARE THE CELTIC SUPPORTERS
We are the Celtic supporters
Faithful through and through
Over and over and over
We will follow you

*(Ian Davison Card Index)*

WE WANT RANGERS
We want Rangers with a rope around their neck
We want Rangers with a rope around their neck
We want Rangers with a rope around their neck
And Celtic goes marching on

Glory glory hallelujah
And Celtic goes marching on

*(Ian Davison Card Index: Rottenrow School;*
*tune: 'John Brown's body'*

WEE JORGEY CADETY
Wee Jorgey Cadety
Has hair like spaghetti
He's got funny knees
And keeps honey bees
Walking in a Cadety Wonderland

*(McVicar Collection: Moray, 2006)*

The informants entitled this 'Cadette'.

2, 4
2, 4, 6, 8, who do we appreciate?
R-A-N-G-E-R-S, Rangers
2, 4, 6 and a quarter
Who do we intend to slaughter
C-E-L-T-I-C, Celtic

*(Ian Davison Card Index: Bellahouston School)*

2, 4, 6, 8, who do we appreciate?
Glasgow Rangers
No we don't, get it right
We support the green and white

*(McVicar Collection: St Robert's PS, Glasgow, 1997)*

# 14
# *Aunty Mary's canary*

## Rude versus polite

> Salvation Army free from sin
> Went to heaven in a corned beef tin
> Corned beef tin began to smell
> Salvation Army went to —
> Helensburgh castle standing on a rock
> If you want to go there you've got to show a —

In Chapter 1 I gave the verse 'Captain Cook was eating soup' that in childhood I thought to be 'rude' because it included the word 'belly'. Another also recalled from Dingwall childhood seemed mysterious rather than 'rude'.

> On top of Old Smokey where nobody goes
> There lies Betty Grable without any clothes
> Up rides Roy Rogers and takes out his c—
> I pity Betty Grable cause it's hard as a rock

How Roy intended to to discomfort Betty with his penis, or why his little appendage had become like stone, we knew not. A few years later, aged twelve, a classmate showed us a sex instruction booklet acquired by stealth from his older brother, an army conscript. We laughed this publication and its crest-fallen purloiner to scorn – it was an obvious and absurd fake, the whole matter physically impossible. We had not yet encountered puberty.

Here are some for those who respond that children never used to know such rude stuff:

> Oor Mary's white drawers
> Oor Mary's white drawers
> A hole in the middle
> To let Mary piddle
> Oor Mary's white drawers

*(Tune: 'Two lovely black eyes')*

O Mary Ann had a leg like a man
And a great big hole in her stockin
A chest like a drum
And a big fat bum
And a hole to shove your c— in

*(Tune: 'The girl I left behind me')*

These two verses are given, along with a version of 'Auntie Mary had a canary' and another explicit song, in James Barke's introduction to *The Merry Muses of Caledonia* (Burns 1970). Barke says 'There were many similar bairns' bawdy rhymes, songs and chants common in West Fife in the first two decades of the twentieth century. Comparing notes with a pious Episcopalian approaching his eighties, I found that the identical bairns' bawdry was common to the city of Perth in the 1880s.'

The 'Auntie Mary' song from my own childhood was clearly one to be hidden from adults, for their own protection. They had more tender sensibilities than we did. We also kept such songs as the following well away from them:

Auntie Mary had a canary
Up the leg o her drawers
When she farted doon it started
Doon the leg o her drawers

When my adult interest in such gems grew I began to find variants. Scots novelist Carl MacDougall gave me the Maryhill version:

Auntie Mary had a canary
Up the leg o her drawers
It pulled a string and began tae sing
And doon fell Santa Claus

Others recalled different versions:

It pulled a string and began tae sing
Ah'm the Cock o the North

and

It wouldna come doon for half a croon
Doon the leg o her drawers

and

It wouldna come doon for half a croon
So we gave it a kick in the jaws

Andy Wilson of Livingston recalled it as

> She sat on the gas and burnt her arse
> And called for Santa Claus

Alex Campbell sang

> She lit the gas and burnt her ass
> And that was the end of the wars

*(Campbell 1964)*

Jenny Suttie had

> It only came doon in the month of June
> Whilst playing among the stars

*(McVicar Collection: Jenny Suttie, Edinburgh, 1999)*

I then began to gather other versions, in which the gallant hero won a medal:

> It flew up the lum and burnt its bum
> And won the Victoria Cross

*(McVicar Collection: Edinburgh University PG student, 1998)*

> She whistled for oors
> An peed in the flooers
> And won the Victoria Cross

*(Margaret et al, early 1990s)*

> It never came doon
> Till the month of June
> And won the Victoria Cross

*(McVicar Collection: source unrecorded)*

In 1992 I was talking with two ladies in a home for the elderly in Stonehouse, Lanarkshire. Both were native to the district and had very similar accents. One said to me she recalled an old song:

> Auntie Mary had a canary
> Up the leg o her drawers
> It whistled for oors
> And oors and oors
> And won the Victoria Cross

Her neighbour, older by some ten years, then said 'No, it whistled for oors, and frightened the Boers [pronounced Booers]', whereupon the younger asked 'Who were the [Booers]?' The older lady made reference to South Africa, and the younger lady said, 'Oh, the [Boars]!'

*(Transcription: Ewan McVicar, from singing of informant; Stonehouse, 1992)*

'Booers' is of course the Afrikaaner way of the word, and it would have been so said at the time of the Boer War in South Africa, but then it became 'Boars'. The change in pronunciation must have happened quite quickly, in South Lanarkshire at least.

A year after my visit, courtesy of royalty, a clear picture emerged. An article in the *Glasgow Herald* commented on a visit by Prince Charles to Islay. At a ceilidh there he had recited his party piece, learned from his Scottish grannie, the Queen Mother:

> Auntie Mary had a canary
> Whistled the Cock o the North
> It whistled for oors
> And frightened the Boers
> And won the Victoria Cross

As well as combining a number of key elements in an elegant fashion, this has the merit of being the first non-rude version of the song I found. The tune consistently used for this song is 'The Cock of the North', which gives a clue as to which versions are probably older.

At last, in *Nicht at Eenie*, I found what felt at the time like the grandaddy of all the Auntie Marys. Except that Auntie Mary herself has disappeared! And the order of the two strains of the tune suggested that what was more recently the single strain tune sung for Auntie Mary was then used for the 'B for Booer' verse.

*(Shelmerdine & Greirson 1932)*

Barnum and Bayley
Had a canary
Whustled 'The Cock o the North'
It whustled for oors
An frichtened the Booers
An they aa fell intae the Forth
B for Booer
K for Krudger
J for General French
The Bri'ish were up at the tap o the hull
An the Booers were doon in the trench

*(Shelmerdine & Greirson 1932)*

Barnum and Bailey were well-known American circus proprietors; Kruger and French were military antagonists in the Boer War. I adore the idea that J stands for General. But why no mention of the Victoria Cross? Surely the very oldest version would have had this? *Nicht At Eenie* then gave this alternative:

Sister Mary had a canary
Whustled 'The Cock o' the North'
It whustled for hoors and frightened the Booers
And won the Victoria Cross

I'm sure the canary was whistling for hours rather than for female company. Sister Mary rather than auntie. Well, I suppose she was younger then. Unless she was a nursing sister in South Africa. Florence Nightingale was the 'lady with the lamp' during the Crimean War, maybe Sister Mary went round the South African wards at night with a little bird on her shoulder to sing to the troops, so she became known as the 'bird with the bird'. Then after that she came home and became an auntie, of course. Eventually she might have become known as the Whistler's Mother? It's as likely as 'Ring a ring a roses' being about the 1665 plague.

I have to tell you, by the way, that there is another claimant for being the original of this song. In an entertaining work, *The General Danced At Dawn*, based on his own experiences serving in the Middle East, the writer George MacDonald Fraser gives a fairly convincing account of the origin of 'Auntie Mary had a canary'. He says: 'There was the little jingle that went to our regimental march, which the children used to sing at play':

> Findlater, Piper Findlater
> Piped 'The Cock o' the North'
> He piped it so loud
> That he gathered a crowd
> And he won the Victoria Cross

Fraser then tells the tale of Piper George Findlater, who won the VC for encouraging his regiment up an Afghan hillside at the Battle of Dargai in 1879 by playing the regimental march, 'The Cock O The North', the tune to which 'Auntie Mary' is invariably sung. Highly convincing – except that Findlater himself apparently always asserted that he in fact had played 'The Haughs o Cromdale'.

In his Author's Note Fraser says 'The incidents [that comprise the stories in the book] have been made up from a wide variety of sources, including my imagination. As to traditions, customs, and one or two pieces of history, these too are a mixture.'

My own opinion is that Fraser's account of the origin of the song draws very heavily on the author's imagination. As with other songs considered in this book, some versions seem to lose the basic song shape entirely:

> Auntie Mary had a canary
> Up the leg of her trousers
> While she was sleeping I was peeping
> Up the leg of her trousers

*(www.mudcat.org, 4/8/98,*
*communication from tjacques)*

The Auntie Mary song has other relatives. When 'The Cock of the North' was played for dancing, the dancers in various places would sing

> Chase me Charlie chase me Charlie
> Lost the leg of me drawers
> Chase me Charlie chase me Charlie
> Kindly lend me yours

*(McVicar Collection: Sheila Gammon, 1999)*

I puzzled over how one can lose one leg of a pair of underpants until Sheila Gammon told me that up until some hundred years ago the garment consisted of two separate legs held together by a drawstring – hence the word drawers. Another song, sung to the tune of 'Comin through the rye', is also related to Auntie Mary:

> Sister Mary bought a canary
> From the butcher boy
> Sister Mary bought a canary
> It was her pride and joy
> But the bird would never whistle
> And she wondered why
> Till she saw the sparrow's feathers
> Comin through the dye

Bob Boulten said this song 'ended up in the first Australian Scout Songbook, which my father worked on'. (McVicar Collection) This song in turn leads to another in which Jean Macpherson dies her hair, but when she goes out in the rain

> All you could see was streaks of grey
> Comin through the dye

There is a different Scottish canary puzzle, arising it would seem from the following song:

> Ah lost ma love and ah dinna ken hoo
> Ah lost my love and ah care na
> The losin of one is the gainin o two
> Fa's the lassie that dare na?

Like 'Chase me Charlie' it was sung to accompany dancing. The tune is often called 'Jock since ever ah seen yer face'. A former writing colleague of mine, Mary McCabe, recalls a Glasgow song from childhood, to the tune of 'For he's a jolly good fellow':

> Ah lost ma wee canary
> Ah lost ma wee canary
> Ah lost ma wee canary
> A humphy dumphy doo

A translation of the last line would be 'An overfat pigeon with a hump on its back'. How can these two verses be linked? I'll show you. Willa Muir, wife of Edwin Muir, in her book *Living With Ballads* (1965), recalls that in a Montrose school playground in 1901, 'Rushing round in a kind of gallop we shouted rather than sang:

> O I've lost my lad and I care-nae
> I've lost my lad and I care-nae
> I've lost my lad and I care-nae
> A ramshy-damshy-doo
> O we'll get anither canary
> We'll get anither canary
> We'll get anither canary
> A ramshy-damshy-doo'

This portion of Willa Muir's book solved a puzzle for the Opies. They had been given the song as 'I lost my lad in the cairnie', and after consulting Scots dictionaries they had 'concluded that, since "cairnie" was a heap or quantity of anything, the lad had been lost in a crowd'. Reasonable enough, but it leads to visions of searching a heap of stones to locate the canary cheeping away within. 'I care nae' means 'I care not', but it can easily become a 'canary' when a child wants to sing the song but comes from another part of Scotland. But what is the 'ramshy-damshy-doo'? A doo is a dove. Ramshy could mean strong or lustful, about damshy I have no clue.

Mary McCabe's song was still being sung by Glasgow schoolchildren in the early 1970s, and it was collected there by teacher Ian Davison. In John Street School it was known as 'I lost ma lad in the cairney'. In Rottenrow School they sang

> I lost my wee canary, canary, canary
> I lost my wee canary, a humphy dumphy doo
>
> I'll need tae get another wan, another wan, another wan
> I'll need tae get another wan, a humphy dumphy doo
> Oh, I met her in the dance hall, dance hall, dance hall
> I met her in the dance hall, a humphy dumphy doo
> Oh, red cheeks and roses, roses, roses
> Red cheeks and roses, a humphy dumphy doo
>
> Oh, this is the one that I choose, I choose, I choose
> This is the one that I choose, a humphy dumphy doo

*(Ian Davison Card Index: Rottenrow)*

Is that not romantic or what?

In my discussion on Katie Bairdie I said I would tell you much later about Cock-abendy. Katie had until late in life a reasonable degree of dignity. In contradistinction, her first cousin Cockabendy, Cockie-bendie or Cockie Bendy seems inherently comic, containing both farmyard and bawdy elements. Cocky Bendie's Castle was the name attached by my mother and her schoolmates to Planes Castle near the Stirlingshire village of Plean where she grew up, because of the risible self-important, small and plump owner of the pile in the 1920s. The castle later collapsed into rubble, but in the last few years it has been totally restored.

The *Scottish National Dictionary* gives the following meanings for cockie-bendie: 'a small, bumptious or rather effeminate man; also applied affectionately to a small boy; applied to a woman in a derogatory sense; the cone of the fir-tree; the large conical buds of the plane-tree; a dance tune'.

As with these conflicting meanings, so the song 'Cockabendy' combines very disparate elements. It offers either the babyish sickly sweet cure of sending 'twenty kisses in a cloot', or the ferocious alternative of sticking a gully knife down his throat. Its other identifying stanza employs basic lavatorial humour. The version which gathers together most of the elements best comes from Vol. 8 of the *Greig–Duncan Folk Song Collection*:

Cockabendy's lyin sick
Guess ye what'll mend him?
Twenty kisses in a cloot
Lassie, will ye send him?
Hi cock, hi cock
Hi Cockabendy
Crack a loose on Jeannie's wame
For a gill o brandy

Dinna gie the lasses drink
Dinna gie them brandy
Gie them sticks o cinnamon
And lumps o sugar candy
Cockabendy had a wife
He didna ken fou to guide her
He put her on a donkey's back
And then sat on beside her

Cockabendy had a wife
Oh but she was a dandy
She gaed in below the bed
And coupit owre the chanty

*(Shuldham-Shaw et al. 2002, no. 1721C)*

This version, from its comparative complexity, length, references to consuming alcohol and to cracking a louse on a female's belly and unique use of a refrain, appears clearly to be an 'adult' version of the song. That said, one could make a reasonable but not I think compelling argument for this being the original form of the song, with shorter versions having split off from it.

The kids' versions start from the 'nursery' message of sending twenty kisses, then turn the instruction into an incitement to casual extreme violence:

> Cocky-Bendy's lyin sick
> Guess ye what'll mend 'im?
> Stap a gully doon 'is throat
> That'll sune end 'im
>
> Half a pound o green tea
> Half an ounce o pepper
> Tak ye that my bonnie lad
> And ye'll sune be better

*(Rymour Club 1911)*

These two stanzas seem to pursue opposite aims for Cockabendy's health. Maybe it is his wife who is intent on doing him harm?

> Coco Bendy had a wife
> She was awfu dandy
> She fell in beneath the bed
> An tumbled o'er the chanty

*(Ian Davison Card Index: Bellahouston School)*

> Coco Bendy he came in
> An smelt an awfu stink
> He went in below the bed
> An had a fizzy drink

*(Ewan McVicar from personal recollection, source not recorded)*

What can one say, chanty humour? Cockabendy seems to have acquired a cow from Katie Bairdie:

> Cokey-Bendy had a coo
> It was yella black and blue
> All the monkeys in the zoo
> Laughed at Cokey-Bendy

*(Ewan McVicar from personal recollection, source not recorded)*

Or did the cow belong to a relative from Greenock, known to Bill Tulloch of those parts?

> Grannie Walker had a coo
> It was yellow black and blue,
> Aa the neighbours danced it through
> Hooch! Cried Grannie Walker
>
> Grannie Walker had a coo
> It was yellow black and blue
> It went un'erneath the bed
> And tum'lt o'er the chanty.

*(McVicar Collection: Bill Tulloch, Edinburgh, 1999)*

Our national treasure Robert Burns was acquainted with 'Cockabendy' and noted the title in his very own handwriting. But he gave no lyrics. The Scottish tune usually applied to 'Cockabendy' is 'Cawdor Fair', a strathspey-style version of 'Four and twenty blackbirds'.

In later times a music hall-style song, with quite a different tune called 'Maggie Cockabendy', emerged. Fife songmaker extraordinaire John Watt used the tune of this latter song for his anthem to bus conductresses, 'The Keltie clippie'.

# Anthology: Rude

> ALL THE DAMES IN FRANCE
> All the dames in France
> Do the Carioka dance
> Crying hey Nellie Nellie
> Put your dirty smelly belly close to mine

*(Campbell 1964)*

> APPLE CRUMBLE
> Apple crumble makes you rumble
> Apple tart makes you fart
> Custard powder makes it louder
> Raspberry jelly makes it smelly

*(Ian Davison Card Index)*

> AS I WAS WALKING
> As I was walking down the street
> I thought I smelt some kippers
> I asked a woman what it was
> She said she peed her knickers

*(Ian Davison Card Index: Rottenrow School)*

BEANS BEANS
Beans beans good for your heart
The more you eat them the more you fart
The more you fart the better you feel
So let's have beans for every meal

Or

The more you sit on the toilet seat

*(Ian Davison Card Index)*

A BIG MEALIE PUDDIN
All of a sudden a big mealie puddin
Came flyin through the air
It hit Mrs Kelly a smack on the belly
And knocked her off her chair
Did she duck? Did she f—
It hit her fair and square

*(McVicar from personal recollection: Dingwall, 1950s; tune: 'Blaze away.')*

In Bathgate the puddin

Missed ma caught pa
Cor blimey, didn't he swear

*(McVicar Collection: Bathgate, 1999)*

BOW LEGGED CHICKEN
I'm a bow legged chicken
I'm a cock a doodle doo
I missed my bus at half past two
I went to the café, to have a cup of tea
I ate too many sausages, whoops, pardon me

*(McVicar Collection: Addiewell, 1996)*

Or

I went ta the café
Ta buy a cup a tea
Ham n egg n sausages
'n' a woopsie, pardon me

*(McVicar Collection: Glasgow, 1993)*

CHAMPIONS
Champions, champions, we we we
Champions, champions, we we we
One two three, who are we?
We are the boys from St Anthony's
Wi a nick nack paddy wack, gie yersel a wash
This old man was puffin hash
Puffin hash, an ah'm nae jokin
[Name] wi her legs wide open

*(McVicar Collection: Glasgow, 1993)*

CHEWING GUM
Chewing gum, bubble gum
Stick it in your mum's bum

*(Ian Davison Card Index)*

DANCE LITTLE NELL
Round about the mulberry bush
Dance little Nell
Down came her father
And kicked up – sugarolly water
Black as the lum
Gather up pins
And ye'll get some

*(Ian Davison Card Index)*

DIAL 999
Dial 999
The police came in time
Caught Wee Bobby
Done a jobby
Dial 999

*(McVicar Collection: Glasgow, 1992)*

DIARRHOEA
I was going to the chippy
And I slipped in something slippy
Diarrhoea, diarrhoea

*(McVicar Collection: Glasgow, 1993)*

I was standing by a tree
When it dribbled down my knee [etc.]

I went behind a bush
I felt a sudden goosh [etc.]

I went behind a tree
And a squirrel laughed at me [etc.]

*(McVicar Collection: Dalkeith HS, 1997)*

I was swimming in the pool
And I felt something cool [etc.]

It stuck to my bum
Like a piece of chewing gum [etc.]

I fell down a trap
And done a wee crap [etc.]

It came out my bum
Like a bullet oot a gun [etc.]

It was lying in my bed
Like a piece of chocolate spread [etc.]

*(McVicar Collection: Glasgow, 1993)*

DOWN IN THE VALLEY
Down in the valley
There lives a wee tally
The wee tally farted
To get his car started

*(Ian Davison Card Index: John St School)*

ELASTICATED NAPPIES
Elasticated nappies
They run on forty batteries
You turn them on (bang-bang)
Bang! The baby's gone
Mum's not very happy
There's something in his nappy
It's big and brown (bum-bum)
It weighs ten pounds

*(Ian Davison Card Index; tune: 'The conga')*

EVERYBODY'S DOIN IT
Everybody's doin it, doin it, doin it
Picking their nose and chewin it, chewin it, chewin it

*(Ian Davison Card Index: Rottenrow School)*

FART FART
Fart fart the beans are calling
Must have been the ones I ate this morning
Up to the toilet, run on the flair
Ma Ma ah didn't mean it
Gies ten bob and ah'll help ye clean it
That's what ye get for giein us
Heinz baked beans

*(McVicar Collection: Bankhead, 1992)*

FRILLY NIGHTIE
Ah wear ma frilly nightie in the winter when it's hot
I wear my jammies in the summer when it's not
And sometimes in the springtime and sometimes in the fall
I jump into my little bed with nothing on at all

*(McVicar Collection: teacher, Bankton PS, 2007)*

HAIL HAIL
Hail hail the Pope's in jail
He wipes his bum on the *Sunday Mail*

*(Ian Davison Card Index: Rottenrow School)*

Hail hail the Queen's in jail
Looking oot the windy playing wi her Sindy
Haa ha-ha ha-haa haa, hoh ho-ho ho-hoh hoh
The Queen's in jail

*(McVicar Collection: Moray, 2006)*

HEY DIDDLE DIDDLE
Hey diddle diddle the cat did a piddle
All over the bathroom mat
The dog had a laugh to see such fun
And piddled all over the cat

*(McVicar Collection: Glasgow, 1991)*

Here comes the bride
Here comes the bride
Forty inches wide
She slid doon the banisters
On her backside

> (Ian Davison Card Index: East Milton School, East Kilbride;
> tune: variant of 'Knees up Mother Brown')

Here comes the bride
All dressed in white
Walking down the aisle
Covered in s—

> (McVicar Collection: Glasgow, 1991)

Here comes the bride
Forty inches wide
See how she waddles
From side to side

> (McVicar from personal recollection: Dingwall, 1950s)

Humpty Dumpty
Humpty Dumpty sat on a wall
Eating a banana
Where do you think he put the skin?
Down the king's pyjamas

> (McVicar Collection: Dalkeith HS, 1997)

I had a little monkey
I had a little monkey
I took it to the country
I fed it on Marshall's Bread
Marshall Marshall
Stick it up your —— (or 'in a parcel')
My wee monkey's dead

> (Ian Davison Card Index; tune: variant of 'Polly Wolly Doodle')

I like you
I like you, I like you
Come up and smell my dirty shoe

> (McVicar Collection: Glasgow, 1991)

JACK AND JILL
Jack and Jill went up the hill
To fetch a pail of water
We don't know what they did up there
But now they've got a daughter

Or

Jill forgot to take the pill
So they had a baby daughter

*(McVicar Collection: Dalkeith HS, 1997)*

Jack and Jill went up the hill
To have some hanky-panky
Jill came doon wi hauf-a-croon
She must've met a Yankee

*(Ian Davison Card Index)*

KEICH BUM
Keich Bum and Toly Fart
Went to the Ally Park
Keich Bum couldnae swim
Toly Fart pushed him in

*(Ian Davison Card Index: Rottenrow School)*

KERMIT THE FROG
Kermit the Frog got slapped on the gob
For messing about with Miss Piggy
He chased her around
And they fell on the ground
And now they have three little friggies

*(Ian Davison Card Index)*

KING BILLY
King Billy slew the Fenian crew
At the Battle o Byne Watter
A pail o tripe came ower the dyke
An hut the Pope on the napper

*(Hanley 1958; tune: 'The girl I left behind me')*

LATE FOR SCHOOL
One day I was late for school
I went in at eleven
The master and the mistress
Were halfway up to heaven

*(McVicar Collection: Glasgow, 1992)*

MICKEY MOUSE
Mickey Mouse was in his house
Pulling down his trousers
He asked his mum to smack his bum
Out pops you

Or

Look mum, dirty bum
Out pops you

*(McVicar Collection: Glasgow, 1991)*

Still popular in East Calder, 2007.

MILK MILK
Milk milk lemonade
Round the corner chocolate's made

*(Ian Davison Card Index: Rottenrow School)*

With 'rude actions'.

MY FATHER AN MITHER WIS IRISH
My father an mither wis Irish
An a wis Irish tee
A bocht a fiddle for achteen pence
An it wis Irish tee
Bit the only tune that it wid play
Wis 'Kittle ma erse wi a barley strae'

Or

'Over the hill and far away'

*(Wilson 1993)*

## My father

My father's a lavatory cleaner
He cleans them from morning till night
And when he comes home in the evening
His shoes are all covered in
Shine up your buttons with Brasso
It's only sixpence a tin
You can get it at Woolworth's for nothing
As long as there's naebody in

*(Ian Davison Card Index: Rottenrow School)*

## My old man

My old man's a Batman
He wears a Batman suit
He farted in the Batmobile
And blew wee Robin oot
My old man's a Batman
He wears a Batman hat
He farted through the letterbox
And paralysed the cat

*(Ian Davison Card Index: Rottenrow School;*
*tune 'Knees up Mother Brown')*

## My Uncle Billy

My Uncle Billy had a 10-feet willy
And he showed it to the girl next door
She thought it was a snake
And she hit it with a rake
And it ended up 5 foot 4

*(McVicar Collection: Dalkeith HS, 1997)*

## Please get off the grass

Please get off the grass
To let the ladies pass
Here comes the policeman
Sliding on his
Ask no questions tell no lies
Shut your mouth and you'll catch no
Fly away Peter fly away Paul
Come back Peter come back
Polly in the kitchen doing a little stitchin

In comes a bogeyman and out pops
She wears red feathers and a hula hula skirt
She wears red feathers and a hula hula skirt
She lives on fresh coconuts and fish from the sea
With a rose in her hair
A gleam in her eye and
Love in her heart for
Me and my teddy bear
Have no worries have no care
Me and my teddy bear
Just play and play all
Daisy Daisy give me your answer do
I'm half crazy all for the love of you
It won't be a stylish marriage
I can't afford a carriage
But you'll look sweet upon the seat
Of a bicycle made for [etc.]

*(Ian Davison Card Index:*
*Rottenrow and other schools)*

Davison notes that 'This can be even longer, but these are the basic songs.' An amalgam of children's rhymes and old popular lyrics.

POPEYE
Popeye the sailor man, toot toot
He lives in a caravan, toot toot
He put on the gas
And blew up his ass
Popeye the sailor man, toot toot

There are many other versions of lines three and four. Here are some:

He put on the telly
And blew up his belly

He went in the lobby
And slipped on a jobby

He went out swimmin
And snogged all the women

*(McVicar Collection: Dalkeith HS, 1997)*

Others collected in Glasgow in 1991 are

He fell down the chimney
And cut off his willy

There's a hole in the middle
Where he keeps his fiddle

He was playing with Cindy
And fell out the windae

He opened the door
And fell through the floor

Davison has

He played the pianner
For two and a tanner

He tickled his granny
She belted his fanny

*(Ian Davison Card Index)*

QUICK, QUICK
Quick, quick, my farts are coming
Must've been the beans I ate this morning
Quick, quick, the toilet paper
Too late! It's on the flair
Teacher, teacher, I didnae mean it
Give me a brush and I'll scrub and clean it
That's what you get for feeding me
On beans, baked beans

*(Ian Davison Card Index;*
*tune: 'The drunken sailor')*

RABBIE BURNS
Rabbie Burns got 60 days
For lookin up a woman's claes
Aa he saw was bugs and fleas
Rabbie Burns got 60 days

*(Ian Davison Card Index)*

RED WHITE AND BLUE
Red white and blue
You dirty kangaroo
You went to a lamppost
And done a number two

*(Ian Davison Card Index: East Milton School, East Kilbride;*
*tune: variant of 'Knees up Mother Brown')*

RIDING IN THE PARLOUR
Riding in the parlour the motherlode I've seen
I throwed her petticoat over her head and seen her magazine
Seen her magazine, seen her magazine
Out of two bare holes hair did grow
And her a— painted green

*(Mary Elizabeth Barnicle-Tillman Cadle Collection, BC 207A: New York, 1940)*

ROMEO AND JULIET
Romeo and Juliet
On a toilet seat they met
Romeo said to Juliet
Pass the paper my bum's still wet

*(McVicar Collection: West Lothian, 2007)*

ROSIE AND JIM
Rosie and Jim, Rosie and Jim
Having it off in a biscuit tin
Rosie said ooh, Jim said aah
Out came baby Cantana

*(McVicar Collection: Dalkeith HS, 1997)*

SALVATION ARMY
Salvation Army free from sin
Went to heaven in a corned beef tin
Corned beef tin began to smell
Salvation Army went to
Helensburgh castle standing on a rock
If you want to go there you've got to show a
Cocktails, ginger beer, two and six a glass
If you don't like it stick it up your
Ask no questions tell no lies
Shut your mouth and you'll catch no

Fly away Peter fly away Paul
Come back Peter come back
Polly in the kitchen doing a little stitching
In pops a bogeyman and out pops she

*(Ian Davison Card Index)*

SEE SEE
See see my bonny
Why won't you play with me
Under the apple tree
That's where I'll always be
And in the morning
When I am standing there
In my underwear

*(McVicar Collection: Dalkeith HS, 1997)*

See 'See see my playmate'.

SINBAD
Sinbad was a sailor, his father was as well
Sinbad went to heaven, his father went to
Helensburgh Castle stands on a rock
If you want to see it you have to show your
Cocktails and ginger 7p a glass
If you don't like it you can stick it up your
Ask no questions get told no lies
That's how Sinbad became paralysed
Mary had a little lamb, she thought it was silly
She flung it up into the air and caught it by the
Willie was a sheepdog lying in the grass
Along came a bumble bee and stung him in the
Ask no questions get told no lies
That's why Sinbad [etc.]

*(Ian Davison Card Index)*

Sinbad was a sailor
His father was one too
Sinbad went to heaven
His father went to
Edinburgh Castle high upon a rock
Every time he goes there
He has to show his
Cocktail ginger

*(McVicar Collection: Glasgow 1991)*

Mary had a baby
Thought it was so silly
Threw it up to the air
And caught it by the
Willy was a sheep dog
Lying on the grass
Along came a bumblebee
And stung it up the
Ask no questions tell no lies
That's how Sinbad got to Paradise

*(McVicar Collection: Glasgow 1991)*

SLABBERY SLABBERY PUDDING PIE
Slabbery slabbery pudding pie
Two dogs tonsils one cats eye
Very very very thick
And gobble it doon wi a hot cup of sick

*(Ian Davison Card Index: Rottenrow School)*

TARTY FARTY
Tarty Farty had a party
All the farts were there
Tutti Frutti did a beauty
They all went out for air

*(Ian Davison Card Index)*

TARZAN
Tarzan in the jungle
Waiting for his mate
Went to the toilet
Psss! too late

*(Ian Davison Card Index)*

THERE WAS A LITTLE MAN
There was a little man
And he had a little gun
And the bullets were made of charcoal
He shot Mrs Brown in the middle of the back
And the bullet came out of her a—

*(Ian Davison Card Index: Bellahouston School)*

THERE WAS A WEE BOY
There was a wee boy from Boston
Who took off his balls to wash them
His mother said 'Jack, if you don't put them back
I'll put them in a bucket and squash them'

*(Ian Davison Card Index)*

THREE WEE DOLLIES
Three wee dollies dressed in pink
One fell down the lavvy sink
Oh oh what a stink
Three wee dollies dressed in pink

*(Ian Davison Card Index: Rottenrow School)*

THREE WEE MEN
Three wee men in Georges Square
Selling ladies underwear [or] Selling knickers a penny a pair
How fantastic no elastic
Only two and six a pair

*(Ian Davison Card Index: Rottenrow School; tune: 'We three kings')*

THREE WHITE HORSES
Three white horses in a stable
Take one out and skin its navel
If another says a word
Hit it wi a horse's turd
Eerie orie eerie orie
You are out

*(School of Scottish Studies archive:*
*Henderson, from Joshua Shaw, Glasgow, 1957)*

See 'Three white horses'.

WHAT DO YOU DO
What do you do if you need the loo
In an English country garden?
Pull down your pants and suffocate the ants
In an English country garden

Pull down a leaf and wipe your underneath
In an English country garden

*(McVicar Collection: Glasgow, 1994)*

Pull down your pants and fertilise the plants
In an English country garden

*(Ian Davison Card Index)*

### WHEN A WIS YOUNG AN HERTY
When a wis young an herty
A hurlit in a cairtie
The cairtie bruk and a fell oot
An skinned aa ma ersie

*(Wilson 1993)*

### WHOEVER
Whoever smelt it
Dealt it
Whoever made the rhyme
Did the crime

*(McVicar Collection: Glasgow, 1991)*

### WEE WILLIE WINKLE
Wee Willie Winkle, ah saw yer pinkle
Wee Willie Winkle, you never saw mine

*(McVicar Collection: Boghall, 2007)*

### ZOOMIN THROUGH
Zoomin through the mo-er way
A huner an four
Maggie Facher farted
In blew af the door

*(McVicar Collection: Glasgow, 1993)*

The interesting spelling is the informant's own.

# 15
# *Who does that tune belong to?*

## Music and copyright

Some of the songs in this book are always associated with particular tunes, but many draw on a limited supply of floating tunes that are amended as they are applied to and shuffled for texts. They include march and dance tunes, music hall tunes and more recent popular song tunes and television advertisements. Most popular tunes have more than one strain; sometimes there is a verse and chorus, sometimes the first strain is repeated then there are eight bars of a new strain – a 'middle eight' – before the first one is returned to. When children's song uses such tunes, usually only the first strain of the melody is employed, sometimes only the first line.

A few tunes that are applied to numerous children's texts have a long Scottish pedigree. The internationally known tune for 'London Bridge' derives from one part of the nine-part 'Gabhaidh sinn an rathad mor' ('We will take the high road') bagpipe march that in the fifteenth century belonged to Clan MacIntyre of Cruachan. 'The merry matanzie,' more widely known as 'The mulberry bush' or 'Nancy Dawson', appears in the Skene manuscript of the 1620s and is first cousin to 'Greensleeves'. The 'Hokey cokey' first appeared in print as 'Hinkumbooby' in Edinburgh in 1842.

Many of the printed sources do not include much if any detail about the tunes used by their informants. Readers were and are usually presumed to know the tunes well already. Chambers pops in a few airs for songs in his *Popular Rhymes*, Ritchie adds a small clutch of tunes to one of his books, the Montgomeries give some tunes in their earlier editions, the Opies include type tunes in *The Singing Game*. We are better served by Maclagan, Gomme, Greig–Duncan and the Rymour Club who give us lots of melodies to consider. There are two other printed music sources that make my pulse quicken.

In Glasgow's Mitchell Library I found the sheet music of *Jing-Ga-Ring Easy Quadrille* by Charles D'Esteve, published in 1883 by James S Kerr of Glasgow. This setting for dancing of sixteen 'Songs and Nursery Rhymes Sung by Children' is the earliest notation I have found for most of the airs included, and in discussion in this book I several times refer to the illumination D'Esteve can provide on the development of the use and application of tunes to texts.

Another richly rewarding publication is the 1933 *Fifty Traditional Scottish Nursery*

*Rhymes*, collected, edited and arranged for voice and piano by Alfred Moffat and published by Augener of London. In his preface he says 'Many years ago I had the good fortune to be allowed access to a manuscript collection of traditional Scottish airs. This manuscript was in the possession of a well-known firm of booksellers in Edinburgh. It was undated and unsigned but must have been written between the years 1845 and 1850. It contained a number of tunes which the compiler had evidently known to be the original airs to many of the songs collected by Dr Robert Chambers in his *Popular Rhymes of Scotland*.' Moffat made use of the manuscript 'to furnish a number of the old rhymes with their traditional melodies', but most frustratingly he does not tell us which of the fifty rhyme tunes are from this manuscript.

Two of the handful of airs given by Chambers are for 'Can ye sew cushions'. He gives the well-known, sweet air that appeared in Johnson's *Scots Musical Museum* (1787–1803), six volumes of songs to which Robert Burns contributed many songs and in part edited. Chambers also includes another, simpler air, from 'a manuscript collection of airs by the late Andrew Blaikie of Paisley'. This may well be the manuscript that Alfred Moffat drew on, but, wouldn't you know it, Moffat does not include 'Can ye sew cushions' in either setting.

One particularly tangled musical tale is of the true tune of 'London Bridge'. Several years ago I was asked by an African musician to teach him a typical Scots tune to play on his flute. I sang him 'Katie Bairdie' to the tune of 'Will ye gang tae Sheriffmuir?'

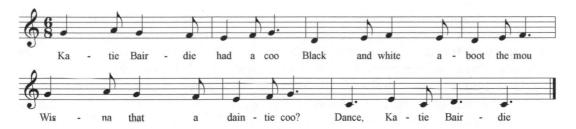

*(Transcription: McVicar, from singing of several informants)*

'I know that one', Amu said, and played the tune back as 4/4 rather than 6/8, making the tune into 'London Bridge is falling down'.

*(Transcription: McVicar, from singing of several informants)*

I was astounded. Which was earlier?

Beginning to look into this, I was further surprised to find that my assumption that the Sheriffmuir tune was universally used for 'Katie Bairdie' was right up the pole: friends from eastern Scotland sang it to 'Whistle o'er the lave o't'.

Ka - tie Bair - die had a coo    Black and white a - boot the mou

Wis - na that a dain - tie coo?    Dance, Ka - tie Bair - die

*(Transcription: McVicar, from singing of several informants)*

I was led into a puzzle of tunes, interlocking, shading and turning into others. Which is the 'original' 'Katie Bairdie' tune? The earlier records are all of 'Whistle o'er the lave o't', but they are not very early. Greig–Duncan no. 1657 has three texts, and text A has the note 'Air – Whistle o're the lave o't'. The earliest printing of tune and lyrics together I have located is in the Montgomeries' *Scottish Nursery Rhymes* (1947), a simplified version of 'Whistle o'er the lave o't'. The next in date is Buchan, 1962, who gives the 'Sheriffmuir' tune.

For earlier song collectors and editors the tune of 'Katie Bairdie' was apparently considered to be either so well known as not to need printing or of insufficient interest and attraction. It probably was 'Whistle o'er the lave o't', another air of antiquity. Some authorities bow to the opinion of Robert Burns that this tune was composed by Highland fiddler James Bruce at the start of the eighteenth century, while others consider the tune older again. Chambers (1842) quotes a reference to 'Chrichty Bairdie' put by Sir Walter Scott into the mouth of King James VI, to show Scott's belief in the age of the tune.

Collinson (1966) says 'the tune of "Katie Bairdie", a nursery song pure and simple, appears in the Rowallan Manuscript circa 1620, and also in the Skene Manuscript (though it is not there recognizable as the same tune.)'

Chambers gives us more detail. He says that ' "Katherine Beardie" is the name affixed to an air in a manuscript musical collection which belonged to the Scottish poet Sir William Mure of Rowallan (the Rowallan MS) and which [the manuscript], there is good reason to believe, was written by him between the years 1612 and 1628. The same tune, under the name of "Kette Bairdie", appears in a similar collection which belonged to Sir John Skene of Hallyards, (the Skene MS) and is supposed to have been written about 1629.'

*(Kindly transcribed by lutenist Rob MacKillop ©*
*for this book from Skene Ms; tune: 'Kette Bairdie')*

In any case, all of the above references are to tunes, without lyrics or any express statement that any lyrics whatever were associated with the tunes. 'Katie Bairdie' as a tune title is older again than 'Whistle o'er the lave o't'. As Collinson says, the tune in the Skene Ms is 'not recognizable' as 'Katie Bairdie'. He does not however indicate what tune he thinks of as 'Katie Bairdie'.

How old is the two strain 6/8 tune 'Will ye gang tae Sheriffmuir?'

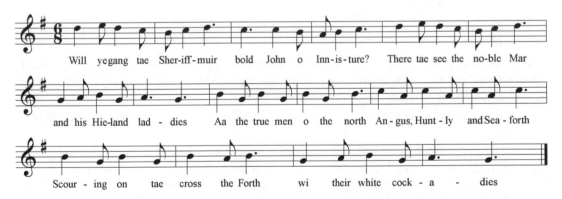

*(Transcription: McVicar, from singing of several informants)*

Emmerson (1971) tells us that in the Gillespie MS, 1768, categorised under Horn-pipes, Jiggs and Reels, item 206 is 'Will you go to Sheriff Moor'. Donaldson (1988) says that 'Will ye go to Sheriffmuir' appears as a song for the first time in Hogg's *The Jacobite*

*Relics Of Scotland* (1819–21) and must in Donaldson's opinion be considered Hogg's own work. In view of the earlier evidence for a tune with the 'Sheriffmuir' title, it is not unreasonable to accept that Hogg followed the same practice often employed by Robert Burns, of selecting a one verse song to rewrite and expand. In *The Songs Of Scotland*, 1859, Graham quotes from Hogg's own note upon the song: 'The air has long been popular, and I have often heard the first verse of the song sung, perhaps the first two, I am not certain.'

But the tune has a Gaelic pedigree older yet. In one of a series of articles in the *Celtic Monthly* on 'The martial music of the clans', Vol 10, April 1902, p131/2, the writer Fionn states that the song 'Gabhaidh sinn an rathad mor', there translated as 'We will take the highway' (though in other music books it is titled 'We will take the good old way') belonged to the MacIntyres of Cruachan. But it was appropriated by the Stewarts of Appin 'as early as the 16th Century', and played by them returning from the Battle of Pinkie in 1547. The Gaelic lyric 'Gabhaidh sinn an rathad mor' relates to the Battle of Inverlochy in 1644. The writer of the article believed this tune was played by the Stewarts at the Battle of Sheriffmuir in 1715, and this caused it to be known among the Perthshire Stewarts as the 'Sherra'muir march'.

*(MacLeod & Boulton 1884; tune: 'We will take the good old way')*

The Gaelic pipe march has in all nine parts. The first two only are used for 'Sheriffmuir'. Many performances of 'Katie Bairdie' to this tune use only the first strain. But Alison Robertson, who attended primary schools in both Glasgow and Edinburgh in the 1950s and 60s recalls singing 'Katie Bairdie' using both strains of 'Sheriffmuir' alternately.

Katie Bairdie is by no means the only Scottish children's song to employ the 'Sheriffmuir' tune. Ones I have found include 'Cat and mouse', 'Hot peas and barley', 'Green peas and barley', 'Oats and beans and barley', 'Off the carpet', 'Two and out', 'Skip the ladder high high high', 'Glasgow ships' and others.

But as my Ghanaian friend Kofi Gift Amu Logotse pointed out, if the first strain of the 'Sheriffmuir' tune is converted from 6/8 to 4/4 time, it becomes the tune now universally used for, and known as, 'London Bridge is falling down'.

The attachment of the 'London Bridge' text to the 'Sheriffmuir' tune appears to have occurred approximately 120 years ago. Prior to that time the tune associated with

'London Bridge' was one usually called 'Nancy Dawson'. Christopher North in an article in *Blackwood's Magazine*, August 1821, lists 'London Bridge is broken down' as one of four songs sung 'in concert' by Edinburgh children 'to the favourite tune of "Nancy Dawson"'. The other three songs were 'We're aa maidens here but ane', 'This is the way the ladies bake' and 'Here we go by gingo-ring'.

*(Chappell 1859; tune: 'Nancy Dawson', transposed from G)*

In his 1908 Rymour Club article on 'Children's Rhymes and Rhyme Games' of 'fifty years ago'(Rymour Club 1911), J L Kelly gives without any tune an older text of 'London Bridge'.

> London Bridge is falling down
> Dan's sister and Lady Ann
> London Bridge is falling down
> With a See, Si, So
>
> We'll build it up wi penny buns [etc.]
>
> The penny buns would be aa eaten up [etc.]
>
> We'll build it up wi silver and gold [etc.]
>
> The silver and gold would be stolen awa [etc.]
>
> We'll get a wee man to watch it at nicht [etc.]
>
> But if the wee man should fa asleep? [etc.]
>
> We'd get a wee dog to bark at his lug [etc.]
>
> *(Rymour Club 1911)*

This lyric does not fit the tune usually thought of as 'London Bridge', but versions given by Gomme (1894) are clearly close relatives. For example:

> London Bridge is broken down
> Dance o'er my lady lee
> London Bridge is broken down
> With a gay lady

Gomme gives three tunes without linking them to any set of words. The tunes are 'The merry-ma-tanzie', the modern 'London Bridge' and a tune from Rimbault's *Nursery Rhymes* that is a version of 'I saw three ships come sailing in' and fits well to the lyric quoted above.

JJ Fuld (1966) says that the first appearance of 'London Bridge' with the modern tune he could find was in 1879, when it was printed with the words in AH Rosewig, *Illustrated National Songs and Games* (Philadelphia).

Chambers (1842) gives two differing texts and descriptions of the 'merry-ma-tanzie' and states that one is sung 'to a pleasing air' and the other 'to the tune of "Nancy Dawson"'. The account of this tune given by Chappell (1849) tells of Dawson, a Sadler's Wells dancer of the 1750s, and says 'the tune became very popular from her dancing.' But the tune was not written for her, it had appeared about 1740 as a dance tune called 'Piss upon the grass', in *Caledonian Country Dances*, printed for J Walsh c.1740.

It should be noted that the tunes listed in the last paragraph are in 6/8 time. When Charles D'Esteve arranged his 1883 quadrille of children's songs he printed the modern 'London Bridge' tune in 2/4 time as the first strain of his 'Broken bridges falling down'. His second strain is an ironed-out 2/4 version of the second strain of 'Sheriffmuir'. We are possibly here on the cusp of the shift from 6/8 to 4/4.

*(D'Esteve 1883; tune 'Broken bridges')*

In the 1890s Maclagan (1901) found a 'Broken bridges' game for which either of two tunes could be used. One was a jaunty widely used march known as 'Bonny laddie, Heilan laddie', to which we sang an irreverent verse in Dingwall:

> See the monkeys kickin up a row
> Bonny laddie, Heilan laddie
> See the monkeys kickin up a row
> Bonny Heilan laddie

*(McVicar from personal recollection: Dingwall, 1940s)*

Maclagan's other tune was the Tullynessle version of 'Glasgow ships', for which I give the text in Chapter 6.

*(Maclagan 1901)*

By the 1900s Rev. JB Duncan was noting the modern tune for texts beginning 'London Bridge is falling down' (Shuldham-Shaw et al. 2002, no. 1566A) and 'Broke bridge is falling down' (no. 1566B).

Did the bounce of 'Sheriffmuir' drive out other tunes for game lyrics, then get ironed out in its turn? The dictum that 'bad money drives out good' can be amended to 'simple tunes drive out more complex ones, and tunes get simplified'. I have found the universally known 'A sailor went to sea' tune applied to quite a few lyrics that formerly were supported by richer airs. Some game tunes were applied to various lyrics and games. I think of the next tune as 'Dusty bluebells', since I recall it in use for that game from childhood, but look at the variety of texts that are sung to it:

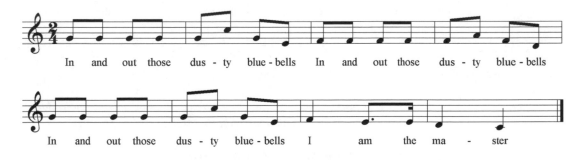

*(Transcription: McVicar from personal recollection, Dingwall 1940s)*

In and out those dusty bluebells
In and out those dusty bluebells
In and out those dusty bluebells
I am the master

*(McVicar from personal recollection: Dingwall, 1940s)*

*(Rymour Club 1911)*

Weary weary waiting on you
I shall wait no longer on you
Three times I've whistled on you
Are you coming out?

*(Rymour Club 1911)*

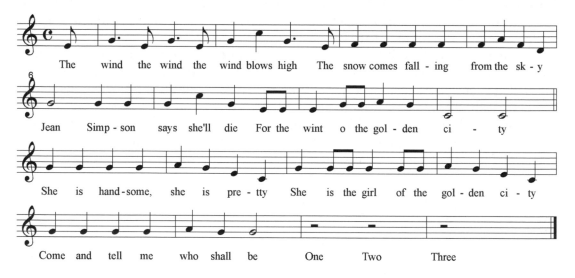

*(Transcription: McVicar, from singing of Craigmillar schoolchildren;*
*School of Scottish Studies archive, Henderson, 1954)*

The wind the wind the wind blows high
The snow comes falling from the sky
Jean Simpson says she'll die
For the wint o the golden city
She is handsome she is pretty
She is the girl of the golden city
Come and tell me who shall be
One Two Three

*(School of Scottish Studies archive: Henderson, Craigmillar, 1954)*

Commercially available recordings of Scottish children's song have been in short supply until very recently. Alison McMorland's 1977 *Funny Family* LP was a very popular gathering together of game songs. In 1983 recordings made by Father Damien Webb OSB were issued as *Children's Singing Games*, and a section of this was recorded in Scotland. The early recordings of Scottish children's show The Singing Kettle in the 1970s featured traditional songs. Then in 2004 Alan Lomax's 1951 recordings of children's song were issued in the USA, and in 2006 *Chokit on a Tattie*, a sampling from the archives of the School of Scottish Studies, was released by Greentrax Records. Although I am named as editor of the latter disc, much of the editing work was in fact done by the general editor of the Scottish Tradition Series, Dr Katherine Campbell. Also in 2006, a book and CD *Hot Peas and Barley-O* was published in the USA. This innovative resource for music educators who use the approach created by Zoltan Kodály combines archive Scottish field recordings with new sample performances by a Scottish children's choir. One remarkable singer's recollection of 'the rich culture of his childhood' in Aberdeen is on traveller Stanley Robertson's double CD *Rum Scum Scoosh!*

These commercial releases of 'traditional' songs raise an issue stuck with thorns. Who owns the songs? If you record the song 'The wind blows high', but title it 'I'll tell my ma', you may end up having to pay arrangement royalties to the Dubliners or the Clancys. If you record 'The hokey cokey', you will certainly be expected to cough up the cash to Jimmy Kennedy's publishers, although he only ever claimed to have written the introductory verses that nobody uses any more. In the original 1942 sheet music he calls it the 'Cokey cokey', and says the song is 'founded on a traditional Canadian Song', and that 'since its introduction here by the Canadian Forces, [the dance] has caught on like wild-fire and bids fair to out-rival some of the most sensational dance successes of the past'.

Peter and Iona Opie in *The Singing Game* (1985) give British versions of this game song under titles like 'Looby loo' or 'Here we go lubin loo' from Lancashire, Newcastle and Farnborough. But they say its 'earliest appearance in print' is as 'Hinkumbooby' in Robert Chambers' 1842 edition of *Popular Rhymes of Scotland* (1842). They believe the game to be far older than this however, and they go on to give old versions from France, Switzerland, the Netherlands, Germany and Spain, plus British troops' versions from both world wars.

In Chambers the lyric begins

> Hinkumbooby, round about
> Fal de ral la, fal de ral la
> Hinkumbooby, round about
>
> Left hands in, and right hands out
> Hinkumbooby, round about
> Fal de ral la, fal de ral la
> Hinkumbooby, round about

The words as you can see are far afield from 'The hokey cokey', but there are echoes in the lines and the actions of the game to show this strong connection. The story of this song goes forwards as well as backwards from 1942. The song did not stop growing when Jimmy Kennedy wrote it down. Internet sources tell me it is still being performed at US football matches and is sometimes known as 'The butcher song': 'You butcher left foot in / You butcher left foot out'.

The word parody presents problems when sharing children's lore with you. If I were to record some of the lyrics I give which are attached to already copyrighted tunes, these would be considered parodies, and I would have to first get permission for any use of each tune from the publisher who claimed the copyright, then pay that publisher all – I mean all – of any royalties received, even the monies earned for new lyrics where no trace of the original words remained. Another possible problem occurs when the original tune has been abandoned, but a line or two of the original lyrics remain.

There are collection societies who control, license and collect cash for the public use of songs on behalf of their members – the songwriters and song publishers. I found when investigating the much recorded and performed songs 'The hokey cokey', 'Coulter's candy' and 'Fitba crazy', that where a songwriter has appropriated, incorporated or rewritten 'traditional' material within a published or recorded work, the collecting societies favour the claim of a known author over that of the vague word 'traditional', and despatch all monies to them, so that an old song is suddenly treated as the property of a new songwriter. Yet 'traditional' means only that a named individual author is not known. The collection societies serve their membership only. The works of an author or composer who is too many years dead to be remembered, or someone who has created only one or two songs and is therefore ineligible for 'society' membership, are of no interest to them. The royalty money earned by very old songs or by occasional songmakers is therefore sometimes held on to by the record company, and sometimes passed on to the collection societies to be put into the pot for their membership to share out. It would be much fairer if this royalty money was used for the general support of Scotland's musical culture.

Here's an example of a small Scottish children's song that holds a large copyright problem:

> I love a sausage, a Co-operative sausage
> And I'm going to have one for my tea
> I went into the lobby to see ma Uncle Bobby
> And the sausage ran after me

*(McVicar Collection: Glasgow, 1991)*

Or

> I love a sausage, a Co-operative sausage
> A hale big sausage tae masel
> Ye eat it wi an ingan, and hear the ingan singin

In other verses, when a cookie is eaten 'Ye squeeze oot the cream, and hear the cookie scream', when an aipple is adored 'Ye cut it up in quarters, an gie it tae the squatters'.

This song uses the tune and a fraction of the lyric of a classic Scots music hall song. The society dedicated to the preservation of the memory of the curly-sticked creator might sue me for breach of copyright should I print the tune, or even the line I have omitted. They have certainly stopped the commercial release of songs using only the tunes the creator made. For example 'I've got a grannie, she's a Hindustani', penned by actor Alex Norton, contains not a shred of the original lyric after the first letter of the first line, but could not be recorded. The music hall singer's protection group pressured a Scottish daily newspaper over the printing of the full 'Co-op sausage' verse I have self-censored, because printing the lyric referred implicitly to the original tune.

Similar copyright problems arise with many lyrics I quote. For example, the following derives from a Hit Parade song of early 1956, 'Pickin a chicken'. All that remains are the tune, the first three words and the last two words of the lyric's first verse:

> Come to the Bendix wash all your clothes
> No need for money no need for soap
> Just press the button and the water will flow
> Come to the Bendix with me
>
> *(Ian Davison Card Index: John Street School)*

For all I know or remember, this may in fact be an intact 1960s or 1970s TV advertisement for the washing machine in question, for which the advertiser negotiated permission, and I am infringing quite a different copyright. It's a minefield out there. Is 'Tipperary' out of copyright yet?

> It's a long way to the pawnshop
> It's a long way to go
> It's a long way to the pawnshop
> Where all our mothers (or someone's name) go (es)
> Goodbye to my jacket
> Goodbye to my watch and chain
> If I don't hang on tae ma troosers
> They'll be gone the same
>
> *(Ian Davison Card Index: Bellahouston School)*

Others are definitely out of copyright, like 'Hark the herald angels sing' – tune by Felix Mendelssohn, 1840, words by Charles Wesley, preacher brother of preacher John, first line drawn from Luke 2:

Hark the jelly babies sing
Beecham's pills are just the thing
They are gentle meek and mild
Two for a man and one for a child
If you want to go to heaven
You must take a dose of seven
If you want to go to hell
You must take the box as well

*(Ian Davison Card Index)*

This must be an adult assault on 'Herald angels', but the parody was a favourite among children in the days when we were a church-going nation. Another over-known hymn for children is 'Jesus loves me', made in 1860 by Anna Barlett Warner. Davison found three separate parody lyrics in Glasgow. The first is obviously adult, the second a rich vignette of tenement priorities, and the third sadly cynical:

Jesus loves me, I don't think
He was the first to give me a drink
He will wash my sins away
A hell of a job for Jesus

Jesus wants me, I'm no gaun
Cause my claes are in the pawn
My shoes as well and though I pray
They won't come oot till next payday

Jesus loves me, yes, I know
Thank you, Jesus, very good show

*(Ian Davison Card Index)*

Where a multi-authored children's rhyme or song has been 'collected' onto tape, and the tape placed in an archive, the issue of who owns what part of the copyright defies clear understanding. The archive preserving the tape has some rights and custodial responsibilities over use of material on it. The collector has rights enshrined in law, but the law, and the commercial collecting agencies who enforce these aspects of the law, are founded on concepts of ownership appropriate to composers of song, not where many anonymous mini-composers have shaped the piece into the version caught on tape that day.

Sometimes the archive has no current contact for the collector or for their heirs. Sometimes the collector was employed by the agency who 'owns' the archive, but sometimes the collector has donated a copy of the recording to the archive for 'study' purposes or in exchange for copies of archive recordings, to be used in turn at the collector's own educational base – where administrators of that archive may then assume or assert rights and responsibilities over their copy of the recording.

The collector got it from the informant. So that informants or their heirs have legal rights over the piece and its use. Except that, again, they did not create the piece. They got it from someone else. They may have changed it, or they may have passed it on untouched. If untouched, the copyright surely belongs to the person they got it from, but that person did not create it either. You have seen in this book how these songs and rhymes grow, transmute, shed and add and mangle and refine. Who made what bit of which? Who owns what of any one of them?

When it comes to commercial exploitation, the law cannot cope, so it hands over responsibility to the big battalions and their lawyers. Where a song is labelled 'folk' or 'traditional' then the recording companies and collection agencies can keep the money it earns for themselves and share it out to their shareholders and members. But this tends to embarrass them as an obvious injustice. If the performer can claim a significant amount of arrangement of the performance the big battalions will usually hand over the copyright fee to them. In former days the battalions were less generous, so in old songbooks you will find the phrase 'new words and music by' attached to the performer's name, though that person has done little or nothing new to the song.

There are notorious examples of the 'folk' label being attached in error to a composed song and the composer earning nothing while the performers claim and get lumps of cash. The Swahili song 'Malaika' has in the last few years been a substantial 'hit' as a 'traditional Tanzanian lullaby' performed by Angélique Kidjo of Benin. But 'Malaika' was a pop song in the Kenya Hit Parade while I lived there in the 1960s. Folk singer Pete Seeger heard it while passing through, learned and recorded it and credited the composer correctly. Other singers heard his recording, assumed it to be 'traditional' and helped themselves to the royalties. In the 1980s the Nordic Copyright Bureau listed seven composers of the song. The generally acknowledged composer, Fadhili William, is one of them. The complexities of international collecting agencies and ownership of publishing companies and record companies are such that it is not known if he received more than a fraction of the royalties. For a full account of this and similar copyright problems read *Big Sounds From Small Peoples* by Wallis and Malm (1984).

# 16
# *Where do they come from,*
# *where do they go?*

## Preserving and recreating

> When grandmama met grandpapa, they danced the minuet
> The minuet was too slow, they danced another step
> With a heel toe heel toe
> Give it a kick, give it a kick, give it a kick
> That's the way to do it

Scottish children's lore has attracted much attention from interested adults, and many fine collections have been published. Robert Chambers was the trailblazer in 1826. The end of the nineteenth century brought a flood — a survey of Golspie in Sutherland in 1897, *Games & Diversions of Argyleshire* in 1901, Robert Ford's general account in 1903. Early in the twentieth century Gavin Greig and the Rev. James Duncan gathered songs from all ages in North-East Scotland, while in Edinburgh the Rymour Club swept up gems and dross. In 1947, William Montgomerie and his wife Norah published the first of several excellent assemblages of *Scottish Nursery Rhymes*, collected from oral and printed sources. At the same time the most productive collector of Scottish children's lore, James T Ritchie, was beginning to uncover and report a wonderful harvest within a single Edinburgh school.

Scottish material is strongly in evidence in the series of seminal books by Iona and Peter Opie. In my introduction I quoted their remarks about 'the Scottish woolbag of oral song'. They have also written (Opie & Opie 1959) that 'Scottish children seem to be in a happy position. They know most of the English child's rhymes . . . and they also have their own *hamely clinky* rarely known to children outside Scotland'.

How numerous? The number is vast. While showing no interest in the topic, Gavin Greig and Rev. James Duncan had 130 children's songs pressed upon them by adults in North-East Scotland in the early twentieth century.

JTR Ritchie collected many hundreds of items from the girls of one Edinburgh school over a thirty-year period. Kenneth Goldstein garnered 183 'games and rhymes' from a few Strichen children in 1960. In the 1960s and 70s, teacher Ian Davison collected over five hundred distinct songs, rhymes and ballad fragments from Glasgow schoolchildren. Lynn Hendry found hundreds of songs in a short 1981 project in primary schools in the Glenrothes area. I have collected hundreds myself. While there is of course much overlap, a startling number of the texts found by these and other collectors are unique in their identity or their combination of elements found elsewhere.

Who were the collectors? Robert Chambers (1802–71) was a native of Peebles. With his brother William Chambers he founded Chambers publishing house in Edinburgh, and wrote many valued books on aspects of Scottish history and culture, including an influential geological work that anticipated Darwin's 'Theory of Evolution'.

In 1826 the first edition of his *Popular Rhymes of Scotland* appeared. His 'only aim' was to 'form an EMINENTLY CURIOUS BOOK, the whimsicality of the design, the oddness of the materials, and the native Scottish humour which pervades a considerable part, are the humble and sole qualities upon which it can found any claim to public notice'.

Editions of his humble work remained in print for over seventy years, and really should still be in print now. This first edition, however, has only a few children's songs and rhymes. His categories are rhymes on localities, characteristics of localities, popular reproaches, families of distinction and their characteristics and slogans, superstitions, and at last a few sample 'Specimens of Unpublished Classes of Popular Rhymes'. These last include the seasons, natural objects and various kinds of children's lore.

He gives 'the names of some [ten] games, upon which our information is already almost complete' and says 'we need not say how imperfect this list is, nor repeat the necessity of enlarging it by contributions from the patriotic and the charitable'. His specimens are given to encourage 'certain individual readers who happen to possess stores of such "legendary lore" to jot down and communicate what may be called to their memory, for inclusion in "the intended second series"'. The 'second series' took a while to appear, because the compiler was occupied by 'other objects, generally of a graver nature'. In 1842 appeared what was termed the third edition, with Scottish children's lore occupying the first 160 pages out of 398. He structured this lore as Rhymes of the Nursery, Fireside Nursery Stories (which often incorporated rhymes), Nursery Riddles, Rhymes Appropriate to Children's Amusements and Miscellaneous Puerile Rhymes.

In this 1842 edition Chambers commented that 'in some instances a remarkable resemblance is made out between rhymes prevalent over Scotland and others which exist in England and Germany'. He expressed the hope that 'the present volume will enable inquirers in France, Holland, Germany, and other countries containing a Teutonic population, to make out such tallies as may exist in those countries'. James Orchard Halliwell was perhaps already at work collecting together *Popular Rhymes and Nursery Tales of England*, but when he published them in 1849 he 'followed in some respects the plan adopted by Mr Robert Chambers in his elegant work'. He found that 'the two collections have not as much similarity as might have been expected. Together, they will eventually contain nearly all that is worth preserving of what may be called the natural literature of Great Britain'. Not much was to be expected from Wales and Highland Scotland, then, and Ireland was left outside the picture altogether.

Indeed, it was long ere a substantial quantity of other Scottish children's rhymes appeared in print. In 1881 Rev. Walter Gregor's *Notes on the Folk-Lore of the North-East of Scotland* was the first published field collection of the London-based Folk-Lore Society. Though this volume had almost no children's games material, Gregor's chapter on Countings-Out gave over fifty rhymes, and he proceeded to contribute substantially to Lady Alice B Gomme's *The Traditional Games of England, Scotland, and Ireland*. (No Welsh informants this time either!)

Volume 1 of Gomme's work appeared in 1894, Volume 2 in 1898. The bulk of the compendious material is English, and most of the Scots entries in 1894 are from Dr Gregor's collecting in Pitsligo, Duthil, Keith, Strathspey and Nairn, though there were other informants in Auchencairn, Biggar and Lanark. By Volume 2 there were twenty-six Scottish locations being served by nine informants, with Dr Gregor reporting from sixteen of them. Lady Gomme, in her introduction to Volume 2, says that the most important circumstance delaying its completion was 'the death of my most kind and learned friend the Rev. Dr. Gregor', because of 'the very special help which he generously gave me for this collection'.

Between the publication of Gomme's Volumes 1 and 2 a rather idiosyncratic approach to collecting came along. The Bodley's Librarian in the University of Oxford, Edward W B Nicholson, went up to Golspie on holiday. He heard children at play in the school playground and became interested in the singing of some of the girls as they played a game. The children noticed his interest, and 'they came and played in a ring in the road' for him. 'I thanked them all and spun up a sixpence for them to scramble for.' Nicholson set up a prize competition for essays on folklore from the local school-children. The resulting book, *Golspie, Contributions to its Folklore*, 1897, is credited to seven students of Golspie School, 'collected and edited' by Nicholson, who commented at such length on the essays, quoting many comparative texts from Gomme and other sources, that most of the book's text is his. He also added a chapter on 'The Place and its Peopling'.

In 1893 the Folk-Lore Society suggested the collecting of county folk-lore, and Robert Craig Maclagan, MD, 'sent a circular to all clergymen, schoolteachers, and some others in Argyle and its attached islands, asking if they would assist. Headings for the various subjects and hints on the best methods of collecting and noting information were given.' The result, in 1901, was *The Games & Diversions of Argyleshire*. Maclagan credits Argyll predecessors Gregorson Campbell of Tiree and Malcolm MacPhail of Kilmartin, and several fellow workers, and says 'This is a further endeavour in the same direction, and it is hoped, while it is, so far as is known, the only collection of nothing but Scottish games, that it may, even if imperfect, form a groundwork for a complete exposition, probably by other observers.' This sentence merits some kind of award for the number of commas used, but despite his self-deprecation the book remains the most complete collection of nothing but Scottish games in print, not least because Gaelic and Scots games and rhymes are freely intermingled on an equal basis. The classification is in forty-seven areas, beginning with Activity (General), Articulation and Auguries, and ending with Throwing Games, Top Spinning and Tossing. Hundreds of rhymes are scattered through the game descriptions, with many notations of tunes. It is a true treasury of folklore.

Robert Ford's 1903 collection, *Children's Rhymes, Games Songs and Stories*, was mostly an uncredited appropriation of Robert Chambers' (by then out of print) *Popular Rhymes of Scotland*, but it has a few attractive additions, in particular Ford's section about 'Wha saw the 42nd' (see Chapter 13).

Ford also edited *Ballads of Bairnhood*, a tooth-rotting collation of the work of Scots Whistlebinkian poets who should have known better, the kind of sickly sentiment that the kids themselves have no truck with. At the end are a dozen anonymous songs taken from Chambers. One of the better pieces is Glasgwegian 'laureate of the nursery' William Miller's 'Wee Willie Winkie', pronounced as 'the greatest nursery song in the world'. Ford redeemed himself for me by editing *Vagabond Songs and Ballads* (1904), a fine collection of neglected songs from the Scottish tradition.

Through the decades illustrated collections aimed directly at children appeared, mostly drawn from other publications but sometimes with a few rhyme versions from the editor's or illustrator's own knowledge. One such was *Scottish Nursery Rhymes* in 1909, compiled by RJ MacLennan and illustrated in lively fashion by Louis MacKay.

Perhaps the richest source came from the Rymour Club, formed in Edinburgh in 1903. The objects of the club were 'the collection, with a view to the preservation and study, and eventually the editing and printing, of ballads, lyrics, and other rhymed material, and of ballad and other tunes, unprinted, or of rarity and in danger of being lost, more particularly such as illustrate Scottish dialect, character, manners, and music in former days'. These objects were condensed into its motto, 'Gader ye the relefis thatt ar left, that thai perische nocht', taken from Murdoch Nisbet's c. 1520 Scots version of the New Testament. Over the next 25 years the club printed, in editions of 250 copies for members only, a wonderful harvest of adult and child rhymed lore. Two of the three volumes were 'issued from John Knox's House, Edinburgh', where many of the club's meetings were held. William J Hay, Curator of John Knox's House, was one of the club's guiding lights.

The membership included collectors and editors Jessie Saxby, Robert Ford and Gavin Greig, plus bookseller James Hay Thin and singer Sir Harry Lauder. Some of the more active children's lore contributors were J Liddell Kelly of Wellington, NZ, Alan Reid of Edinburgh, J Home, the Duchess of Sutherland and Gavin Greig-informant Annie Shirer of Mintlaw.

During the first two decades of the twentieth century two collectors, schoolmaster Gavin Greig and Rev. James B Duncan, amassed thousands of texts and tunes from singers and song preservers in Scotland's North-East, now at last in print in eight large volumes through the heroic efforts of Emily B Lyle and many others. Volume 8 of *The Greig–Duncan Folk Song Collection* has a mish-mash of children's songs. They were pressed upon the not very interested collectors, who nonetheless preserved several fine items.

Norah and William Montgomerie's first collection of *Scottish Nursery Rhymes* was published in 1942. In it they draw in part on the 1935 collection *Nicht At Eenie, The Bairns' Parnassus* of 1935, which has much of the same material, and identical musical transcriptions using a diamond shape instead of the usual oval for each note. One of the two editors of *Nicht At Eeenie*, JM Shelmerdine, created these music line blocks. Rev. AAW Ramsay is stated to have 'suggested the enterprise and supplied the nucleus of the collection. Most of the rhymes were sent by people who had heard them in the nursery.'

The *Scottish Nursery Rhymes* selection of rhymes in vibrant Scots culled from the Montgomeries' own collecting as well as many printed sources ran through several editions, eventually being published by the Chambers publishing house that Robert and his brother had created. In 1952 they made an early field recording of thirty children's game songs (School of Scottish Studies archive: 1952) that adds substantially to our store of tunes. I should like to have included several pieces from the Montgomeries' collecting, but contractual problems intervened.

A source of shortlived and localised versions of rhymes is the booklet or monograph published by a local paper drawing on the column contributions of a local writer. Jean C Rodger's *Lang Strang*, 'a mixter-maxter of Old Rhymes, Games, etc' of the town of Forfar, without a publication date but stated by the Opies to be 1948, is the best of these I have seen, rhymes on local characters and businesses, hand games, descriptions of rope and singing games, tongue twisters and more. In an article in the *Scots Magazine*, January 1974, Ms Rodger further enriches us with a fine description of the town contexts of the rhymes.

I have repeatedly in this book expressed my debt to the key labours of Peter and Iona Opie. From 1947 on they created volume after volume of essential works on aspects of British children's culture. They are the one key source for information.

While the Opies raided the libraries of the world, and enlisted an army of informants, Edinburgh science teacher James TR Ritchie showed what could be harvested from the female pupils of a single school. Alerted by a second-hand copy of Chambers' *Popular Rhymes*, Ritchie began in the 1930s to collect from pupils of Norton Park School. In 1951 he and other Norton Park teachers created a film, *The Singing Street*, with astonishingly evocative scenes of children at play. The famous documentary filmmaker John Grierson called it 'the best amateur film I ever saw'. Ritchie went on in the 1960s to create two excellent books of his collected material, *The Singing Street* and *Golden City*. Both have been reprinted in the last few years. In 1951 Ritchie and one of his best informants, Peggy MacGillivray, were interviewed by visiting American folklorist Alan Lomax. Much of the interview is on the Rounder CD *Singing in the Streets*. Lomax also recorded children at play in Edinburgh and Aberdeen and in choir mode in South Uist, along with the reminiscences of English born Scot Ewan MacColl and of Hamish Henderson.

Perthshire-born Hamish Henderson learned the basics of field recording while acting as one of Lomax's guides in a 1951 jaunt round Scotland that garnered astonishing riches of song and music. Hamish Henderson went on to be the senior collector of song and story for the School of Scottish Studies, the discoverer of many key tradition bearers, a poet, a songwriter and a towering figure in the Scottish Folk Revival. His recordings for the school archives of children singing in Edinburgh and Campbeltown, and of adult informants, are always illuminating and at times joyous. Another eminent American folklorist, Ken Goldstein of the University of Pennsylvania, recorded several tapes of children's lore from youngsters and adults in Strichen and Fettercairn on a 1960 visit, and gave copies of his tapes to the School of Scottish Studies, as Alan Lomax had before him and as have many subsequent collectors.

In the 1960s and 1970s Glasgow teacher of English and songwriter Ian Davison followed the track laid down by Ritchie and got the pupils, arriving in the secondary schools where he taught, to write down the lyrics and rhymes they had learned in primary school. He created a card index of what he found, and though he used some of the material for teaching purposes he published none of it. He kindly lent me this card index, to be eventually deposited in the archives of the School of Scottish Studies. Another Glasgow-based songwriter and teacher of English, Adam MacNaughtan, a contemporary of Davison, has done much work on Scottish children's games but published little so far.

'A pot-pourri of Games, Rhymes and Ploys of Scottish Childhood' is the subtitle of the 1975 book *Dae Ye Min' Langsyne?* collected and edited by Amy Stewart Fraser. Through appeals in Scottish newspapers and magazines she recruited over a hundred and fifty named informants and sewed together variant rhyme versions and detailed descriptions.

In Maureen Sinclair's 1986 fine monograph *Murder, Murder, Polis,* which collects together 'songs and rhymes which have been sung by Glasgow children for many years', she laments that the material has vanished from the street, not knowing it was still to be found in the playground.

A key collector of adults' recollections of children's lore working in the School of Scottish Studies is Emily B Lyle. Of particular note are her collecting trip to Australia in 1974 and her interviews with several douce Lowland ladies, as can be heard on the CD *Chokit on a Tattie.*

For a time an optional task for undergraduate students at the school in the 1970s and early 1980s was to collect the children's lore of their native localities, and the papers they wrote are an under exploited seam. One such 1981 student, Lynn Hendry, titled her work 'A comparative look at children's lore in Glenrothes New Town and the surrounding villages'. The vitality of the associated playground rammy recordings she made is intoxicating.

I myself from 1990 to 1997 collected hundreds of songs and rhymes from many school classes in Scotland's central belt. Sometimes the children wrote them down for me, sometimes I circulated speedily around the room with a small handheld recorder. After 1997 I made no organised investigation in schools till 2006. On a 2004 trip with David Rowan of *The Times Saturday Magazine* we found much material alive and kicking in schools in Glasgow and the Mearns, but I was startled to find one school in the Angus Glens where the children had no rhymes or small songs at all, though they did have dance routines and new-minted games spawned by TV shows and films – *Big Brother*, *Pop Idol* and *Lord of the Rings* – plus old running and chasing games.

Over the course of three days in June 2006 I visited seven primary schools in Moray – Alves PS, Applegrove PS in Forres, Dallas PS, Findochty PS, Mosstodloch PS, Portessie PS and St Geraldine's PS in Lossiemouth. I hoped to find at least forty different songs and rhymes in use. I collected over a hundred and twenty. About ninety of them were either found only once or in almost identical texts in different schools. The other thirty varied notably from school to school.

In March 2007 I took a last-minute dip into the repertoires of classes in West Lothian. One hour in East Calder Primary, West Lothian, in March 2007 produced a welter of counting out rhymes, versions of clapping routines, verses about baked beans, football songs, vigorous brownie action songs and more. Five of the items have been with us for over fifty years at the least. One of them gave advice on how to safely buy a horse by counting how many white feet it has. The class also proudly performed poems by Hugh McDiarmid and JK Annand.

On a visit to Boghall PS three days later P6 girls were impressively fast and adept as they clapped and did the actions for their songs. They made no distinction between playground songs and ones learned in class for performances or competitions. They were pleased to share them all.

Two P6 classes in Bankton Primary, Livingston, showed me how the priorities of key students can shape interests. P6A had enjoyed their week in 'camp', and the performance enthusiasts in the class shared some of the American style 'camp songs' they had learned with gusto and elan: 'I'm a nut in a rut', 'Tarzan was swinging on a rubber band', 'Peel banana, peel peel banana', 'Oh wayla', an 'African' song, 'The old brown cow went poop on the cabbages', and 'Have you ever seen a penguin just like me?' The P6B performers preferred to show complex hand-clapping routines. Both classes had a full range of other children's lore.

When I am collecting from a class as a group, the more extrovert dominate. A final visit, to Springfield After School Care scheme in Linlithgow, allowed me to gather direct from quiet little groups over orange juice and biscuits. They gave me the following and twenty more:

'Coulter's candy', 'A sailor went to sea sea sea', 'My boyfriend gave me an apple', 'Double double this this', 'Cinderella dressed in yella', 'Teddy bear teddy bear', 'Ye canny shove yer grannie', 'Rockaby baby' and 'Twinkle twinkle little star'.

Each of my brief West Lothian visits produced text variants I'd not met before and Brownie and camp songs I did not know. The latter, plus a few older pieces that a young informant told me had been learned in the library or from a grandparent, and a couple of small gems recalled for me by teachers from childhood, reminded me again of the way adults inject old and new material into the rushing stream of child lore.

The above sources focus strongly on children's lore, but there is useful and informative material in all kinds of places. In *The Complaynt of Scotland* of 1549, the list of 'sueit melodius sangis' sung by shepherds includes 'The frog cam to the myl door'. The first chapter of Willa Muir's 1965 study *Living with Ballads* considers her own North-East childhood songs and games. Jessie ME Saxby's gathering of *Shetland Traditional Lore* in 1932 includes puzzling rhymes in a mixture of Shetlandese and Old Norn. Cliff Hanley's sparkling account of Glasgow life, *Dancing in the Streets*, has several gems. The collections *Scotscape* (1978) and *Scotsgate* (1982), edited by Hendry and Stephen, include sections on children's rhyme and song. Careful scholastic collections of the repertoire of noted source singers include the children's material they recalled, with tunes: *Jeannie Robertson, Emergent Singer, Transformative Voice* (Porter and Gower 1995) has twelve 'Songs of Childhood' and *Till Doomsday in the Afternoon* gives twenty-five 'Children's Rhymes' from the Stewart family of Blairgowrie. The short autobiographical account of a well-known Revival singer, *Frae Glesga Toon, Songs and Stories of Alex Campbell* (1964), includes several children's rhymes.

Three key educators and animateurs are credited with kickstarting the Scottish Folk Revival of the 1960s and 1970s – Morris Blythman, Norman Buchan and Hamish Henderson. Through initial work by them and many others, songs – ones that had been preserved and held within their own communities by a few older singers or by Scotland's travellers, or had grown dusty lying in neglected books – were brought into wider life and were learned and sung at hundreds of folk clubs throughout the land. A handful of Scots children's songs thus became widely popular – the few that had enough length and depth to interest an adult audience that was used to songs shaped by the 3 minute, 78 revolutions per minute disc.

Blythman does not feature in this book though he inspired many including me to engage with Scottish song, and I have written about him in *One Singer One Song* (1990). The work of Henderson and Buchan features repeatedly here. Norman Buchan's *Weekly Scotsman* song column, and his 'wee red songbook' *101 Scottish Songs*, provided much of the key repertoire and standard texts of the early revival. Included under the category 'Children's Songs' were 'Katie Bairdie', 'The Tod', 'Coulter's candy', 'I've a laddie in America', 'Wee gallus bloke' and several more. The only one from Buchan's 'Children's Songs' section that I have never heard performed by anyone is the most eerily atmospheric. Buchan found it in Moffat's *50 Traditional Scottish Nursery Rhymes*:

As     I    went   by    the    Luck-en-booths  I    saw   a    la-dy  fair   She

had   long  pen-dles  in    her   ears   and    je-wels  in    her   hair   And

when  she   cam   to    oor   door,  she   spiered  at    wha   was   ben        'Oh,

hae   ye   seen   my    lost   love   wi    his   braw Hie-land  men?'

*(Moffat 1933)*

As I went by the Luckenbooths I saw a lady fair
She had long pendles in her ears and jewels in her hair
And when she cam to oor door she spiered at wha was ben
'Oh, hae ye seen my lost love wi his braw Hieland men?'

The smile upon her bonnie cheek was sweeter than the bee
Her voice was like the birdie's sang upon the birken tree
But when the meenister cam out her mare began to prance
Then rade into the sunset beyond the coast of France

The Luckenbooths of Edinburgh Old Town were cleared away in 1817. Moffat says
this song 'appears to have been much beloved of children of the 17th and 18th centuries',
but does not tell where he got it from. Other rhymes have a far-reaching pedigree. From
the Rymour Club comes what is stated to be a 'counting out rhyme':

Can ye mak a Hielandman?
Yes indeed, and that I can
Just as weel as ony man
He rumbled it, he tumbled it, he gied it sik a blow
Oot jumped a Hielandman, crying Trootcho

*(Rymour Club 1911)*

In Rymour Club Vol. 3 there is a 13-line version of 'As I gaed up the Brandy Hill'
which includes the following three lines:

> Can ye shape a Hielandman oot an auld wife?
> He rummelt her, he tummelt her, he gied her sic a blow
> That oot cam the Hielandman, cryin troot show

'Trobhd so' is Gaelic for 'Come here!'
Maclagan (1901) reports as a 'Nursery Rhyme'

> Whaur are ye gaun, my wee Johnnie Hielanman?
> I'm gaun awa steal a wee coo
> You'll be hanged, my fine Johnnie Hielanman
> What do I care if my belly be fu?

These three verses are reworked from the first part of a poem recorded in 1568 in the Bannatyne MS (Watson 1995), that tells 'How the first heilandman of God was maid of ane horss turd in Argylle, as is said'. Or else the Bannatyne poem quoted in part below might just have been reworked from the same source as the above three smaller verses.

> God and Sanct Petir was gangand be the way
> Heiche up in Ardgyle quhair thair gait lay
> Sanct Petir said to God in a sport word
> 'Can ye not mak a heilandman of this horss turd?'
> God turnd owre the horss turd with his pykit staff
> And up start a heilandman blak as ony draff
> Quod God to the heilandman, 'Quhair wilt thow now?'
> 'I will down in the lawland, Lord, and thair steill a kow'
> 'And thow steill a kow, carle, thair thay will hang thee'
> 'Quattrack, Lord, of that? For anis mon I die'

I named above some of the children's songs that Norman Buchan brought back to the repertoire of adult singers. This involved at times the selection and respectful editing together of various versions he found. The same process has always been used by some singers, child or adult. Some performers strive to present the song exactly as they heard it, though the tricks played by memory and the processes involved in performance often make subtle changes over time. Other singers take what they want, cut and shunt, weld and polish. If done without respect the result can be jarring; if properly handled the effect can be entrancing.

The Opies (1985) tell us that in Aberdeen in the mid nineteenth century it was 'no uncommon sight to see two or three hundred mill girls coming up the Justice Port at night from the Bog Mill, singing [a song called 'The salmon fishers'] with a kind of cheerleader in front of them. All recordings are from the north-east of Scotland.' Indeed, in *Greig–Duncan* (Shuldham-Shaw et al. 2002, no. 1607A and B) there are two different tunes with variants of this verse:

Cam ye by the salmon fishin?
Cam ye by the roperie?
Saw ye my ain sailor laddie
Sailin on the ragin sea?

*Greig–Duncan* no. 1607C has another four lines of half-remembered text, while the Opies give us another twelve lines. Earlier, Rev. W Gregor had contributed three lengthy sets of lyrics to Gomme's *Traditional Games* (1894). The longest, from Rosehearty, conflates at least five narrative elements that I treat elsewhere in this book as belonging to specific 'songs':

Cam ye by the salmon fishers
Cam ye by the roperee?
Saw ye a sailor laddie
Sailing on the raging sea?
Oh dear (girl's name) are ye going to marry?
Yes indeed and that I am
Tell to me your own true lover
Tell to me your lover's name
(boy's name) is a bonnie lad
(boy's name) is a bonnie fellow
Oh he's a bonnie lad
Wi ribbons blue and yellow
Stockings of blue silk
Shoes of patent leather
Points to tie them up
A gold ring on his finger
Did you see the ship he came in?
Did you see it comin in?
Every lassie wi her laddie
Every widow wi her son
Mother, struck eight o'clock
Mother, may I get out?
For my love is waiting
For to get me out
First he gave me apples
Then he gave me pears
Then he gave me a sixpence
To kiss him on the stairs
Oh dear me I wish I had my tea
To write a letter to my love
To come back and marry me

The other two versions given by Gregor, of sixteen and twenty-two lines, assemble different again song couplets after the first three or four lines.

In 1985 Nigel Gatherer edited a book of *Songs and Ballads of Dundee* and included two versions of 'The sailor laddie'. One is *Greig–Duncan* no. 55 from volume 1 of the collection, with a tune and two verses. The second text has four verses, collected by Maurice Fleming from a singer who 'claimed that this song originated in Dundee'. The six verses are clearly part of the same song family as 'The salmon fishers' though they do not include the salmon and roperie verse. They are considered to belong to Dundee, not to the North-East. But here is a version of the same children's song preserved by adults. More than preserved. The tune of the first text is bell-like, and the two texts have been combined and sung with slightly amended words, most notably by one of our best traditional singers, Christine Kydd, who has recorded and performed her version widely. Further, she has taught it to adult song groups and classes of children all around Scotland. So a slumbering song has come back to life.

> I've been east and I've been west
> And I've been in Dundee
> And the bonniest lad that ever I saw
> He ploughs the raging sea
> So away with my sailor laddie
> Away with him I'll go
> I've been east and I've been west
> And I've been in Montrose
> And the bonniest lad that ever I saw
> He wears the tarry clothes
> He rows upo' the ocean
> And he sails across the sea
> And the sailor wi the curly kep
> Oh he's the lad for me
> He bade me aye cheer up my hert
> He bade me ne'er be dull
> He bade me aye cheer up my hert
> He wid tak me fae the mull

*(Gatherer 1985)*

In the 1970s, the first recordings of top Scottish children's show The Singing Kettle popularised particular versions of many traditional Scottish children's songs. For a little time these would have been the orthodox 'correct texts' of the old material, and widely disseminated through the land. But the living oral process reasserts itself again over the frozen nature of tape and disc. Some parts will have lived on, much will again have dropped out of sight.

In this book I have investigated and tried to solve some puzzles and problems and considered the jawdropping entanglements of some song chains and themes. Children are essentially 'green' in their approach, pragmatically stitching together and reutilising song elements, using them for games, activities and amusement while they are fruitful, eventually discarding them ruthlessly. Sometimes no longer understood words and phrases are carefully preserved, more often they are remade into new 'sense', although the assemblies of rich language and striking phrase are often surreally humorous in effect.

There is a process of continuous re-creation. Chapters 2 and 3 have rhymes or songs used by adults with babies and very small children, and these tend to be stable. But all the rest are from the folklore and culture of children themselves, first heard from their pre-teen elders, learned along with their peers aged seven to ten, to be abandoned when puberty strikes. Some of these children's songs travel the globe and live in multiple guises. Others are so short lived they droop and wither before they can be collected and preserved. Those that survive adapt to local languages and conditions, and versions multiply just like the Child Ballads, the old anonymously made ballads that had for centuries been sung, hacked about, remade and preserved by adults through the English-speaking world, till in the nineteenth century they were edited and examined in five volumes by FJ Child of Harvard, whose name is now used to label them. And like these, the children's songs are created and re-created as they are adapted, remade, glued together and chopped into fragments. They drop their tunes and become rhymes, other tunes are then applied to them, sense becomes nonsense and is rewritten to become sense again.

Their basic use is for developing language and physical co-ordination. Children utilise many of them to accompany physical play activity: for group or individual selection for games ('counting out' and elimination), for group game songs, for use with a ball and for skipping, hand-clapping, elastic ropes and so forth. Others are used for performance and include wordplay and parody verses, or narrative ballads of more than one stanza.

In general, the girls learn and use the play songs. Some of the performance songs and ballads are performed in common by girls and boys. The boys sing the songs of football and violence and earthy bawdy songs and rhymes. Many songs and rhymes of all types exist in bawdy and 'polite' versions but children still seek to protect tender adult ears from the 'rude' versions.

Variants of songs and rhymes blossom like a flower meadow, however children and adults are often assertive about which text is the 'correct' one, about the associated activities and where the songs originated. Localised texts of widely known songs abound in child and adult lore, but here is a song where the name of the locality has created the new ingenious verses, which are dependent for effect on mime actions.

> A sailor went to sea sea sea
> To see what he could see see see
> And all that he could see see see
> Was the bottom of the deep blue sea sea sea
>
> *(McVicar Collection: from every school I ever asked)*

This is the most widely known of all small action songs. In this original verse you lift your hand to shade your eyes. Subsequent verses can replace 'sea' with 'knee', 'toe' etc., with appropriate action, then the three can be combined to make 'A sailor went to sea knee toe'. In the USA 'Columbus went to sea'. What makes this appropriate for a book on Scots rhymes? In the early 1990s I heard from Glasgow schoolkids a verse 'A sailor went to diz diz diz', the action being a forefinger twirled at the temple. This reminded me of my mother's criticism of some daft action, 'You're a dizzy juck'. In 1990s Glasgow touching the knee and the ground followed, and the combination verse became 'A sailor went to diz knee land' – Disneyland.

I then tried with no success to think of any other Scottish location with a three syllable name to use. In 2002 I met two small siblings amusing themselves during a concert break in a Linlithgow church, and they showed me 'deep', 'sea' and 'world', which combines as Deep Sea World, a very popular centre in North Queensferry, just across the river Forth from Linlithgow. In East Calder Primary in 2007, the teacher recalled from childhood the sequence and movements for 'arm', 'sterr' (stair) and 'dam' – touch an arm, hands climb a stair, hands hold something back – which combined as Amsterdam.

The children's impulse to reknit old pickings is perennial as the grass. When collecting from a class I am always trying to spot the rehashes cooked up on the spot for me. I expect there are a couple in this book that only sprang into life the day I visited that school and died at the end of the session. Though some lyrics live long, in general the rate of change and variation is speedy indeed. As is the rate of sudden demise of games and much-loved songs and rhymes. The kids keep them carefully, then drop them like the unwanted teddy they deny ever having loved, while the onlooking adult mourns the loss.

Where do they come from, how old are they, how does the process of unpicking and recreating them happen, what makes some die out, who makes the new ones and what are they for? I have advanced a few possible answers, but all in all I speculate cautiously and undogmatically – or just scratch my head in wonder, and laugh.

The greatest blessing I find in our children's lore is the humour. Yes, the infectious energy and enthusiasm of the games is enticing, but the greatest gifts we have are love and laughter. And these we get best from our children.

My last few old rhymes show how puzzling and obscured language is valued and preserved by some adults. Like me.

> I sat upon me humpie birlie
> An I lookit doon troo da humpie dirlie
> An I saw the Ree-Raw
> Cairryin da Lintie's pipes awa
> An I swore be mi nittie nattie
> That I wid tak mi wittie wattie
> An mak the Ree-Raw
> Pey for cairryin da Lintie's pipes awa

*(Saxby 1932)*

As I went up by Humber Jumber
Humber Jumber jiny o
There I met a hokum pokum
Carrying off Capriny o
Oh, if I'd had my tit my tat
My tit my tat my tiny o
I would have made my hokum pokum
Lay me down Capriny o

*(Chambers 1842)*

The rhyme is usually stated to be a riddle and variously explained as a tod stealing a hen, a wolf stealing a lamb or a hawk catching a little songbird. The speaker is a farmer, a shepherd, or just an indignant observer. His weapon can be a stick, a stone or a gun, or he may wish he had his dog with him.

The following related rhyme was called by MacLennan (1909) a 'Yule rhyme', not a riddle. Chambers (1842) said it 'alludes to the Man in the Moon'. MacGregor (1948) explains it as a child sitting on its buttocks, looking through its crossed fingers at the Man in the Moon.

I sat upon my houtie croutie
I lookit owre my rumple routie
And saw John Heezlum Peezlum
Playin on Jerusalem pipes

And two that combine counting out, riddling and puzzling words, character, animal, movement, music, rhythm, and rhyme are

Minty tinty halgulum
Mortal portal piel a gum
I saw the laird o Eastle Weastle
Jumpin owre Jerus'lum steeple

*(Rymour Club papers: Rev. Finlay)*

Tootie tinty, henery memory
Bawptie leeritie, hover dover
Saw the King o Hale Pale
Gruppin at his cuddy's tail
Jumpin ower Jerusalem dykes
Playin on his wee bagpipes
One two three
Oot goes he

*(Rymour Club 1928: Dumfriesshire)*

Oot goes me.

> Noo my story's endit
> And gin ye be offendit
> Tak a needle and a threid
> And sew a bit t' end o't

*(Rymour Club 1919: Forfar)*

# Glossary

*aboon*: above
*airay*: basement area
*alearie, aleery*: crooked
*ava*: at all

*backin rock*: distaff for scraps of wool etc.
*baloo*: comforting sound made to a baby; lullaby
*baps*: bread rolls
*baudron*s: affectionate name for cat
*bawbee*: ha'penny
*beck*: curtsy
*begood*: began
*bellises*: bellows for blowing air on a fire
*big*: build
*birken*: birch
*birl*: whirl round
*bogle*: ghost
*bosie*: bosom
*boukie*: body
*bowster*: bolster
*bowsy-leggit*: bow-legged
*bree*: liquid in which something has been boiled or soaked
*breeks*: trousers
*brenty*: smooth
*brinkie*: smooth
*brod*: sharp-pointed thing, spur
*brose*: oatmeal mixed with boiling water or milk
*brosy, browsy*: stout
*brunt*: burnt
*bubbie*: breast
*bubbly-jock*: turkey cock
*bummin*: bragging, boasting
*buss*: bush

*cadger*: hawker, especially of fish
*cahoutchie*: rubber (F. caoutchouc)
*caller*: cool, fresh
*canles*: candles
*canny*: lucky, skilful
*canty*: cheery, pleasant, neat
*carle*: man, fellow
*carlin*: (old) woman, witch
*castock*: cabbage
*caup*: cup or bowl, often wooden
*champit tatties*: mashed potatoes
*chanty*: chamber pot
*chap*: knock
*chapsies*: way to claim exemption from forfeit in a game
*cheetie*: cat
*chick*: clicking sound made to a horse
*chicki naigie*: dandling game where child rides the adult's knee or ankle; see also *chick* and *naig*
*clamjamfry, clanjamfrie*: rabble
*clash-piety, clash-pyotie*: telltale
*clout*: cloth
*cob*: beat or strike
*Cocky Breeky*: small boy in first trousers
*cods*: testicles
*coffed*: bought
*coft*: bought
*collop*: slice of meat
*coost oot*: fell out, disagreed
*corbie*: raven, crow
*craigie*: neck
*Cripple Dick*: lame person
*croby*: Scots Irish for *corbie*, crow
*croodin doo*: wood-pigeon, term of affection

*cuddie*: donkey
*custock*: cabbage or kail stalk
*cutty sark*: short shirt, undergarment

*dang*: knocked
*deuk's dub*: duck pond
*dicht*: wipe
*die*: toy, trinket
*dight*: prepared, wiped
*dirk*: Highland weapon, short knife worn in the belt (n); to stab or prod (v)
*doo*: dove
*doup*: bottom
*dowt*: cigarette end
*draff*: refuse of malt after brewing
*drawers*: underpants
*drow*: drizzle

*failie*: bit of turf
*fair, fairing*: gift bought at a fair
*far*: where
*farden*: farthing
*fat*: what
*fat maks*: what matters
*file*: dirty
*fite*: white
*flailsoople*: tool for beating out grain
*fog*: grass left in the field to over-winter
*furliemajigger*: whirligig or showy ornament
*fyle*: dirty

*gallus*: bold, cheeky
*garten*: garter
*gate*: road, way
*gauge*: measure; template for the mesh of nets
*gem*: game
*gerse*: grass
*gib, gibbie*: tom-cat
*gled*: hawk
*gleyt*: squint
*glowerin*: scowling
*gouk, gowk*: cuckoo; fool
*greet*: cry, weep
*grice*: pig

*gully*: big knife
*gutty*: rubber
*gweed*: good

*haddy*: haddock
*hallow o straw*: sheaf
*hap and row*: cover and wrap around
*harns*: brains
*Harry Wraggs*: Partick Thistle
*haufers*: half shares
*heddle*: tool used in weaving
*herdie*: person who herds and protects sheep or cattle
*herry*: harry, rob
*herry pie, herries*: tough Glasgow working-class girls
*hinkumbooby*: silly, stupid person
*hirplin*: limping, walking unsteadily
*hotch*: cause to move jerkily
*howlet*: owl
*humphy*: having a hump, hunchbacked
*hun*: derogatory term, from German tribe
*hurcheon*: hedgehog
*hurlit*: rode on something with wheels

*jaurie*: marble
*Jenny*: country girl, woman
*jiggin*: dancing
*jimp*: close-fitting, neat
*juck*: duck

*kailpot*: cabbage pot
*kaim*: comb
*kale*: kind of cabbage
*Katy Beardie*: name for a woman with facial hair
*keek*: peep
*keetles*: cattle-beasts
*keich*: excrement
*kent*: known
*kerseckie*: overall, pinafore
*kick the can*: like hide and seek – the seeker tries to stop the rest getting back to base and 'kicking the can'
*kist*: chest, large box

*kit*: small tub
*kittle*: tickle
*knowe*: hillock
*kye*: cattle

*laid*: mill-lade, bringing water to a mill
*lanny*: cheap powerful wine
*lave*: rest
*laverick, lavrick*: lark
*law*: rounded hill
*led me them hame*: carried them home for me; transported harvest of any kind from the fields
*leefu-lane*: all by myself
*leerie*: lamplighter
*leese me on*: I like, blessings on
*leman*: sweetheart
*licks*: physical punishment
*lift*: steal
*lillie, lily*: beautiful
*lintie*: linnet
*list*: desire
*loose*: louse
*loot*: let out
*loup*: leap, jump
*low*: fire, glow
*Luckenbooths*: (Edinburgh) covered stalls which could be locked
*lum hat*: top hat (like a chimney)

*mavis*: songthrush
*meal-poke*: oatmeal bag
*mend a pen*: sharpen a quill
*midden*: dungheap
*midgie man*: bin-man
*minnie*: mother
*monyfauld*: ruminant's third stomach
*mools*: the grave
*moudiwort*: mole
*moup*: nibble
*mutch*: headgear for married women
*my lane*: all by myself

*naig*: horse
*nappie*: bumpy

*neb*: nose, beak
*neuk*: corner
*nib*: nose, beak
*nieve*: fist

*okey pokey*: ice-cream
*onion bag*: football net
*oo*: wool
*ouks*: weeks
*oxter*: armpit

*pappie*: breast
*peedie*: little
*peelins*: potato peelings
*peenie*: pinny, apron
*peerie*: little (adj.); spinning top (n)
*pickle*: a little
*pinky*: little finger
*plick*: pluck
*pock*: bag, small sack
*points*: laces for shoes or boots
*pouther*: powder
*powe*: head
*preen*: pin
*puddock-stool*: toadstool
*pyat, pyot*: magpie

*quattrack*: what matter

*rackled*: rattled
*rammy*: boisterous row
*rickle*: loose collection or heap
*rift*: belch
*riftin fu*: full to bursting
*rodden*: rowan
*rossen*: roasted
*row*: wrap
*rumples*: rump, haunches

*sark*: man's shirt, woman's shift
*scroggs*: brushwood, undergrowth
*shin*: shoes
*shoo*: sew
*shoon*: shoes
*siccar*: safe

*skailed*: spilled
*skelp*: slap
*smoch, smock*: thick fog
*sneck*: latch of a door
*souple*: tool for beating out grain
*sowens*: food made by steeping oat husks and meal and fermenting that liquid.
*Spangi, Spaingie*: Spanish
*speel*: climb
*stank*: gutter grating
*starns*: stars
*staw*: stole
*stot*: bounce
*stoter*: smasher, bouncing blow
*sugarallie*: liquorice
*sugarellie hat*: top hat
*sugarollie*: liquorice
*sinsyne*: since then
*souple Tam*: jointed wooden doll
*strides*: trousers

*tanner*: sixpence
*tartan*: (of skin) mottled by sitting too close to the fire

*tearie*: rage, spree
*thrapple*: throat
*thrifty*: moneybox
*thumle*: thimble
*tift*: gust of wind
*tine*: prong
*titlen*: meadow pipit
*tod*: fox
*toly*: lump of excrement
*tone*: buttocks, bottom
*trig*: trim
*trowies*: fairies, mischievous spirits
*tyke*: dog

*wall*: well, standpipe
*wame, wamie*: stomach
*ware*: spend
*wat*: know
*wean*: small child
*whitterit*: weasel or stoat
*wummle*: auger, gimlet
*wyte*: blame

*ya bass*: used in slogans as short-hand for 'You bastard'

# Bibliography

## Published works

Alburger, MA (1996) *Scottish Fiddlers and Their Music*. Edinburgh, The Hardie Press

Anderson, JA (1933) *The Cleikum*. Galashiels, Border Telegraph office

Anonymous (nd, 1960s) *Carlton Folk Songs*. Glasgow, Mozart Allan

Anonymous (nd, 1850s) *The Lyric Gems of Scotland*, First and Second Series. Glasgow, John Cameron

Bett, H (1924) *Nursery Rhymes and Tales*. London, Methuen & Co.

Berg, L (1997) *Flickerbook*. London, Granta Books

Bronner, SJ (1988) *American Children's Folklore*. Arkansas, August House

Buchan, N (1962) *101 Scottish Songs*. Glasgow, Collins

Burns, R (1970) *The Merry Muses of Caledonia*. London, Panther

Campbell, A (1964) *Frae Glesga Toon*. Woodham Walter, Essex, Folk Scene Publications

Cass-Beggs, B & M (1969) *Folk Lullabies*. New York, Oak Publications

Chambers, R (1826, 1842, 1847, 1870) *Popular Rhymes of Scotland*. Edinburgh, W & R Chambers.

Chappell, W (1859) *Popular Music of the Olden Time*. London, Cramer Seals & Chappell

Cheviot, A (1896) *Proverbs, Proverbial Expressions and Popular Rhymes of Scotland*. Paisley, Alexander Gardner

Cluer, A (1976) *Walkin' the Mat*. Aberdeen, Lantern Books

Collinson, F (1966) *The Traditional and National Music of Scotland*. London, Routledge & Kegan Paul

*Concise Scots Dictionary* (1985). Aberdeen, Aberdeen University Press

*County Folklore – Fife*, 1912. London, Folk Lore Society

Crawford, T (1979) *Society and the Lyric*. Edinburgh, Scottish Academic Press

D'Esteve, C (1883) *Jing-Ga-Ring Easy Quadrille*. Glasgow, James S Kerr

Dick, JC (1903, 1962) *The Songs of Robert Burns and Notes on Scottish Song by Burns*. Hatboro, Penn, Folklore Associates

*A Dictionary of the Older Scots Tongue* (1931–2002), 12 vols. Oxford, Oxford University Press

Donaldson, W (1988) *The Jacobite Song*. Aberdeen, Aberdeen University Press

Dorson, RM (1968) *The British Folklorists*. London, Routledge & Kegan Paul

Emmerson, GS (1971) *Rantin' Pipe and Tremblin' String*. London, J M Dent & Sons

Fionn (1902) 'The Martial Music of the Clans', *Celtic Monthly*, April

Ford, R (1903) *Children's Rhymes, Games Songs and Stories*. Paisley, Alexander Gardner

Ford, R (nd) *Ballads of Bairnhood*. Paisley, Alexander Gardner

Fraser, AS (1975) *Dae Ye Min' Langsyne?* London, Routledge & Kegan Paul

Fraser, GM (1970, 1972) *The General Danced at Dawn*. London, Barrie & Jenkins & Pan Books

Freemont, V & N Barbaresi (1992) *Counting-Out Rhymes*. New York, Dover Publications.

Fuld, JJ (1966) *The Book of World Famous Music*. New York, Crown Publishers

Gatherer, N (1985) *Songs and Ballads of Dundee*. Edinburgh, John Donald

Gilchrist, AG & L Broadwood (1915) *Journal of the English Folk Dance and Song Society*, Children's Game-Songs. London

Gomme, AB (1894, 1984) *The Traditional Games of England, Scotland and Ireland*. London, Thames and Hudson

Gosset, ALJ (1915) *Lullabies of the Four Nations*. London, De La More Press

Gregor, Rev. W (1881) *Note on the Folk-lore of the North-east of Scotland*. London Folklore Society

Halliwell, JO (1849, 1970) *Popular Rhymes & Nursery Tales of England*. London, John Russell Smith and the Bodley Head

Hanley, C (1958) *Dancing in the Streets*, London, Hutchinson & Co.

Haynes, DK (1973) *Haste ye Back*. London, Jarrods

Hecht, H (1904) *Songs From David Herd's Mss*. Edinburgh, WJ Hay

Henderson, H (1992) *Alias MacAlias*. Edinburgh, Polygon

Hendry, ID & G Stephen (1978) *Scotscape*. Edinburgh, Oliver & Boyd

Hendry, ID & G Stephen (1982) *Scotsgate*. Edinburgh, Oliver & Boyd

Herd, D (1776, 1973) *Ancient & Modern Scottish Songs*, Vol. II. Edinburgh, Scottish Academic Press

Hogg, J (1821) *The Jacobite Relics of Scotland*. Edinburgh, Wm Blackwood

Johnson, J & R Burns (1787-1803) *The Scots Musical Museum*. Edinburgh, James Johnson

Kidson, F (1891) *Traditional Tunes*. Oxford, C Taphouse & Son

Kidson, F (1916) *100 Singing Games*. London, Bayley & Ferguson

Knapp, M & H (1976) *One Potato, Two Potato*. New York, W W Norton & Co.

Lawson, M (1997) *Guid Auld Galashiels*. Galashiels, Margaret Lawson

Leyden, M (1989) *Belfast, City of Song*. Dingle, Brandon

Locke, M (1981, 1988) *Sail Away*. New York, Boosey & Hawkes

Lomax, JA and A (1934) *American Ballad and Folk Songs*, New York, Macmillan

MacColl, E & P Seeger (1986) *Till Doomsday in the Afternoon*. Manchester, Manchester University Press

MacGregor, F (1948) *Scots Proverbs and Rhymes*. Edinburgh, Moray Press

Maclagan, RC (1901) *The Games & Diversions of Argyleshire*. London, David Nutt for the Folklore Society

MacLennan, RJ (1909) *Scottish Nursery Rhymes*. London, Andrew Melrose

MacLeod, AC and H Boulton (1884) *Songs of the North*. London, JB Cramer & Co.

Mactaggart, J (1824, 1876, 1981) *Scottish Gallovidian Encyclopaedia*. Strathtay, Cluny Press

McVicar, ER (1990) *One Singer One Song*. Glasgow, Glasgow District Libraries

Margaret, M & Florence & Lynne (early 1990s) *Jinkin An Joukin*. Bathgate, Albus Project

Moffat, A (1933) *Fifty Traditional Scottish Nursery Rhymes*. London, Augener

Montgomerie, N & W (1947) *Scottish Nursery Rhymes*. London, Hogarth Press

Muir, W (1965) *Living With Ballads*. London, Howarth Press

Monro, A (1996) *The Democratic Muse*. Aberdeen, Scottish Cultural Press

Munro, N (1992) *Para Handy*. Edinburgh, Birlinn

Nicholson, EWB (1897) *Golspie, Contributions to its folklore*. London, David Nutt

North, C (1821) 'The Voyages and Travels of Columbus Secundus', *Blackwood's Magazine*, August

Opie, I (1993) *The People in the Playground*. Oxford, OUP

Opie, I & P (1951, New Edition 1997) *The Oxford Dictionary of Nursery Rhymes*. Oxford, OUP

Opie, I & P (1959) *The Lore and Language of Schoolchildren*. Oxford, OUP

Opie, I & P (1969) *Children's Games in Street and Playground*. Oxford, OUP

Opie, I & P (1985) *The Singing Game*. Oxford, OUP

Palmer, R (1979) *A Ballad History of England*. London, Batsford

Partridge, E (1961–84) *A Dictionary of Slang and Unconventional English*. London, Routledge & Kegan Paul

Phillips, R (1995) *Music for the Lute in Scotland*. Temple, Kinmor Music

Porter, J & H Gower (1995) *Jeannie Robertson, Emergent Singer, Transformative Voice*. East Linton, Tuckwell Press

Ritchie, JTR (1964) *The Singing Street*. Edinburgh, Oliver & Boyd

Ritchie, JTR (1965) *Golden City*. Edinburgh, Oliver & Boyd

Robertson, JDM (1991) *An Orkney Anthology, the Selected Works of Ernest Walker Marwick*. Edinburgh, Scottish Academic Press

Rodger, JC (nd) *'Lang Strang'*. The Opies give 1948 as a date. Forfar, Forfar Press

Rodger, JC (1974) 'The Singing Streets of Forfar', *Scots Magazine*, January. Dundee

Rymour Club (1911) *Miscellanea of the Rymour Club Edinburgh*, first published in parts 1905–1911, as Volume 1 in 1911. Edinburgh, from John Knox House

Rymour Club (1919) *Miscellanea of the Rymour Club Edinburgh*, published in parts 1912–19, as Volume 2 in 1919 and reprinted 1973. Edinburgh, from John Knox House

Rymour Club (1928) *Miscellanea of the Rymour Club Edinburgh*, published in parts 1920–28, as Volume 3 in 1928 and reprinted 1973). Edinburgh, from the Outlook Tower

Sandburg C (1927) *The American Songbag*. New York, Harcourt, Bracey & Co.

Saxby, JME (1932) *Shetland Traditional Lore*. Edinburgh, Grant & Murray

*Scottish National Dictionary* (1931–76), 10 vols. Edinburgh, Scottish National Dictionary Association

Seeger, P & E MacColl (1960) *The Singing Island*. London, Belwin-Mills Music

Shaw, F (1970) *You Know Me Anty Nelly*. London, Wolfe Publishing

Shelmerdine, JM & F Greirson (1932) *Nicht At Eenie*. Warlingham, Samson Press

Shuldham-Shaw, P & EB Lyle & S Douglas (1997) *The Greig–Duncan Folk Song Collection, Volume 7*. Edinburgh, Mercat Press

Shuldham-Shaw, P & EB Lyle & K Campbell (2002) *The Greig–Duncan Folk Song Collection, Volume 8*. Edinburgh, Mercat Press

Sinclair, M (1986) *Murder Murder Polis*. Edinburgh, Ramsay Head Press

*Tocher 36/7* (1982). Edinburgh, School of Scottish Studies.

Wallis, R & K Malm (1984) *Big Sounds From Small Peoples*. London, Constable

Watson, R (1995) *The Poetry of Scotland*. Edinburgh, Edinburgh University Press

Wellington, S (1997/98) 'Women Work and Song', *Locscot*, Vol 3 No. 8

Williams, RV & L Lloyd (1959) *The Penguin Book of English Folk Songs*. Harmondsworth, Penguin Books

Wilson, WM (1993) *Speak o' the North East*. NES Publications

# Unpublished sources

Ian Davison Card Index of songs collected by him from Glasgow schoolchildren, 1960s/70s, currently in the possession of Ewan McVicar

Frank Kidson Collection in Mitchell Library, Glasgow

MacFarlan Ms, 2085 in the National Library of Scotland, Edinburgh

McVicar Collection: manuscripts written by schoolchildren and adult informants, emails, recordings and printed copies from Internet sources, 1990–2007, held by Ewan McVicar

McVicar, ER (1998) 'Singing in the Playground', MSc thesis, University of Edinburgh

Rymour Club Minute Book of 1913–20, in National Library of Scotland, Edinburgh

Rymour Club papers, 1904–7, in National Library of Scotland, Edinburgh

School of Scottish Studies Card Indexes, George Square, Edinburgh

Skene Ms, Adv. MM.5.2.15 in the National Library of Scotland, Edinburgh

# Recorded sources

## Commercial recordings

*The Carter Family, Anchored in Love*, (1993) Rounder CD 1064

*Children's Singing Games* (1983), recorded and edited by Father Damien Webb, Saydisc Records CD-SDL 338

*Chokit on a Tattie, Children's Songs and Rhymes, Scottish Tradition 22* (2006) Greentrax CDTRAX9022

*Ma Maw Says*, unnumbered cassette issued in late 1980s by the WEA for Castlemilk People's History Group, Dougrie Drive, Glasgow

*Rum Scum Scoosh, Traveller Traditions of North-East Scotland No. 2* (2006) Elphinstone Institute, Aberdeen

*Singing in the Streets: Scottish Children's Songs*, Rounder CD 82161-1795-2

## Recording archives

Mary Elizabeth Barnicle-Tillman Cadle Collection, East Tennessee State University archives, Johnson City, Tennessee

Alan Lomax archive, Association for Cultural Equity, New York

School of Scottish Studies Recordings archive, George Square, Edinburgh, tape recordings by: Argo, A (1960) Glasgow; SSS SA1960/245. Henderson, H (1954) Craigmillar; SSS SA1954/139-42. Henderson, H (1956) Campbeltown; SSS SA1956/171-2. Henderson, H (1957) Glasgow; SSS SA1957/99. Henderson, H (1960) Leven; SSS SA1960/241. Hendry, L (1981) Glenrothes; SSS SA1981/13. Montgomerie, N & W (1952) Dundee; SSS SA1952/44-6. Neilsen, E (1961) Stenness, Orkney; SSS SA1961/83. Neilsen, E (1961) Lerwick, Shetland; SSS SA1961/89. (Headlee) Williamson, L (1976) Montrose; SSS SA1976/111.

# Index of titles and first lines

# General index